PLAINS HISTORIES

JOHN R. WUNDER, *SERIES EDITOR*

ALSO IN PLAINS HISTORIES

America's 100th Meridian: A Plains Journey, *by Monte Hartman*

American Outback: The Oklahoma Panhandle in the Twentieth Century,
by Richard Lowitt

As a Farm Woman Thinks: Life and Land on the Texas High Plains,
1890–1960, *by Nellie Witt Spikes; edited by Geoff Cunfer*

Children of the Dust, *by Betty Grant Henshaw; edited by Sandra Scofield*

The Death of Raymond Yellow Thunder: And Other True Stories from the
Nebraska–Pine Ridge Border Towns, *by Stew Magnuson*

From Syria to Seminole: Memoir of a High Plains Merchant,
by Ed Aryain; edited by J'Nell Pate

"I Do Not Apologize for the Length of This Letter": The Mari Sandoz Let-
ters on Native American Rights, 1940–1965, *edited by Kimberli A. Lee*

Nikkei Farmer on the Nebraska Plains: A Memoir,
by The Reverend Hisanori Kano; edited by Tai Kreidler

Railwayman's Son: A Plains Family Memoir, *by Hugh Hawkins*

Rights in the Balance: Free Press, Fair Trial, and
Nebraska Press Association v. Stuart, by Mark R. Scherer

Ruling Pine Ridge: Oglala Lakota Politics from the IRA to Wounded Knee,
by Akim D. Reinhardt

Where the West Begins: Debating Texas Identity, *by Glen Sample Ely*

Indigenous Albuquerque

Indigenous Albuquerque

Myla Vicenti Carpio

Foreword by P. Jane Hafen

Texas Tech University Press

This book is typeset in Monotype Amassis. The paper used in this book meets the minimum requirements of ANSI/NISO Z39.48–1992 (R1997). ♾

Library of Congress Cataloging-in-Publication Data

Carpio, Myla Vicenti.

Indigenous Albuquerque / Myla Vicenti Carpio ; foreword by P. Jane Hafen.

p. cm. — (Plains histories)

Includes bibliographical references and index.

Summary: "Investigates the complexities of urban American Indian life in Albuquerque, New Mexico. Examines Indigenous experiences in the city, focusing on identity formation, education, welfare, health care, community organizations, and community efforts to counter colonization"—Provided by publisher.

ISBN 978-0-89672-678-9 (hardcover : alk. paper)

1. Indians of North America—Urban residence—New Mexico—Albuquerque. 2. Indians of North America—New Mexico—Albuquerque—Social life and customs. 3. Indians of North America—New Mexico—Albuquerque—Social conditions. 4. Albuquerque (N.M.)—Social life and customs. 5. Albuquerque (N.M.)—Social conditions. 6. Albuquerque (N.M.)—Ethnic relations. I. Title.

E78.N65C27 2011

305.897'078961—dc22   2010052106

Parts of chapter 5 have been published elsewhere: "Countering Colonization: Albuquerque Laguna Colony," *Wicazo Sa Review* 19:2 (2004).

Printed in the United States of America

11 12 13 14 15 16 17 18 19 / 9 8 7 6 5 4 3 2 1

Texas Tech University Press | Box 41037 | Lubbock, Texas 79409–1037 USA

800.832.4042 | ttup@ttu.edu | www.ttupress.org

Contents

Illustrations   vii

Plainsword   ix

Acknowledgments   xiii

Introduction   xvii

ONE

Urban Movement, Urban Dilemmas   3

TWO

Paak'u, Alburquerque, Albuquerque
The Politics of Settlements   24

THREE

Indians in Albuquerque
Political, Economic, and Physical Recognition   48

FOUR

Maintaining Our Lives
Organizations, Music, and Programs   73

FIVE

"Let Them Know We Still Exist"
The Laguna Albuquerque Colony   94

SIX

Decolonizing Albuquerque   115

Appendix   129
Notes   131
Bibliography   159
Index   175

Illustrations

PHOTOGRAPHS

1. From relocation pamphlet   xxii
2. From relocation pamphlet 2   xxii
3. American Indian enclave in Albuquerque, 1912   38
4. Pueblo tribal members visiting Albuquerque Indian School   42
5. Young Albuquerque Indian School girls   44
6. Albuquerque Indian Center   81
7. Albuquerque Indian Center (rear)   84
8. Indian Pueblo Cultural Center Travel Center / Smoke Shop   86
9. Indian Pueblo Cultural Center entrance   88
10. Indian Pueblo Cultural Center east entrance / restaurant   89
11. Development near Petroglyph National Monument   123
12. The 8.5 acres excluded   124

MAPS

1. Map of American Indian population in U.S.   4
2. American Indian population in New Mexico   29
3. Reservations surrounding Albuquerque   53
4. American Indian population in Albuquerque   56

TABLES

1. Indian Health Service User Population   16

2. Language Groups and Pueblos in New Mexico   28

3. Albuquerque's Largest Employers   51

4. American Indian Populations in Albuquerque   53

5. Top Ten Specified Tribal Affiliations in Albuquerque   55

6. City of Albuquerque, 1995 and 1996, Applicants   63

7. Albuquerque School District: Graduation / Dropout Rates   68

|| ILLUSTRATIONS ||

Plainsword

IN THE CUARTO CENTENARIO sculpture garden outside the Albuquerque Museum, on the corner of 19th Street and Mountain Road NW, is a monumental bronze collection of life-sized horses, riders, wagons, oxen, and other animals. This assemblage is titled *La Jornada* by Betty Sabo and Sonny Romero. Its eighteen human figures depict the colonizers of New Mexico, and they are led by Don Juan de Oñate. Down the sidewalk on Mountain Road is a large black-and-white, free-standing mural (*Que Vive San Felipe* by Leo Romero) with what appears to be a nineteenth-century procession and celebration of a Catholic saint. Noticeable only to those who are looking carefully is an earthen installation between the two, *Numbe Whageh: Our Center Place*, by Nora Naranjo-Morse (Santa Clara Pueblo). Constructed with indigenous plants, local rocks, and water, *Numbe Whageh* restores the land and celebrates the survival of Native peoples.

The development of this artistic space was fraught with controversy and conflict. The Hispanic Culture Preservation League and the Hispano Chamber of Commerce wanted to glorify Oñate who, as Myla Vicenti Carpio points out in *Indigenous Albuquerque*, is viewed by Native peoples "as a symbol of Spanish colonization and brutality toward Indigenous people." To those accustomed to having power, financing this public art with public funds justified an emphasis on the traditional narrative of conquest and the textbook history of New Mexico. That history of colonization, as Vicenti Carpio illustrates, erases much Indian experience.

Despite the conflicts, even including opposition from some Pueblo peoples, the project proceeded and Naranjo-Morse was able to see fulfillment of her artistic vision informed by the traditional values of her Pueblo heritage:

> It's feminine in its approach, . . . which is reflective of the Pueblo matrilineal culture. It speaks of old things, old ways and our traditions, yet also raises issues of race, politics, history and respect for the environment that we have been confronting for over 400 years. I wanted to use natural materials in a way that reflected our worldview before European contact. It has become, again, our place. This is not a work driven by art market values, but rather by our cultural values. I have slept, ate, dreamed, breathed and thought of this project for six years. It taught me tremendous lessons and has been a very exciting, creative challenge. It has been a gift to me, and now I give it back to my people and all visitors.[1]

To experience *Numbe Whageh*, the observer cannot simply stand and look, as is possible with many closely situated statues, visual representations, and *La Jornada*. To simply look, one would see only the rim of landscape. The attentive observer must follow a spiral path that leads down into the center of the installation. No longer surrounded by conquistadores, traffic, or other elements of the surrounding environment, the "Center Place" becomes a spot of refuge and peace. This "Center Place" represents renewal and continuance, "a sacred wholeness" (Naranjo-Morse).[2]

In the center of contemporary Albuquerque, right next to narrative representatives of cultural hegemony, is a patch of what Gerald Vizenor (White Earth Ojibwe) would call "survivance"—survival and endurance. The installation also decolonizes the surrounding narratives through Indigenous resistance, in its presence and in its construction against political opposition. As Diane Reyna (Taos Pueblo) notes, *Numbe Whageh* represents "perseverance through adversity," not only in a historical sense, but in its contemporary struggle to be completed.[3] Kathy Friese states:

> It is impossible to look at *Numbe Whageh* and not understand that Naranjo-Morse is commenting not only on the past but also on the future.

The land, as it has been condensed into a spiral form, is disappearing. The land, as visitors walk the approximately fifty steps into the center of the piece, may not exist next time they return to visit this piece of art. Certainly, the piece will not exist in precisely the same form, which contributes to its shifting interpretive qualities. The plants will have grown or died. The stones on the path will have moved. The water will flow differently.[4]

The evolution of the piece and experiencing its changes distinguishes it from other static or plastic arts. When the observer emerges from "Numbe Whageh," the conflicting narratives seem even more marked in their contrast. Naranjo-Morse retells history experientially and communally, and the dominant narratives are refuted and reconsidered. One cannot exit the installation without an awareness of the complicated relations of Indigenous peoples and their surroundings.

Like the *Numbe Whageh*, this volume, *Indigenous Albuquerque*, represents survival, reconstruction of historical narrative and decolonization. Vicenti Carpio (Jicarilla Apache/Laguna and Isleta Pueblo) does not accomplish this undertaking through artistic creation and public art like Naranjo-Morse, but through detailed research and scholarship. Unlike other volumes that have discussed contemporary Indians in urban settings and in general terms, she addresses a specific place and specific history. She calls on her own experience of maintaining her sense of Native self while surrounded by tribal and non-tribal others. She offers a new narrative reconstruction of the history of New Mexico in general and Albuquerque in particular. By discussing and analyzing federal policies, she looks at social and economic displacements of Indian peoples. The strongest contribution of this book is the close examination of particular organizations and events that create an Indian community in the metropolis of contemporary Albuquerque.

Vicenti Carpio has inculcated the ideas of contemporary Indigenous theorists who have spelled out decolonization as a strategy of resistance and recovery. Influenced primarily by Maori scholar Linda Tuhiwai Smith, a number of American Indian scholars have applied this Indigenous methodology to understanding and explaining histories and literatures, and to creating a space of resistance. This analysis is especially evident in her discussion of the Laguna Colony in Albuquerque. Like *Numbe Whageh*, the Laguna Colony is visible as a center of power to those who are looking and retells its own story about survival in Albuquerque.

Additionally, Vicenti Carpio's study speaks to the fundamental principles of American Indian studies: land, language, and sovereignty. She covers ideas of place, urban spaces, and historical Indigenous spaces. She acknowledges that urban Indians have ties to their homes and places of origin. English is the language of the colonizers, along with Spanish in New Mexico, but English is also the reclaimed language of survivors. Vicenti Carpio's readings of historical, federal, and policy documents gives way to usages of English as a decolonizing mechanism. Finally, through the detailed study of individual and tribal populations, she acknowledges that not all Indians are alike, but asserts their tribal affiliations. She also looks at the specific interactions of affiliated tribes with government-to-government entities, such as the All Indian Pueblo Council and local municipalities.

Another important contribution to contemporary Indian scholarly discourse is Vicenti Carpio's deconstruction of essentialist ideas about identity. Often a political quagmire that ranges between policing blood quantum to emotional claims to descent from distant Indian relatives to a reservation litmus test, identity issues are difficult at best. Vicenti Carpio effectively shows that "real" Indians exist and survive in urban settings.

Indigenous Albuquerque offers the reader new insights to Native peoples in Albuquerque, New Mexico. Through historical narrative, policy analysis, careful examination of documents and statistics, and through decolonizing methodologies, Vicenti Carpio recovers the past while setting the stage for future understanding. Because this study is a careful examination of specific peoples in a specific place, it serves as a model for other scholars. Vicenti Carpio guides the reader to new understandings, just as Naranjo-Morse guides the observer to the *Numbe Whageh: The Center Place.*

P. JANE HAFEN

Acknowledgments

THE PROCESS OF WRITING a book is much like a book itself, with different chapters. This project began as a dissertation in the history department at Arizona State University (ASU) and is ending in American Indian studies at ASU. I would like to thank my dissertation advisor Peter Iverson for his patience, kindness, and persistence. Many thanks to my dissertation committee members James Riding In, Chris Smith, and Margaret Connell-Szasz for their many comments and years of support. This manuscript has gone through many phases and it has been a long road completing this book, but it could not have been possible without those individuals who generously gave their time to be interviewed and talk with me. I especially acknowledge Larry and Lynn Martin, who always shared materials and asked about the book. This work is built on the knowledge of many; however, any and all mistakes are mine alone.

Throughout graduate school I was blessed with a support network of people who made graduate school bearable, but thankfully we remain supportive, humorous, and loving friends—Melissa Dyea-Purley, Amy Lonetree, and Waziyatawin. May we keep "Staying Alive." Many thanks also go to Elizabeth Carney, Leah Glaser, Maryann Villareal, J. Wendel Cox, Michele Curran, Stephan Amerman, and Andy Fisher.

The long process of revision meant numerous readings and comments from patient and honest souls. An enormous thanks to Ann Hibner-Koblitz

for reading and providing insightful comments on numerous versions of the
entire manuscript; Susan Miller for her sharp editing skills; Karen Leong for
her constant readings; James Riding In for comments on Chapter 5; Nandhini Gulasingam, Cynthia Brewer, and Mike Medrano for the great maps; John
Wunder for seeing the potential of this manuscript in its earlier stages; and
Judith Keeling for believing in this project and seeing it through even in the
midst of extraordinary circumstances. Also, thanks to the anonymous re-
viewers for their generous comments.

As many of us know, archivists are essential in assisting historians with
our research. I am truly appreciative of the archivists whom I have encountered and admired for their vast knowledge of the records. I want to thank
Mary Alice Tsosie (now at Indigenous Nations Library Program at the University of New Mexico [UNM]) and Nancy Brown-Martinez at the Center for
Southwest Research at UNM, Eric Bittner at the Rocky Mountain Region of
the National Archives, Joe Sabatini at Special Collections in the Albuquerque
Public Library, and Paul Wormser at the National Archives Laguna-Niguel. I
also want to acknowledge the financial support provided by the Jicarilla
Apache Nation Scholarship, assistantships by the history department at ASU,
and the DIGS Grant from the College of Public Programs at ASU.

I want to thank all the students who took my Issues in Urban Indian
Country classes in American Indian studies at ASU. Through those lectures
and students' questions, comments, and patience, I was able to rethink and
formulate some of my understandings of urban Indian issues.

Also at ASU I am grateful to my colleagues who have provided unyield-
ing support and intellectual community: Karen Kuo, HQ, Crystal Griffith,
Tisa Wegner, Elizabeth Archuleta, Karen Leong, Ayanna Thompson,
Michelle McGibbney, Louise Baca, James Riding In, Carol Lujan, Susan
Miller, Simon Ortiz, Michelle Hale, Sara Peña-Lee, Tamara Underiner, Barbara Shaw-Snyder, Kenja Hassan, Seline Szkupinski-Quiroga, Lisa Anderson,
Jackie Martinez, Serena Freewomyn, and Randilynn Boucher. I am thankful
for my two teaching assistants, Elise Boxer and Kishan Lara, who are not just
colleagues but friends. Special thanks to Vicki Ruiz—while I was never formally her student she has provided amazing mentoring and encouragement.
Much appreciation goes to Mary Rothschild, an incredible mentor and advocate.

Thanks to my wonderful friends Lynn Abeita, Kathryn Manuelito, Carol Takao, and Sherril Tomita, who because of my seemingly constant work on this manuscript understood when I could not come out to play. Also, to Jeffrey Shepherd and Cynthia Bejarano, I am immensely grateful for your friendship and do not have the words to express what you both mean to me.

During this project I was diagnosed with cancer. I want to acknowledge those individuals whose medical expertise has been instrumental to my recovery: Dr. PenniAnn Whitten, Dr. Christi Bourne, and Rachelle Marmor. Thank you to my oncologist Dr. Marvin Chassin and especially to the chemo nurses at Desert Oncology who consistently showed amazing compassion, humor, and care during one of the more difficult times in my life.

Finally, I am deeply grateful to my families in Dulce and Laguna for their continual support and guidance. They never cease to show me which way is up and keep me grounded. I owe a debt of gratitude to my grandmother, Elizabeth H. Roberts, and my mother, Thurza Vicenti. While my grandma is no longer here to share this achievement, I carry her love, support, and admiration always within my heart and memory. My greatest debt and appreciation go to my mother. Beyond her great financial sacrifice and unrelenting support, I have learned, by her example, what it means to successfully live within different worlds while maintaining an inviolable cultural integrity. Lastly, my utmost thanks to Karen and Maitlyn for reminding me that there is much more to life than academia. I am fortunate to be the recipient of Karen's unwavering love, compassion, devotion, and laughter in sickness and in health.

Introduction

WHEN I WAS FOUR YEARS OLD, my mom decided to leave the Jicarilla Apache reservation, and our nation helped us move from Dulce, New Mexico, to Denver, Colorado. My mother moved for personal reasons, not for the "economic opportunities" promised in the Bureau of Indian Affairs Indian relocation program propaganda. At that young age, I had no idea that so many others had taken a similar path in moving to the cities. We moved mostly without the aid of the relocation program, but the program did find us an apartment and day care. Even at four, I understood the change in environment and landscape that came with moving from the beautiful mountains of northern New Mexico to the Mile High City. Our move took us away from our relatives, our reservation, and the clean air. More than forty years later, I would once again relive that move, this time as an Indigenous historian.

The move to Denver located me outside my Indigenous cultural environments on the Jicarilla Apache reservation and the Laguna and Isleta pueblos. In Denver, I went to elementary school with only one other Indigenous classmate. Living near the projects, I had mostly Mexican-American, African-American, and white classmates. I was immersed in the mythology of American greatness and the ideologies of freedom and democracy by teachers who glossed over the cost in Indigenous lands, cultures, and lives.

In the Independence Day play, I was a Massachusetts delegate who supported the new constitution, a constitution (and mindset) that excluded Indians. In school, I was recognized as an Indian only at Thanksgiving.

Fortunately, while all this indoctrination was going on, my mother never let me forget who I was: a Jicarilla Apache, a Laguna, and an Isleta. She never let me forget the history of my family and my people, even when I did not want to be Apache because we were portrayed so brutally on the television show *High Chaparral* (among other shows). Eventually, my mother moved us back to Albuquerque, New Mexico, to be closer to the Jicarilla reservation and to ensure that I would grow up knowing what it meant to be Jicarilla Apache, Laguna, and Isleta. I know I was not the only Indigenous person in Denver, nor was I the first to come to the city and then leave.

Most scholarly research on "urban Indians" has produced a history and narrative that refers to urban Indian migration as a recent phenomenon. These narratives begin their discussions about Indigenous urban migrations relative to European and American urban development. For instance, in *The American Indian in Urban Society*, James E. Officer "demonstrates how . . . governmental actions have, in so many ways, been significant forces behind the eventual movement of Indians to urban centers, or to small-town colonies, or enclaves nearer their reservations or centers of aboriginal distribution."[1] Moreover, in *The Urban Indian Experience in America*, Donald Fixico focuses on urbanization "caused by WWII and continuing to the present."[2] Yet for millennia, Indigenous peoples of the Americas had already lived "urbanized" lives in Indigenous cities. To say that Indigenous peoples have only recently become urban ignores the many large, complex civilizations that existed before the European invasion, and privileges colonial views of urban migration and Indigenous history. Indigenous peoples of the pre-colonial Americas thrived in both urban and rural cultures.

Jack Forbes portrays urbanization not as a new concept for Indigenous peoples, but rather as a longstanding part of our lives. Indigenous nations have "gone through periods of de-urbanization and re-urbanization," and myriad Indigenous peoples have lived "highly urbanized" lives for thousands of years.[3] Forbes defines urban areas not by the presence of densely placed structures, but rather as the "intimate interaction of substantial numbers of people in a given geographic space."[4] Large, complex urban centers guided by sophisticated cultures greatly affected the regions in which they were situated. Such cities were part of trade networks that covered great distances throughout the Americas. Some of these early metropolises were analogous in importance to the large cities of today.

Indigenous North American cities such as Cahokia, Mesa Verde, and Chaco Canyon, as well as various Central and South American cities, illustrate long traditions of urbanization. Cahokia, known for its impressive size and number of mounds and considered the largest pre-Columbian site within what is now the United States, had an estimated population at about A.D. 1100 between 10,000 and 20,000, with the highest estimate at 25,500.[5] This does not include the thousands of inhabitants surrounding Cahokia who remained under the authority of the central community. The urban center of Cahokia in what is now Illinois is considered a "presence on the world stage," as a global illustration of a well-planned, complex society where the "view of humanity's relationship to the spirit world was formulated."[6]

Just as the Cahokians forged an influential urban center in the Midwest, the ancestral Pueblo people (formerly called the Anasazi) at Mesa Verde and Chaco Canyon and the Huhugam of present-day Arizona built urban centers in the Southwest. The Huhugam numbered in the tens of thousands and had great irrigation canals upon which Phoenix, Arizona, would later be built.[7] The ancestral Pueblo people lived in large urban areas with outlying communities that are best known for their many apartment-style dwellings; some of the largest great houses stood four to five stories and contained more than 650 rooms. It is apparent from the primary complex at Mesa Verde National Park that the cultural centers were large and sophisticated.[8] The ancestral Pueblo used Chaco Canyon and its outlying communities as cultural, spiritual, and commercial centers, whose trade routes reached well into modern-day Mexico. Other sites as far away as ninety miles in all directions also exhibit features and influence of the Anasazi.[9] Mexico and South America are, of course, known for large Indigenous metropolises such as the Mayan city of Nakbe, Teotihuacán in the Valley of Mexico, the Aztec capital Tenochtitlán, and the Incan capital Cuzco.

Today's Indigenous urban life is an "intimate interaction" of Native peoples in an urban landscape with few physical boundaries such as specific neighborhood areas.[10] Unlike the ethnic enclaves typical in large American cities, such as the Bronx's or Brooklyn's Little Italy in New York City, or Kaisertown in Buffalo, New York, most Indigenous peoples in urban areas do not tend to occupy distinct neighborhood areas, and most cities do not have distinct boundary areas considered Indigenous. Susan Lobo comments that, "in the 1990 Census there was an assumption that all Indian people in urban areas lived in congregated communities, such as Chinatown, but in reality the majority of Indian people live dispersed throughout cities."[11]

Early scholarly studies from the 1950s to the 1970s focused primarily on Indigenous urban migration and settlement in a way that pathologized Indigenous urban community life and cultural loss. As with much of the American historical record of Indigenous peoples, scholars wrote from colonizing perspectives using colonizing methodologies, defining success, failure, levels of assimilation, and lifestyles from American theoretical perspectives. Focusing on experiences, behaviors, and cultures, they probed factors relating to the relocatees' maladjustment. Using polarized assessments to evaluate urban Indigenous residents as either American *or* Indian, scholars generally accepted a maladjustment model where, accordingly, Indigenous people failed when they did not fully assimilate or integrate into American society.[12]

In the 1960s and 1970s, assimilation, integration, and acculturation remained at the center of scholarly and policy discussions. Seeking to increase the rates of successful urban integration, scholars focused on presumed characteristics that facilitated assimilation and social integration into white society. Successful relocatees had Western educations, were integrated with whites socially, and distanced themselves from their cultural beliefs.[13] Sociologist Robert Weppner, in a study of urban economic opportunities for Navajos in Denver, suggested that the government avoid relocating Navajos not suited or qualified for the city, and focus instead on Navajos trained in trades and wage-labor work, who could speak better English. Often, such people had already lived away from the reservation.[14] Even relocation program placement officers felt that were only a few "ideal" applicants.

> . . . [W]e should recognize that the ideal type of person who presents excellent occupational qualifications, good moral background, a reasonable

degree of education, perhaps 8th grade or better, currently, for the most part, is gainfully employed and needs no assistance in so far as our program is concerned. There are perhaps a few of such people described above who are on reservations who find themselves unemployed at this time. I believe that some of the men we have sent, perhaps may fall in this group, and if our placement program were designed to deal exclusively with this group and ignore others, we would have no particular problem.[15]

In the attempt to highlight the "success" of a relatively small number of Westernized Indians in the city, an image of failure of the majority was emphasized and dramatized by the image of the drunk on skid row. This category of drunken, poverty-stricken urban Indians contributed to furthering negative stereotypes and images that continue to shape policy and attitudes. These images also define "good" Indians and "bad" Indians. The portrayals blame Indigenous people for their own hopelessness and destitution, instead of looking for causal relationships and disempowerment.[16]

Most studies of Indigenous urban residents focused on the costs of urban life for American Indians, emphasized social and economic problems, and rarely commented on positive outcomes or strategies for cultural organizing and survival. According to the paradigm of assimilation, moving to cities for employment, gaining and holding employment, and staying away from the reservation were deemed positive and successful.[17] Figures 1 and 2 present pages in a relocation program pamphlet. Indians are portrayed as childlike, indecisive, and in need of help. A stairway leads up the ladder of success, presumably away from the reservation. The Indian is not fully clothed until he is successful; then he wears a shirt and tie.[18]

Early scholars focused on the social, economic, and psychological problems that Native peoples faced in the urban setting. They interpreted the existence of these problems as evidence of pathology in Indian culture without considering how institutional prejudice against Indigenous peoples was at the root of these problems.[19] Indigenous people were viewed as failures for not coping with the urban environment.

These early studies influenced how the larger society perceived urban Indigenous people and how Indigenous people viewed themselves. Many scholars since have focused on questions about Indigenous identity and

Fig. 1 From relocation program recruitment pamphlet, ca. 1955

Fig. 2 From relocation program recruitment pamphlet 2, ca. 1955

urban life, such as Who are urban Indians?, Is "Indianness" maintained in an urban setting?, and How do Indians survive the urban environment? Instead of such assimilationist questions, I ask how relationships develop between non-Indigenous and Indigenous citizens and how these institutionalized relationships reflect and perpetuate Indigenous struggles with colonization in urban living. Moreover, I examine ways in which important interactions between urban and reservation communities exist.

While many studies have catalogued the problems that Indians face in urban environments, my goal in this book is to address more clearly some of the issues that urban Indians have had to negotiate with various levels of government, including health care, welfare reform, relations with city administration, and relations with one another and themselves. I focus on the historical ramifications and the political, economic, and social dilemmas of Indigenous people living in one urban area—Albuquerque, New Mexico. I argue that the Indigenous urban experience in Albuquerque has its own distinct narrative that is nonetheless intertwined with the reservation experience. This differs from previous studies of urban Indian life insofar as those studies have centered their discussions on pan-Indian identities where powwows, churches, and Indian centers gather Indigenous people from diverse nations into communities.[20]

The "Indian" or pan-Indian identity may be a reality for some cities, but it is not completely the case in Albuquerque. Growing up in Albuquerque, I saw a different version of urban identity. In some cases, Indigenous people acknowledged "being urban" only in terms of a current address, but maintained a determined focus on tribal and reservation ties. Many engage in a pattern of constant movement between the reservation and the city, maintaining specific tribal identities despite their urban addresses. Understanding this relationship is intrinsic to understanding the experiences and issues of Indigenous people in Albuquerque.

This monograph is not a community history. Instead, it examines the changing relationship between the City of Albuquerque and Indigenous populations, with attention to community and political organizations. Only a few people have studied Albuquerque. It has a unique location in that twelve Indigenous nations, mostly Pueblo, are within a 50-mile radius. This creates an unusual environment for Indian urbanization and distinct relationships between Indians and the City. I argue that the urban Indian experience cannot be viewed as distinct from the reservation because it is integrally connected not only through cultural, religious, political, and economic spheres, but also through federal reservation policies. I also examine how Indigenous people in Albuquerque have structured their development of urban Indigenous communities and organizations to counter federal goals of assimilation.

Significantly, I position my manuscript not within American Indian history, but within the discipline of American Indian studies. Dakota scholar Elizabeth Cook-Lynn states that American Indian studies focuses on and defends Indigenous sovereignty and indigenousness itself.[21] Like histories of American Indians that document the past and analyze change over time, I discuss the historical context of how the past informs the present. However, I also seek to address what is at stake in what is memorialized as "the past" and what is "forgotten." I examine the relationship between "urban" Indians in Albuquerque and the city of Albuquerque within the context of colonization, and the dilemmas confronting urban Indians as a result of this colonized past. I assert that "urban" as a lived experience does not occur in isolation from either Indigenous communities' survival or the legacies of Euroamerican colonization.

One particular aspect of the legacy of Euroamerican colonization has been not only the exclusion of Indigenous history, but the lack of access to certain sources. It is evident that the federal government diligently recorded all aspects of the relocation program. While records concerning housing and job placement, income, relocation officer evaluations, and other topics are numerous, many of the records kept by the relocation office officials contained private information such as Social Security numbers, addresses, and medical information about individuals. Many of these records are restricted for 75 years, and therefore information concerning relocation and relocation officers' attitudes is missing from the urban Indian historical memory. Albuquerque was not a major relocation center, although it was an area for training; for example, the Albuquerque Business College provided secretarial training for Indigenous women.

When relocation policy was first implemented, most relocatees left Albuquerque by bus or train to designated relocation cities. Therefore, much of the information on relocation centers and individuals must be attained by oral interviews or the government policy records of the relocation program.[22] These sources—governmental policy records and selected oral histories of urban Indian activists and organizations—are primarily what I have relied upon in this study to begin to document the challenges faced by and the accomplishments of urban Indian organizations in Albuquerque.

Indigenous people's relationships with each other and with the city, and the development of community institutions, reflect the legacies of European and American colonization. These legacies are an important factor in the way Indigenous people in urban areas interact with the city and how the city interacts with them. I examine the complexities of Indigenous life in the city and concentrate not just on identity (which has been the conventional focus of scholars), but on education, welfare, health care, community organizations, efforts to counter colonization, and some actions toward decolonization. I also attempt to illustrate ways in which Indigenous Albuquerque residents express and continue their tribal culture.

Chapter 1 recontextualizes the federal relocation program of the 1950s and 1960s as a continuing form of colonization that still affects both urban and reservation Indigenous people in the United States. Although the impact of federal Indian policy has been most conspicuous in terms of reservations and loss of land, it also has profound implications for the political and economic realities of urban Indian life. I examine how Indians contend with the new political, cultural, and social battlegrounds confronting them in the city, and how they build bridges between their urban communities and their Indian nations. Moving to a city produces a new set of difficulties involving social services, political recognition, and internal and external identities. In this chapter, I address how these difficulties are manifest in the everyday lives of Albuquerque Indians.

Chapter 2, "Paak'u, Alburquerque[23], Albuquerque: The Politics of Recognition," traces the history of Albuquerque from Indigenous roots (Paak'u) to Spanish colonization (Alburquerque) to American subjugation (Albuquerque). I demonstrate a continuous Indian presence throughout the city's history, although, as I discuss in chapter 3, the city government did not politically acknowledge an Indigenous presence until the 1990s. Chapter 3 illustrates how this relationship has played out in lack of recognition and in hiring practices. I examine how the contemporary Indian community in Albuquerque developed through organizations, programs, and activism. In Chapter 4, I argue that a concept of pan-Indian identity limits our understanding of the lived reality of urban Indigenousness. Instead of concentrating on the division between the reservation and the city, I focus on the intersection where urban Indian organizations develop community while maintaining and nurturing connections with reservation life and culture. The history of the Laguna colonies in Chapter 5, particularly the Laguna Colony of Albuquerque, illustrates the intersections of urban and reservation life and the dual landscapes where Indigenous people counter colonization. Instead of assimilating the dichotomy of "reservation" and "urban Indians," the members of the Laguna colonies live outside their reservation home while maintaining their cultural connections through the colonies. Chapter 6 concludes this study with an exploration of ways in which some organizations, such as the SAGE Council, are attempting to move beyond tribal identities and build coalitions to influence urban political processes. Many dilemmas face Indians when they move to the city, problems relating not only to identity, but also to health, education, and finance.

My work thus engages Duane Champagne's vision that American Indian studies as a discipline focused on "understanding and preserving Native rights, understanding Native communities, and helping preserve Native culture, language, land, and government."[24] I emphasize that urban Indians are another Native community with concerns that overlap those of with their home communities but also with concerns unique to the urban setting. My hope is that this study about how Albuquerque's multitribal Native community has negotiated federal, state, and city politics, and developed its own organizations, constitutes a step toward a more inclusive American Indian studies, and a deeper analysis of urban Indian experiences and institutions.

Indigenous Albuquerque

ONE

Urban Movement, Urban Dilemmas

MANY URBAN HISTORIES have viewed current Indigenous urban migrations in America as primarily a post–World War II (WWII) phenomenon. But Indigenous people have been moving to urban areas for jobs, education, or personal reasons, and in response to federal policies, since the 1920s. The recent main waves of migration have occurred during the post–WWII and Cold War eras. Increasingly today, Indigenous people are moving in and out of the city, affecting American Indian social, religious, political, and economic lives. These migrations are multifaceted, and their reverberations may encompass loss of identity and difficulties in urban life. Besides loss and difficulties, migration also involves survival, especially in terms of cultural and political perseverance within the urban structure. Indigenous people are different; their cultures, many times, are vastly at odds with American culture(s). How, then, do individuals from very different worldviews maintain their cultural integrity and thrive in an urban environment? How does one live in two, three, four, or more worlds while maintaining a delicate equipoise of wholeness and cultural integrity?

According to the 2000 U.S. Census, over one-half of the American Indian population is urban, with the three largest Indian populations located in

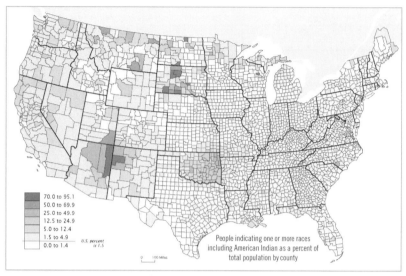

Map 1 **American Indian Population in United States.**
(From U.S. Census Bureau, 2000 Census.)

New York, Los Angeles, and Phoenix.[1] Map 1 illustrates the population of Indigenous peoples across the nation. These statistics reveal a demographic transformation that is shifting constructions of American Indian identity and relationships between American Indians and federal, state, and city governments. Urban complexities produce sometimes tenuous relations between Indians and the cities in which they live. These conditions are not only part of the colonial context—they also illustrate the dilemmas faced by Indigenous peoples.

To protect their lands and sovereignty, Indigenous nations fought and continue to fight difficult battles against American colonialism. Since the European invasion, Indigenous leaders have made difficult decisions in order to maintain their sovereignty/self-determination and lands for future generations. The U.S. government's vision of relations with the tribes varies continually, creating a roller coaster ride of federal Indian policies. Meanwhile, Indigenous nations continue to adhere to political, economic, spiritual, and cultural beliefs so as to remain Indigenous. Scholars of American Indian studies and history have focused mostly on reservation issues, such as economic development, political struggles, jurisdictional issues, and cultural continuity. Meanwhile, Indigenous people in urban environments face struggles not encountered on reservations and have interests that may not accord with some reservation political and economic structures. Nonetheless, a dynamic relationship exists that connects the reservation and urban Indians, despite what is sometimes viewed as an "urban divide."

This perceived divide, usually understood as an urban/reservation dichotomy, has been used in different ways for particular ideological purposes. Proponents of relocation positively depict this divide as progress, with Indians moving away from the past (reservation/culture) toward the future in the urban environment as self-sufficient citizens. Some Native people, on the other hand, describe their experience of this divide as living in two distinct cultures—the reservation on the one hand, and urban environments on the other. Significantly, many of these people note that this divide is not only cultural but also spatial, consisting of the distance between their urban location and the reservation, which they still consider home. These views have developed and shifted throughout the processes and waves of relocation.

However, a more accurate analysis focuses less on the relocatees as exclusively urban and more on the distinction, separation, and ongoing relationships between urban and reservation entities and environments. I propose that relocation and its changing impacts on Indigenous lives can best be understood in three waves, or periods, that are not always chronologically defined. These periods of change may evoke the way immigrants are defined by generations, and in some cases these terms do apply.[2] I look at American Indian urbanization in three periods distinguished by their experiences of urban life, the physical and psychological distance between reservations and city life, and the extent of urban Indian community development.[3]

The first period of American Indian urbanization constituted a mostly new experience for relocatees, and many of the subsequent waves of relocatees benefitted from the wisdom of existing urban residents. As more Indians migrated to the cities, they were met with the experience of other Native residents, as well as developing their own social, cultural, and political communities. Moreover, as Native urban residents returned to the reservation, they brought with them social and political knowledge and experience from the cities. This continued cyclical migration, to and from the city and reservations, diminished the separation between the urban and reservation environment.[4]

While movement to the cities occurred not only through the relocation program and with relocation funding and assistance, the beginning of relocation as a policy illustrates that a clear distinction was expected between urban and reservation life and issues. During the first wave of relocation, distance (physical and cultural) between the city and reservation was greater. Traveling home to visit family was rare or near impossible. Freeways were not as developed and not everyone owned cars. Home was a long bus or train ride away, sometimes lasting days as opposed to a few hours today on an airplane. Contact with home was mostly by U.S. mail, which may have taken days or longer to reach its intended party, unlike quick email or immediate text messaging. For many, transportation, time constraints, and differing cultural values made the urban environment a truly brand-new experience.

The second wave of relocation brought the reservation and city closer; many relocatees during this wave already had contacts in the cities, including friends and family. Connections with people, work, housing, and "urban" dwellers with lived experience helped to build informal relationships between Indigenous urban and reservation residents. Sharing lived experiences helped people to transcend intertribal differences. The development of Indian centers provided a space for social interactions and cultural support. Dances, powwows, bars, and the commonalities of survival and struggle brought Indigenous people together, crossing tribal lines. Political activism and community organizing helped develop, strengthen, and define many urban Indian communities.

Time and technology have brought the reservation and urban areas into closer spatial and cultural proximity. The third wave of relocation benefits from today's technology. Television brings the outside non-Indigenous world into the Indigenous world's own "intimate" personal and cultural spaces, where it must compete. Urban styles can now be seen in rural areas, such as in changing fashions, hair styles, language uses, music, attitudes, and behaviors. Instant communications such as email, text messaging, and cell phones now reduce—although they do not eradicate—the distance from home. The shrinking of the urban/reservation divide has impacted the reservation environment. The introduction of gangs on reservations illustrates not only a decreased divide, but mutual impacts.

Youth gangs in Indian country have direct urban-reservation connections. The migration of youth gangs to Indian country illustrates the reduction in the psychological as well as the spatial distance between the reservations and urban circumstances. For many Indigenous urban residents, disconnections from cultural homes, feelings of not belonging, economic hardship, and violence in urban environments, lead them to return to the reservation.[5] This return to the reservation also means that they bring part of the city with them.[6] Youths involved in city gangs return to the reservation bringing the activities, mindset, or actual gangs from the cities. Moreover, youth who already had encounters with the law may be sent to the reservation in the hopes of keeping them out of further trouble.[7] In a recent article, James Bell and Nicole Lim comment:

> Today, the urban environment and its slow engulfment of the imagination of Indian youth undermine parental and communal influence over young Native Americans. Youth are drawn to the flashy lifestyle of the street, and that attraction weakens the strength of their ancestors' voices. For too many young Indians today, gangs are the only place they belong.[8]

While Indigenous urban residents face distinct issues within an urban setting, they also share many of the concerns reservation communities are dealing with, such as health care, economics, and education.

In this chapter, I address some of the issues faced by Indigenous people in urban areas today, such as lack of access to health care and education, and the harmful effects of welfare reform and census undercounting. Urban Indigenous reality consists of complex interactions and intersections of colonialism, survival, and empowerment. I attempt to address the distinct dilemmas encountered by urban Indigenous peoples in general and subsequently in Albuquerque.

First, we must understand the complexities that urban Indians experience in leaving the reservations to live in a non-Indian urban world. In particular, we must address and understand the unique qualities that make up Indigenous communities and their structures.

HISTORY OF RELOCATION—URBANIZATION

Before contact with the West, Indigenous nations engaged in viable, sustainable cultural, economic, religious, and political systems. Since the late fifteenth century, European imperialism has systematically sought to dismantle Indigenous nations' viable worlds. Colonial expansion, especially as articulated in the nineteenth-century American ideology of Manifest Destiny, put forward the belief that God predestined control of and supremacy over North America for Christian Euro-Americans. This ideology legitimized the purposeful destruction of Indigenous economies to create reliance upon the U.S. government.

American federal policies further impoverished Indigenous lands and usurped Indigenous sovereignty. Federal political, legislative, and judicial governmental branches each participated in this process, placing Indigenous peoples under the State in a position of "pupilage" as "domestic dependent nations."[9] Supreme Court Justice John Marshall stated in his opinion for *Cherokee Nation v. The State of Georgia* that "their relation to the United States resembles that of a ward to his guardian."[10] Thus, the federal government had a responsibility to protect Indigenous lands and resources; this stance further institutionalized colonialism over Indigenous peoples.

This trust responsibility, mostly administered through the Bureau of Indian Affairs under the Department of Interior, has not, however, been carried out with the benevolence implied by Marshall's words. In reality, Indigenous lands, resources, and peoples have been subject to capricious policies, corrupt officials, and rapacious outside interests. After the publication in 1885 of *A Century of Dishonor*, Helen Hunt Jackson's damning account of flawed and corrupt Indian policies, a call for reform caused the Department of Interior to initiate an inquiry.

Little changed, however. By the 1920s, reform was still in order, and Secretary of the Interior Herbert Work commissioned a comprehensive survey of Indian country. On February 21, 1928, the Brookings Institution presented Work with an 872-page report, *The Problem of Indian Administration*. Better known as the Meriam Report after lead investigator Lewis Meriam, the study focused on health, education, general economic conditions, family and community life and the activities of women, migrated Indians, legal aspects of the "Indian problem," and missionary activities among Indians. The Meriam Report was a scathing commentary on the failures of U.S. Indian policy. It illustrated the destructive consequences of American colonization on Indigenous peoples by detailing the impoverished conditions visited by U.S. policy upon most reservations. Adverse health factors included unsanitary conditions, little or no running water, and high rates of mortality, tuberculosis, and trachoma.[11] Economic conditions were no better. On some reservation lands, the federal government still encouraged agriculture as a viable economic venture, although the rest of the nation was moving from agriculture into an industrial economy, and in any case agriculture was not appropriate for most of the reservations. Policies favoring agriculture were unrealistic in many arid environments where water was scarce and irrigation impractical. In addition, much Indigenous land was too remote for wage labor activities and suitable only for grazing. The Bureau of Indian Affairs (BIA) mishandled and manipulated leases to benefit non-Indigenous ranchers instead of individual Indian landholders or tribes. Lack of economic development on the reservations drove many Indigenous people to the cities in hopes of improving their economic prospects.[12]

The Meriam Report addressed the early migration of Indigenous people to the urban environment, where their prospects varied. Some viewed their urban migration as temporary until their tribes' claims were settled before the Indian Claims Commission, or until they secured fees patent to lands from allotments or built enough capital to live on reservation lands.[13] Others considered their move to the city as permanent. They sought economic and educational opportunities rather than a return to reservation life. Many found employment and became permanent urbanites, purchasing homes, developing social circles, and realizing educational opportunities.[14]

In New Mexico, a combination of natural disaster and economic losses on the Diné (Navajo) reservation was the catalyst for the beginning of the federal relocation program. In 1947 and 1948, a severe blizzard hit the Diné in Arizona and New Mexico especially hard.[15] Many lost their livestock leaving them without means of subsistence in an already dire economic environment. The federal government took steps to improve economic conditions with the establishment of a local job placement program. The BIA would relocate mostly male, employable Indians from the Diné reservation to urban areas.

This small program became even more important when, in 1950, Dillon S. Meyer replaced John Nichols as Commissioner of Indian Affairs.[16] Truman's appointment of Meyer came as a surprise, not only to Indigenous nations who were never consulted, but also to the sitting Commissioner John Nichols. Indigenous people, as well as those sympathetic to Indigenous issues, met Meyer's appointment with great opposition. During WWII, Meyer had directed the War Relocation Authority. As director, he was in charge of the forced relocation of thousands of Japanese Americans into internment camps. Ironically, two of the internment camps were located on Indian reservations—the Gila River (about fifty miles southeast of Phoenix, Arizona) and Colorado River (near Poston, Arizona) communities. Meyer was known not to consult Japanese Americans and to discourage cultural activities in the camps.[17]

After the war, non-Indian politicians sought, again, to end the trust relationship. The federal government wanted to withdraw federal services and federal protection from Indian communities under the pretext of "liberat[ing] Indians from their shackles of paternalism and culture."[18] Meyer's appointment indicated a move in that direction.

For U.S. officials, a primary purpose of the "liberation" of Indians was to decrease funding to tribes and thus offset the increasing expense of the Cold War.[19] This liberation of the U.S. government from its trust responsibility to tribes made possible both increased funding for foreign policy initiatives and increased access to natural resources on reservations. In 1952, Meyer, addressing the Western Governors' Conference in Phoenix, Arizona, commented that "in the light of this historical pattern of responsibilities carried by the Bureau of Indian Affairs and the complex problems that have developed, the question which naturally arises is what are the next steps that should be taken looking to the ultimate elimination of the special agency of the Federal Government providing services on a segregated basis for Indians."[20] In 1953, the termination policy was made official with the passage of Concurrent Resolution 108.

The small relocation program of the late 1940s was in a sense the counterpart of the termination policy. The federal government utilized the relocation program and services for the terminated tribal members. Terminated tribal members could "take advantage of relocating on the Vocational Training Program," before their tribe was terminated.[21] After termination they were no longer eligible for services because of the "discontinuance of Federal trust supervision of the tribe . . . and the ending of special Federal service to the tribal members because of their status as Indians."[22] Relocation moved Indigenous people off reservations so that they would merge into urban society, while termination took Indigenous lands out of trust status. If Indians moved away from the reservation, so did their need for federal trust responsibility and federal funding. Thus, relocation would soon join with termination as aspects of the larger federal policy goal of assimilating American Indians by encouraging them to "live like other Americans without federal trust restrictions."[23]

In 1951, Meyer pushed for funding for a program that would encourage and expand the recruitment of American Indians to relocate to cities throughout the United States. The program's first annual budget was slightly more than $500,000. The next year, Congress allocated funds to expand the program.[24] Although he received only part of the funding he had requested, Meyer pressed vocational training and employment assistance as the primary objectives of relocation programs. They were to focus on young, adult Indian males, who usually left families behind until they found jobs and housing.[25] By early 1952, the Chicago and Denver relocation offices had opened and the relocation program had processed 442 applicants for employment in Chicago, Los Angeles, and Denver.[26] By the end of 1953, the program had placed 2,600 Indians in permanent jobs in various cities and had given financial assistance for 650 families with working applicants to move. In 1954, the San Francisco relocation office opened, and the total number of relocatees reached 2,163, including 400 family units and 514 single male and female relocatees. An estimated 6,200 of a possible 245,000 Indians relocated from reservations.[27] By 1956, San Jose, California and St. Louis, Missouri opened relocation offices, and a total of 12,625 Indians from the reservation had gone to the cities under the program.[28]

Approximately 54 percent of Indigenous relocatees came from areas served by the Aberdeen, Billings, and Minneapolis offices, and the remaining 46 percent were processed through the Anadarko, Gallup, Muskogee, and Phoenix areas.[29] The program relocated Indians to twenty states. Los Angeles and Chicago received the largest new Indian populations.[30] In Chicago, relocation workers (similar to War Relocation Authority workers with Japanese Americans during WWII) contacted area employers, such as Carnegie Steel, Mattison Machinery, U.S. Steel, and Linberg Engineering, to encourage them to hire Indians.[31] Some companies showed interest, and relocation officers went to the Great Lakes Consolidated Indian Agency to interview prospective relocatees.[32]

The numbers of applicants continued to increase, and the Bureau soon opened additional offices in Dallas, Cleveland, Oklahoma City, and Tulsa. In response to this promising showing, support increased for vocational training and general services, such as on-the-job apprentice-type training, work training in factories on or near reservations, and instruction in specific occupational areas such as carpentry and plumbing. Direct employment subprograms soon provided urban job information and employment opportunities near reservations,[33] and the federal government began encouraging companies to locate on or near reservations.

Overall, between 1945 and 1957, more than 100,000 Indians left their reservations. Significantly, 75 percent of these did so without government assistance. The federal government portrayed relocation as a "New Deal" for Indians, or what Grant Arndt called an "imagined landscape" of success.[34] Relocation propaganda sold the city environment as an opportunity to improve economic status. The program did not, however, anticipate urban Americans' unwillingness to accept Indigenous people into the melting pot. Despite some of its success on paper, relocation was another colonialist program meant to accompany termination efforts, and thus abrogate government trust responsibilities while providing cheap labor for the post-WWII industrialization of western cities.[35]

This initial wave of the relocation stimulated migration. When American Indians moved to urban settings, they confronted a number of difficulties. For many new relocatees, moving to the city was their first time off the reservation. Once arriving in a designated city by bus, train, or automobile, relocatees found themselves in a strange, large urban setting. Many modern conveniences were new and foreign—stop lights, telephones, clocks, elevators, and public transportation. Regardless of their previous experience, the sheer speed of life in the city was overwhelming.[36] Moreover, what they encountered was far different from the picture presented in BIA propaganda. Other problems compounding the strangeness and unfriendliness of the city included inadequate paychecks, unreliable employers, insufficient transportation, and scarce housing.[37]

Bureau of Indian Affairs officials often placed relocatees in the harshest ghettos in the largest cities. Sometimes they placed entire families in high-rent one-bedroom apartments.[38] When my relatives arrived in Oakland, they were housed in run-down hotels until they could find an apartment.[39]

World War II veterans and others with more experience outside the reservation faced fewer problems than the less educated and experienced. The program provided very little training or orientation about their new home environments. For example, the program offered Alaska Native relocatees a brief tour, gave a few instructions, and then within a week of the relocatees' arrival (two weeks in Seattle), placed them in whatever housing was available.[40] In Los Angeles and Chicago, relocatees were placed in "true slum dwellings," motor courts, and semi-slum areas.[41] Others were just told to show up, placed in housing, given addresses for interviews, and left to find their own way.

As with most federal Indian programs, the work of the relocation program was hampered by chronic funding problems. Employment trends throughout the country also influenced the program. In 1958, Los Angeles field relocation officer George M. Felshaw reported that "there were mass layoffs in the aircraft industry and in all industries allied with aircraft production. As the year progressed, automobile manufacturers and steel producers began cutting payrolls. The competition [for] . . . available jobs became keen."[42] The program began relying on public employment agencies that placed people in seasonal work, the lowest-paying and least secure positions. With low-paying jobs and poor wages, ghettos soon emerged. Many relocated people moved to other cities or back to their reservations.

One strategy to alleviate estrangement in cities was the creation of American Indian centers. Initially, the Indian centers and relocation offices communicated needs and referrals for relocatees. Their informal relationships eventually disintegrated over disputes about federal policy goals.[43] Many of the centers provided counseling, temporary shelters, and other assistance to newly arrived Indigenous people or helped more established residents. Other survival strategies arose through pan-Indian movements and identities or multitribal organizations focused on issues of urban life. The American Indian Movement (AIM), the best known of these organizations, formed in Minneapolis to help urban Indians, and many other groups formed around urban Indian centers.

DILEMMAS—FEDERAL TRUST RESPONSIBILITY, HEALTH, WELFARE

Scholars have written much concerning tribal sovereignty and federal trust responsibilities.[44] Yet many do not seem to acknowledge that when one leaves the reservation, those services afforded on the reservation are no longer available: the federal trust responsibility ceases to exist in its most practical form. As a result of PL 93–580, the American Indian Policy Commission was established and through task forces compelled to study "the legal aspects, policies, and procedures with respect to the relationship between the Federal Government and Indian Tribes, compile data for the understanding of Indian needs, [and] consider of methods to strengthen tribal governments while preserving individual rights."[45] The Commission was required to submit recommendations in a final report to Congress within six months.[46] On August 18, 1975, Task Force No. 8 was "activated" under Section 4(a) of PL 93–580 to conduct a "comprehensive review of the historical and legal development underlying the urban and rural non-reservation Indians relationship. . . ." Task Force No. 8 was charged with conducting a comprehensive appraisal of the historical and legal developments underlying the urban and rural nonreservation Indians' relationship with the federal government.[47]

The report reiterated many known facts, such as the economic factors propelling Indigenous people to urban areas.[48] As with other publications of that time, the Task Force stressed that many urban Indians could not make the necessary transition from reservation to urban life due to limited support from the federal government and indifference and misunderstanding on the part of the communities where Indians chose to live:

> These policies were poorly administered and unsuccessful in attaining their goal. The United States bears some liability for the effect of these policies on Indian people, yet today Indian people who live in cities find it extremely difficult to avail themselves of the minimal federal services they would readily receive on reservations.[49]

The Task Force understood quite clearly that the federal government relinquished responsibility when an Indian left the reservation.

The relocation policy thus created a cultural and legal paradox in which Indians were neither reservation nor urban and neither culturally stable nor assimilated.[50] The final report's findings stated that the federal government simply transferred the crisis from one location to another, from the impoverished and undeveloped reservations to perhaps even worse conditions of the poorest parts of the city.[51] Moreover, the lack of clear service jurisdiction left Indigenous people in urban areas without any access to social services. The Task Force investigation highlighted the difficulties facing urban Indians in 1976; but over thirty years later, many of those same problems have not been addressed, let alone resolved.

To further complicate an ambiguous and complex situation, state and local governments denied or provided only limited services when an Indian arrived.[52] Each believed that the other had the primary responsibility for Indian citizens. Because the Relocation policy was established with the intent of assimilation, federal, state, and local governments never anticipated these social service jurisdictional quandaries. The federal government assumes little or no responsibility once an Indian leaves the reservation, yet the state and local governments believe that the federal government continues its social service jurisdiction over Indians off the reservation.

Health care is a good example of this paradox. Many Indigenous people see federal Indian health care as a right obtained through negotiations, exchange of lands, and the loss of many lives. It also has discernible ties to the federal trust responsibility. The basis for Indian health care is derived from

treaties. The 1921 Snyder Act first authorized health services and appropriations, and the 1955 Transfer Act placed Indian health programs under the
Public Health Service. The 1975 Indian Self-Determination and Education
Assistance Act (PL 93–638), the 1976 Indian Health Care Improvement Act,
and amendments (PL 94–437) further defined federal responsibilities for
health care.[53] More than half of the American Indian population uses the Indian Health Service (IHS).

TABLE 1   Indian Health Service User Population, FY 2003

Area Office	User Population
Tucson	29,879
Nashville	81,992
Billings	60,686
Albuquerque	85,409
Portland	165,670
Bemidji	97,604
California	137,113
Alaska	113,812
Aberdeen	106,995
Phoenix	156,417
Navajo	229,031
Oklahoma City	329,725
IHS Total	1,564,454

Source: Indian Health Service, "Trends in Indian Health 2000–2001: Part 2, Population Statistics" (U.S.
Department of Health and Human Services Indian Health Service Office of Public Health Office of
Program Support Division of Program Statistics, 2004), 1.

The IHS provides two types of health care: direct and contract. Direct
health care includes all health services provided directly by IHS hospitals,
clinics, and health centers. Contract health care refers to services provided
by non-IHS hospitals or other health care institutions that IHS facilities lack,
such as cardiac testing and MRIs. The IHS contracts and pays for these services. For instance, if a patient has a heart attack and needs an arterial balloon
procedure that the IHS facility does not provide, the patient's IHS physician
refers him or her to a non-IHS facility. In order for the IHS to be responsible
for payment, such care must be authorized.[54] Moreover, the patient first must

use all other resources available to pay for care since IHS is the payer of last resort.[55]

For those living on the reservation, IHS health care eligibility is straightforward. Once an Indigenous person leaves the reservation and needs contract services, however, issues of eligibility become almost insurmountably complicated. IHS has specific policies and regulations to determine who is eligible for contract services when off the reservation. While any member of a federally recognized tribe may receive care at an IHS hospital or clinic, those who leave the reservation are no longer eligible. In order to receive contract health service, the patient must show proof of Indian descent, live on or near their own reservation, and/or live within a contract health service delivery area (CHSDA).[56]

After leaving the reservation, potential patients retain six months of contract health eligibility, but once those six months end, the dilemma begins. For example, a Hopi person leaving the reservation to move to Phoenix can use the Phoenix Indian Medical Center (PIMC) or drive four hours back to Hopi to his or her home service unit. A patient whose condition requires treatments unavailable at the IHS facility, however, may not be eligible for contract service. Therefore, the patient must utilize personal health insurance, visit the county hospital, incur all costs at PIMC, or forego medical treatment. A patient who returns to a reservation must wait for the six-months residency requirement to pass. Treatment is even more problematic for a tribal member from a distant reservation—Wisconsin, for example—who lives in the Southwest.

The IHS will pay for emergency services if notified within seventy-two hours of treatment. Since many urban Indigenous people do not have health insurance, or live outside their CHSDA, their primary health care provider has become the emergency room. Moreover, Medicaid has allowed lower-income families, especially those in urban areas, to pay for needed health care.[57] Although Indian health care amendments have provided for the establishment of urban centers to make health centers more accessible to urban Indigenous residents, the decline in appropriations, increased need, and PL 93–638 have limited federal funding for IHS hospitals and urban Indian health centers.

The problems of funding and unmet needs have greatly contributed to a health and welfare crisis in Indian country. According to the U.S. Commission on Civil Rights report, *A Quiet Crisis: Federal Funding and Unmet Needs in Indian Country*,

> After 1985, per capita Native American and general population spending did not increase at the same rates, resulting in a wide gap. The Native American population has grown at a faster rate than the U.S. population as a whole; therefore, overall spending increases have not translated to equivalent per capita spending increases.[58]

In addition, many Indian health centers and programs in cities are losing money because of PL 93–638. The Act authorized the Secretary of Health, Education, and Welfare (now Department of Health and Human Services) to contract out the functions of the IHS to tribal organizations.[59] While many rightly heralded the Self-Determination Act of 1975 as a boost for tribal sovereignty and self-determination, it has begun to hurt urban Indians. Many Indian nations have opted to create their own health clinics, which has meant that large Indian health care facilities are losing funds to tribal health facilities, such as the PIMC, the Albuquerque Indian hospital, and numerous other urban health care centers. Many tribes have elected to exercise their right to run their own clinics and take their allocation of IHS appropriations to create or continue funding their own facilities. Although tribes are looking out for their members on the reservations, a division between urban and reservation results. The problem arises when federal, state, and local government officials erroneously view urban Indian health care as completely covered by the IHS.

PL 93–638 has created a fundamental difficulty: PIMC, for example, is set up to serve reservation Indians, but except for Diné and Tohono O'odham, more than half their clientele are urban Indians.[60] They are not receiving funds for the additional usage, and congressional appropriations have not increased. Because of case overload and the increasing tribal tap on appropriations, services at this facility have declined. The overload caused the PIMC dental clinic to close, and then later it reopened with limited services focused on children aged six years and younger. A similar problem occurred with the dental clinic at the Southwestern Indian Polytechnical Institute (SIPI) in Albuquerque. Set up for the school and surrounding communities, the dental clinic was closed because of the loss of federal appropriations and increased patronage. Although a few tribes in that area, such as Jemez and Isleta, have established their own dental clinics, many tribal people in that region have lost access to dental care. Recent lobbying for increased and continued appropriations provided $1 million for the SIPI dental clinic. Because there are no separate accounts for urban monies, however, the depositing of these earmarked monies into IHS coffers has led to a minor struggle for those funds with other urban health clinics.[61] Only 1 percent of IHS funds go to urban facilities, although recent estimates indicate that more than 60 percent of the Indigenous population is urban.[62] According to Norman Ration, director of the National Indian Youth Council in 2008:

> What we found is that $3 billion are provided to service 1.6 million Native Americans. The thirty-four clinics that are off reservations get only $34 million and typically provide service for 75 percent of Native Americans . . .
>
> This is how we looked at it: on-reservation health care get[s] $2,000 to $3,000 a [person]. For off-reservation, urban, we get $2 a [person]. In Albuquerque, we get $8 and that's because the money that First Nations gets. And if you take that $2,000 that's for on-reservation, [and] you gave everybody that $2,000, we'd need about $14 billion. And then you do the comparison between Indian health care, which is almost at the bottom of the scale, you get $2,000, prisoners get $6,000, . . . people in other . . . health care [systems] get $8,000 per head. . . . [S]o what's wrong with that picture?[63]

EDUCATION

Another issue that arises among Indigenous urban residents is access to adequate education. Many students are involved in the public school system and forced to absorb a curriculum that mostly neglects Indigenous cultures and histories. Indians are often the smallest minorities within student populations.

School locations affect dropout rates, test scores, and overall student success. For many Indigenous urban families, living in poor neighborhoods means attending schools that are poorly funded and staffed, factors that ultimately impact student preparation, achievement, and retention rates. Some urban Indian students fall through the cracks or leave school ill prepared. In many cities, Indian students have high or the highest dropout rates and low or the lowest test scores.

The National Indian Youth Council created an advisory group to address failing academic status, truancy, and homelessness of many Indigenous students.[64] In recent years, Indigenous residents of Albuquerque began to meet with the Albuquerque Public Schools (APS) superintendent and have helped him realize the issues that American Indian students are facing, including that many dropouts leave Albuquerque and go back to school on the reservation. A few recommendations by the 1995 Task Force on Education in Albuquerque suggested increased hiring of Indian counselors and teachers in the APS district.[65]

In other cities, charter schools, such as the Little Red School House and Heart of the Earth in the Minneapolis public school system, combat Indian alienation and dropout rates.[66] In August 2006, a new charter school in Albuquerque, the Native American Community Academy (NACA), was opened to serve the Albuquerque Indigenous population.[67] Principal Kara Bobroff comments, "The lessons at the charter school meet state standards while giving a top priority to the culture and traditions of the students as well as their health."[68] NACA is further discussed in Chapter 3.

WELFARE

In 1996, sweeping welfare reform took place. Temporary Assistance for Needy Families (TANF) replaced Aid to Families with Dependent Children (AFDC), Emergency Assistance (EA), and Job Opportunities and Basic Skills Training (JOBS). Welfare reform was purportedly intended to extricate individuals from welfare by requiring work in exchange for time-limited cash assistance, a requirement that assumes welfare recipients choose not to work, but rather are exploiting the welfare system. By presuming that "marriage is the foundation of a successful society,"[69] the Personal Responsibility and Work Opportunity Reconciliation Act (PRWORA) of 1996 also limited the use of funds to the specific goals of reinforcing and promoting heterosexual marriage and families.

Welfare reform also affects urban Indians and urban migration. Since the passage of PRWORA, more Indians have moved to urban areas to find work. Title I specifically includes Indian people. It requires state TANF programs to include certain mandatory work-, education-, and job-related activities (including job training and job search) for the purpose of moving people off of welfare to self-sufficiency, and it is supposed to provide Indians with equitable access to that assistance.[70] Not only does TANF aim to prevent out-of-wedlock pregnancy and reduction of out-of-wedlock births in the overall U.S. population, but it also sets up broader options for American Indians and Alaskan Natives. The PRWORA also gave "federally recognized tribal nations the authority to design and administer their own TANF programs either individually or as part of a consortium" instead of receiving benefits and services from state TANF programs. Nations also have more flexibility than states in program development in order to meet TANF requirements.[71]

Tribes and Alaskan Native villages with approved TANF plans receive direct funding to operate their own welfare programs with requirements similar to those imposed on state residents, including work requirements and time limits for receipt of welfare-related services for adults living on reservations or in Alaskan native villages.[72] PRWORA also makes available other grants for Indian tribes that conducted JOBS programs in fiscal year 1995 to enable them to make work activities available to tribal members. At the same time, Tribal Job Opportunity and Balanced Budget Basic Skills programs were replaced with the Native Employment Works (NEW) program. The Department of Labor is authorized to provide welfare-to-work funds to states, federally recognized tribes, and local communities.[73]

In running their own programs, Indian nations have the flexibility to delineate their service populations and service areas, job participation rates, and time limits, as well as to define what constitutes a family. Welfare caseloads on many reservations have not decreased,[74] mainly because of the "scarcity of jobs on reservations, [and] the difficulty residents have accessing work supports they need, [such as] . . . job training and child care."[75] Importantly, the scarcity of jobs and inadequate job skills and training force many Native people to urban areas, although this is not always a permanent solution. Emmett Francis, liaison for Indian affairs to Albuquerque Mayor Jim Baca (1997–2001), commented,

> Recently, welfare-to-work requirement [brings Indians to the city] because reservations lack employment. Many reservation Indians are moving to the cities, especially single-parent families. . . . Without economic development, more individuals will come to the cities. Even though they come, they still have trouble making ends meet, with two jobs to pay the rent. It's not always easy to come to the urban areas, [and it is] harder for those that have to come because of welfare-to-work.[76]

American Indians in the urban setting often have limited education and job skills. They are at greater risk than most urban dwellers, and they add to the strain on municipal services. In most cases, cities and Native people need more programs designed specifically for urban Indians.

UNDERCOUNTING IN THE U.S. CENSUS

Related to federal and state appropriations for these and other programs is the problem of undercounting certain populations—typically socioeconomically disadvantaged people—in the U.S. Census. The census undercount affects everyone in the United States, because officials use it to determine, for example, the amounts of congressional appropriations; the scale of social service needs on federal, state, and local levels; and the size of a state's congressional delegation. Undercounting has far-reaching consequences in most minority communities and in poor areas of the country. It affects American Indians on and off reservations in the form of inadequate health care, social service monies, education, and political awareness about Indian people. In the 1990 census, estimated undercount percentages were as follows: Hispanics, 5 percent; African Americans, 4.4 percent; Asians, 2.3 percent; and American Indians, 12.2 percent.[77] In the 1990 census, an estimated 2,550 reservation Indians and 379 other Indians living in Albuquerque were not counted. University of New Mexico Regents' Professor Theodore

Jojola (Isleta Pueblo) stated that 13 percent of American Indians in surrounding reservations and 4 percent in the city of Albuquerque were missed.[78]

Various factors shape the undercount. Among American Indians and other minority groups, language barriers and distrust of the U.S. government (and particularly its use of personal information) can influence the count.[79] Recent attempts to improve the count have involved hiring census workers from underrepresented communities. This measure has helped increase the accuracy of the count and the information gathered from hard-to-reach populations.

Geographic mobility is another reason for the undercounting of Indians. Indian people tend to be mobile, moving not only within cities, but also to and from reservations. This mobility is a major factor in the undercounting of Indians in the Albuquerque area, where numerous reservations surround the city, and Indian people travel back and forth or move from city to city. Homelessness or residence in hotels contributes to the undercounting of Indians on reservations and in cities, especially when American Indians are overrepresented among homeless persons.[80] Further, some Indigenous peoples simply refuse to participate in a governmental project.

Indian people in urban areas face specific issues that are as complex as those on reservations, yet are ignored or unrecognized by federal, state, and local governments. In Albuquerque, officials have only recently begun cultivating a relationship with Indian residents. Although Albuquerque Indians share many of the same challenges that confront urban Indians throughout the United States, their experiences differ from those of Chicago, Los Angeles, and Minneapolis, which have been studied more intensely. Moreover, Albuquerque is unique in the number of Indian nations that surround the city. A recent and tenuous relationship between these nations and the city has created dynamics specific to Albuquerque. The numbers of Pueblo nations around Albuquerque, moreover, have shaped the social and political dynamic of the Albuquerque Indian community and its relationship with the city government.

TWO

Paak'u, Alburquerque[1], Albuquerque

THE POLITICS OF SETTLEMENTS

WHEN DRIVING FROM THE WEST on Interstate 40, you know immediately when you cross the New Mexico state line. The border is littered with signs proclaiming, "See a Real Buffalo" and "Indian Jewelry Wholesale." There is a large tipi shop with a fort that holds "real" buffalo, and statues—a bear, an elk, and an eagle—perched on the rugged cliffs nearby. Rampant commercialism seeks to exploit the fact that Indigenous people have been here for centuries. And Indigenous peoples persist here, living in the hogans seen in the distance. On the horizon, you can see Mt. Taylor, an old volcano that has left evidence of its ancient eruptions across the flatlands. Its sacred status has not changed over time: Diné, Lagunas, and Acomas still revere it.

From the highway you can see distant rock hills among the juniper, cedar, and piñon trees. As you continue eastward, Acoma's Sky City Casino looms close to the road on your left, followed by Laguna's Dancing Eagle Casino on your right. In the midst of this modern economic growth of casinos, gas stations, and convenience stores, exists the oldest inhabited city in the country, Acoma's Sky City.[2] The interstate then takes you near the Pueblo of Laguna, with its six villages right off the Rio Puerco and the To'hajiilee turnoff. From there, you pass through Sandoval County and then Bernalillo County, coming quickly upon Nine Mile Hill. What was the site of once numerous Pueblo villages is now a city that boasts a population of more than half a million. The largest city in New Mexico, Albuquerque sits at the crossroads of Interstates 40 and 25, accessible from the four directions—east, north, west, and south.

Centuries before I-40 and I-25 became major highways, the Indigenous people of these lands traveled these routes. The Anasazi, ancestors of the Pueblo peoples, followed these roadways as far as South America for trade with numerous Indigenous peoples. Later, Diné, Pueblo, Apache, and other Indigenous peoples used these familiar pathways in economic, political, and social pursuits. The petroglyphs near the roadways further illustrate inhabitance by Indigenous peoples and their sacred relationship to the area.

In the more recent past, European invaders entered the area from the four directions. Seeking gold, glory, and god, the Spanish traveled the Camino Real from Mexico to Santa Fe. The Santa Fe Trail brought easterners to the west, eager Anglos entering "new territory," later citing Manifest Destiny as their justification to take Indigenous lands and seek a share of the American Dream through trade.

With its beautiful red rock, mountains, river valleys, and flat lands of the south, New Mexico became known as "the Land of Enchantment" by the turn of the twentieth century, before it became a state. It has since acquired the moniker "the tri-cultural state," a reference to the Indigenous, Spanish, and Anglo cultures represented there. Although recently a growing African-American population has contested the tri-cultural classification, the term also is misleading because it implies that all three cultures are equally recognized in state and local affairs.

In actuality, mapped against the lava rocks, mountains, and metropolitan sprawl is another landscape, one in which the city of Albuquerque constitutes the nexus of an intersection of peoples, politics, and cultures. These formations—not of sandstone or lava, but of racial ideologies and power—continue to shape Indian interactions with non-Indians, the city, and the state. These formations, a legacy of multiple colonizations, manifest themselves even today in Albuquerque's spatial organization and political struggles and alliances.

To understand the experiences of Indians in Albuquerque, we must first understand the formation of Albuquerque as a racialized and politicized urban space. Traditional histories of Albuquerque rely on records of the conquistadors, soldiers, and missions. To truly understand Albuquerque as a dynamic landscape, however, one must see it from perspectives of those who interacted with the landscape well before the arrival of Europeans. I begin this chapter, therefore, from the ground up, providing an overview of the various communities that occupied this landscape and ultimately renamed it: from Indigenous origins to Spanish domination, Mexican possession, and U.S. imperialism. Through all these political shifts, Indigenous peoples are a constant presence as sources of conflict, labor, and resources, integrated constantly into local, state, and national economies. I seek to counter the dominant historical narratives that suggest that Indigenous peoples were "passive onlookers to progress" by demonstrating how they have sought actively to shape and negotiate changes throughout the course of their colonization. I conclude this chapter with a discussion of how Albuquerque's industrial economy and demography have shifted from the 1940s and into the Cold War with the advent of nuclear testing and technologies, and the effects on the nearby Indian communities and the Indians residing in Albuquerque.[3]

PAAK'U

Many Indigenous nations populated the New Mexico region long before the arrival of Spaniards, Mexicans, and finally, Americans. Oral histories and other traditions acknowledge Indigenous ancestors' origins and settlement. According to the Pueblos, Apaches, and Diné, their ancestors arrived millennia ago from underground worlds. These lands are their origins, and each nation's oral traditions designate specific geographic areas that hold religious, social, and cultural importance. This sacred connection and the responsibility to these lands are critical to understanding how Indigenous peoples have responded to invasion and occupation. Although these lands have been occupied, exploited, and commercialized, such connections continue to have relevance and importance in contemporary Indigenous societies.

Just as many Indigenous people have been disconnected from their lands, colonial forces have also disconnected Indigenous people from much of their traditional histories by largely ignoring or negating them in the colonial historical record. Therefore, I privilege scholarship that has documented histories of Indigenous peoples as preserved by their own communities. This overview of the Indigenous nations who inhabited and cultivated the area that is now known as Albuquerque reflects these voices and silences.

Like all Native peoples, the Pueblos have complex social, political, and religious lives. Religion remains at the core of their universe and their social and political lives are interconnected and highly spiritual, not separated from religion. Religious beliefs have greatly influenced the political realm in that many political leaders are involved in some aspect of religious leadership. The invasion of Spanish Catholicism and eventually, the American system, forced many changes, but adherence to their cultures and syncretism with outside practices have allowed the Pueblo peoples to survive.

Pueblo people entered this world at a place called Shipapu from the underground via a lake. Led from place to place, they eventually settled in what is now known as the Four Corners area.[4] The Great Spirit came with them at the time of their emergence and taught them the culture of their daily lives during their travels.

All Pueblo peoples have similar origin stories, though they vary somewhat, illustrating the uniqueness of each group. Laura Bayer with Floyd Montoya and the Pueblo of Santa Ana, in their book *Santa Ana: The People, the Pueblo, and the History of Tamaya* tell of the Hanu (the People) who emerged from Shipapu, northwest of where Tamaya is now located.[5] They saw that this world was abundant, and they set out on their journey traveling south to Kashe K'atreti (White House). Settling there, they established the foundations of their political and social lives, creating a governing system headed by the Tiyamune (leader) who governed the people. He appointed the Mase'ewi (war chief) and U'uye'ewi (assistant war chief) for religious ceremonies and religious life.[6] There they resided before journeying to the east side of the Sandia Mountains.[7] The group split, one group staying and founding the village of Paak'u and the other traveling west and then south before returning to Paak'u. They met with other Pueblos: the Acume (Acoma People), the Tsiiya (Zia), the Kwiisti (Laguna-Paguate),[8] and the Hemishiitse (Jemez).

After their journeys, the Pueblo people became more sedentary and agricultural, growing corn, beans, and squash, and gathering various other plants, while also hunting deer and smaller animals. The people of Paak'u prospered from the numerous resources of the mountains and the Río Grande Valley and the crops they grew in the region from Corrales to Angostura (Bernalillo).[9] When the Tamayame (Santa Ana people) reunited, their settlements of six or more villages stretched from modern-day Albuquerque to Angostura along the Río Grande. Eventually, the Tamayame founded the Kwitste Haa Tamaya village west of Bernalillo, where they are now located.[10] Living in separate villages, each Pueblo speaks a different dialect of five distinct languages (Table 2), but their worldviews and economic systems are similar.

TABLE 2   Language Groups and Pueblos in New Mexico

Keres	Acoma, Cochiti, Laguna, San Felipe, Santa Ana, Kewa (formerly Santo Domingo), Zia
Towa	Jemez
Tewa	Nambé, Pojoaque, San Ildelfonso, Ohkay Owinghe (formerly San Juan), Santa Clara, Tesuque
Tiwa	Isleta, Picuris, Sandia, Taos
Zuñian	Zuñi

Source: Marc Simmons, *New Mexico: An Interpretive History* (Albuquerque: University of New Mexico Press, 1988), 46; Bertha P. Dutton, *American Indians of the Southwest* (Albuquerque: University of New Mexico Press, 1983), 15–16.

Later, the Paak'u region was occupied by Tiwa people and eventually, by Spanish and American Albuquerqueans.[11] Contact with Europeans changed the number of Pueblo villages and some of their locations. Eventually, smaller Pueblo groups joined larger villages, creating the modern-day nineteen Pueblos.[12] Each Pueblo governs itself as a sovereign people and nation. Today, most of the Pueblo Indians of New Mexico live along the Rio Grande.

The Pueblos also interacted with other Indigenous nations that thrived in the southwestern United States, including the Diné and the Jicarilla and Mescalero Apaches. Their social and economic relationships involved various geographic areas including the Albuquerque region. The Diné live in the

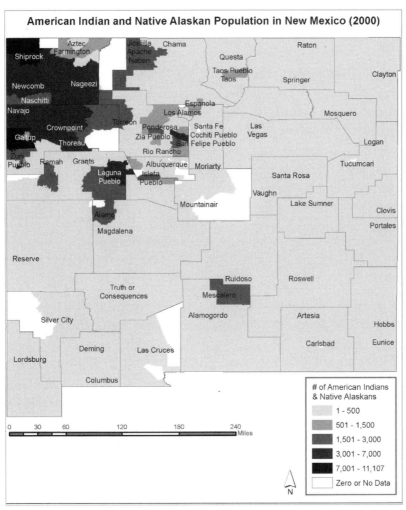

Map 2 **American Indian population in New Mexico.** (Based on 2000 U.S. Census data. Courtesy of Nandhini Gulasingam, Chicago, IL, April 2010.)

Four Corners region, northeast of the Pueblos. The Diné entered this region through four worlds. In what today is called North America exists the fourth world where First Man and First Woman formed the four sacred mountains. First Man and First Woman discovered Changing Woman. After she matured, she bore twin boys with Sun. These twins are known as Monster

Slayer and Child Born of Water. Eventually, four clans were created, and the holy people designated a home for the Diné within the area surrounded by the four sacred mountains.[13]

In the Four Corners region with its varied environment, the Diné hunted large and small animals, gathered numerous plants, and participated in certain agricultural pursuits. They lived in separate small communities or families in a matrilineal society. The Navajos' interaction with the Pueblos was marked by tensions, for the Navajos at times raided their Pueblo neighbors to the south. Their continued interactions also influenced the practices of each group.

The Mescalero Apaches lived in southern New Mexico and northern Mexico. They attribute their origins to the "Killer of Enemies," who placed them in the "vicinity of White Mountain," the twelve thousand foot mountain now called the Sierra Blanca. Their vast homeland encompassed the Sacramento and Guadalupe Mountains on the southern New Mexico-Texas state line and the Davis Mountains in the Big Bend of the Rio Grande in southwestern Texas and northern Mexico.[14] The name *Mescalero* comes from a Spanish word meaning mescal-makers. It refers to their use of the mescal plant, a large agave with thick, fleshy, green leaves armed with flesh-tearing spikes.[15] The Mescalero Apaches survived by hunting and by gathering berries, nuts, and plants. They lived in small groups with organized social and political systems and strong religious convictions.

My people, the Jicarilla Apaches, occupied northeastern New Mexico, southern Colorado, and the easternmost sections of Oklahoma and Texas. Our origin narratives describe us as emerging from our underground world to a place near the center of the earth. That center, in today's geographic terms, is surrounded by four rivers. The Jicarilla Apache author Veronica Velarde Tiller describes the area as "bordered by the Arkansas River in Southeastern Colorado, the northeastern plains region drained by the tributaries of the Canadian River, the flat lands of the Pecos River Valley and the area northwest to the Rio Grande in the Chama River Valley of New Mexico."[16] Living in a "dual-band system," the Jicarillas occupied the mountainous regions of northern New Mexico and southern Colorado and the western plains of Texas and Oklahoma. In 1700, Spaniards classified the two bands as Apaches of Xicarillas—later to be known as the Jicarilla Apaches. The Jicarillas had relationships with the Comanches and northern Pueblos. Before and after the Pueblo Revolt of 1680, some northern Pueblo people sought refuge with the Jicarillas. They still maintain this relationship, especially with the Taos and Picuris Pueblos, attending each other's feast days and foot races.[17]

Indigenous nations of New Mexico had varied economies based on their regions and relationships with one another. The Apaches and Diné, for example, established camps according to the seasons and the climate. This transhumance practice allowed communities to use a variety of foods for subsistence. Groups followed a pattern of movement to the mountains in the spring and to lower areas in the winter. This practice also protected each environment from overuse. In contrast to the Apache and Diné pattern, the Pueblo people lived in permanent villages, which Spanish colonists termed "Pueblos" (towns). The Pueblo lifestyles reflected cultures that could support larger populations.

These varied Indigenous peoples interacted in diverse ways. Some sustained harmonious relationships, while others' interactions were marked by conflict. The common interaction, however, was trade. All the Indigenous communities of the region were connected by an intricate network of trade routes. As historian Marc Simmons writes, "Albuquerque is situated roughly in the center of this old native kingdom. . . ."[18]

ALBU*R*QUERQUE

Indigenous interactions would change dramatically during Spanish colonization. The wealth of the Aztec people inspired Spaniards to imagine similar riches among the communities of the Southwest. Stories of treasure motivated searches for the Seven Cities of Cíbola and Gran Quivira. Among the first Spaniards to reach this region was Fray Marcos de Niza. His travel guide and companion, Esteban, a black Moroccan slave from Azamore, was one of four survivors of a failed attempt to settle Florida in 1528.[19] Those survivors traversed what is now Texas to the Rio Grande, and then on to present Chihuahua, Mexico, on an eight-year journey. They told stories of riches to be found at the mysterious seven golden cities of Cíbola, and Spanish colonists, desperate to find another gold or silver mine, blindly believed them.[20]

In March 1539, Esteban guided Fray Marcos de Niza and a small party that included Native guides into their "New World" of possibilities. At a place called Vacapa, de Niza stopped and sent Esteban with the guides to seek treasure. Esteban, instead, found Hawikuh, a Zuni village that denied him entrance.[21] Various stories exist about the death of Esteban, but as Joe Sando informs us, Esteban insulted the Zunis by introducing himself through a "colorful calabash (rattle) with some rows of feathers, on red and on white."[22] The Zunis rejected the gift and ordered him not to enter their town. Esteban again insulted the people at Hawikuh by demanding gifts and women. He told them that he arrived in advance of a larger party, and the Zunis killed him to protect their location and themselves. The Pueblos say, "The first white man our people saw was a black man."[23]

This first interaction between Spanish explorers and Zunis foreshadowed subsequent interactions between Spaniards and Indigenous people in Albuquerque and surrounding areas. De Niza reported Esteban's death to Viceroy Mendoza and also reported his sighting of Hawikuh, which he called Cíbola, a large city, and presumably one of the fabled seven golden cities. This story inspired another Spanish expedition to the region. In the late summer of 1540, Francisco Vásquez de Coronado's expedition, consisting of hundreds of men, horses, and a few Franciscan priests, searched for the Cíbola and for the Gran Quivira.[24] Their exploration for riches took them on well-established Native roads to the Tiguex region, where Spaniards had their first contact with the Pueblos in the area that would eventually become Albuquerque. Coronado observed that the people were more "intent on farming than war."[25] In this first encounter, the Tiwa Pueblo people gave gifts of food, blankets, and skins, and received some small articles in return.[26]

The conquistadors were not well prepared for the winter. As they experienced the harshness of the season, they quickly violated Pueblo trust and hospitality with continuous demands for food, shelter, blankets, and women. Eventually, they overran Kuava Pueblo, at the site of the present town of Bernalillo. Pueblo people fled in protest to other Pueblo villages, leaving their village to the Spaniards in the dead of winter. Soon the Spaniards inflamed their anger further by demanding more supplies. The Tiwas fought back by attacking a guard detail and taking the Spaniards' animals. The Spaniards retaliated by attacking another Pueblo village, Arenal, burning captives at the stake.[27] They continued their rampage by sacking another

Pueblo and then waited out the winter at Alconfor Pueblo. After searching for Gran Quivira in present-day Kansas, the Spaniards finally left for home in the spring.[28]

The events of this first year of contact had long-lasting consequences in the area. They gave Indian inhabitants a view of things to come: more exploration and settlement, exploitative and colonizing attitudes toward the Pueblos and other Indigenous inhabitants, and eventually, the rise of the largest city in New Mexico: Alburquerque, founded under the Spanish Crown.

The initial failure to find gold did not halt invasions by Franciscan friars and conquistadors, who wreaked havoc on Indigenous life. In 1598, Juan de Oñate created the first permanent Spanish settlement in New Mexico right across the river from Oke Owinge, or San Juan Pueblo.[29] Thus began the Spanish use of colonial settlements to exploit Indigenous homelands and peoples. Oñate immediately established a new Spanish colony, awarded noble titles and imposed a new political and social order involving exploitative systems that taxed Pueblo goods, labor, and lives.[30] Titled Spaniards participated in the subjugation of Indigenous peoples through the *encomienda* and *repartimiento* systems.

The *encomienda* system meant that Spaniards awarded titles required heads of Indian households to pay yearly tributes in corn and blankets.[31] The repartimiento system forced Pueblos to till Spanish fields and tend Spanish livestock. Spanish landowners would apply to the governor for a body of laborers, and then the governor would establish a levy of as many as a hundred Native people from a nearby Pueblo.[32] Although landowners were supposed to pay workers daily wages and rations, many refused to pay wages, withheld rations, and increased work hours illegally.

Within the colonial system, Pueblo people had no recourse. Franciscan priests, moreover, used them to further missionary endeavors by forcing Pueblo laborers to build churches, furnish food and supplies, and proselytize "heathen" Pueblo people.[33]

The violent relations that Spaniards maintained with Indigenous people of New Mexico are reflected in a stark difference in perceptions of Oñate today. Some contemporary Hispanos claim Spanish "blood" to identify with a Spanish colonial past and claim a connection to a land and history based on colonial conquest. Claims to Spanish blood are "a convenient tool for fashioning and deploying collective memory."[34] Thus, people of Hispanic origin admire Oñate as the founder of New Mexico. Pueblo people, however, see Oñate as a symbol of Spanish colonization and brutality toward Indigenous people.

The history of colonization still informs relations between Indian people and Hispano and Anglo populations in New Mexico. One example of Spanish brutality that is still recalled nearly four hundred years later occurred during Oñate's raid on Acoma Pueblo in early 1599. The Acomas had killed Oñate's nephew, Juan de Zaldívar, when his troops attacked them, demanding food and clothing. In retaliation, Oñate's forces attacked the Pueblo. After killing hundreds of resisters, taking captives, and leveling the Pueblo, the Spaniards punished the Acoma people in February 1599 by cutting off the right foot of all men aged twenty-five and older and sentencing them to twenty years of servitude.[35] They placed remaining males between twelve and twenty-five and all adult women into servitude, and apportioned out the children to monasteries.[36] They even punished two men from Hopi who happened to be visiting Acoma, by chopping off one hand each and sending them home as an example to the other Pueblo peoples.

The historical record, passed down orally, recalls the brutality of the Spanish leader and settlers, as well as of Catholicism. This legacy exploded in January 1998, when a bronze statue of Oñate was found minus the right foot north of Española. While the perpetrators remain unknown, it is clear that the historical memories of Spanish and Indigenous peoples differ, setting the stage for continued divergent viewpoints.

By the mid-1600s, the European competition for empire had planted the oppressive seeds of Spanish government and culture in Pueblo lives. The Franciscans had also made some headway in their missionary and conversion efforts, for they boasted about thousands of baptisms. The conversions for the most part proved to be illusory: Pueblo residents had grown tired of the brutality, levies, and ongoing attempts at religious conversion, so they feigned compliance. In reality, Pueblo religion was completely intertwined with Pueblo life. Every aspect of existence was infused with the sacred, from the food they ate to their ceremonies centered on tradition and belief, and on keeping a balance with their environment.[37] For many Pueblo leaders and community members, the destruction of the kivas and the Franciscan insistence upon replacing their Pueblo religion with a foreign system were intolerable.

Oñate's brutal attack on Acoma together with other incidents throughout the seventeenth century fueled the 1680 Pueblo Revolt. The revolt is significant because it illustrates the continued resistance on the part of many Indigenous peoples to the onslaught of brutal colonization. For Indians in New Mexico, the revolt remains a hallmark of cultural survival and persistence, as well as a symbol of the continued need to fight against the oppression that would take various forms over the next four hundred years.

Many of the Pueblo people understood that the only way to return to their grandfathers' way of life was to rid themselves of the Spaniards. The difficulty was that some of the Pueblo people had positioned themselves with the Spaniards and some had converted to Catholicism.[38] At this time, a Pueblo war captain named Popé, who showed the qualities of a strong leader—compassion, respect, cultural and religious convictions, wisdom, and strength for his people—emerged to lead a revolt against the colonists.[39] Raised in the Ohkay Owingeh (San Juan) culture, he practiced the religious and cultural beliefs that the Spaniards were trying to destroy.[40] Understanding the challenges confronting them, he planned with other Pueblo leaders, including Luis Tupatú of Picuris and Catití of Santo Domingo, to rid their lands of their unwelcome guests. In meetings held at night in secrecy, the northern Tewas invited southern Tiwan leaders from Tuei (Isleta) and Keresan leaders from Tamaya (Santa Ana) and Tsia (Zia) to join them. Together, the leaders came to the same conclusion: they would have to resort to war to gain their freedom. Under Popé's leadership, the confederacy devised the first successful American revolution, involving an intricate system of covert communication among the Pueblos.[41]

As rumors of the uprising began to spread, converted Indians and Pueblo leaders sympathetic to Spanish rule began warning of the revolt. Fray Fernando de Velasco, the pastor from Pecos, was informed of messengers meeting with war chief Diego Umbiro.[42] He, as well as Galisteo and Taos officials, notified Governor Otermín of this activity. When the governor sent soldiers to investigate and arrest the young messengers, many Pueblo people were further enraged.[43] On August 10, 1680, the Pueblo Revolt against the Spaniards commenced.[44] Leaders targeted the clergy in particular for persistent persecution of the Pueblo religion, brutality toward Pueblo people, and exploitation of Pueblo people and resources. A Tetsugeh pastor, Padre Pio, returned to hold mass and found the village deserted. When he found the villagers hiding and armed in the nearby hills, he was killed.[45] The revolt spread as planned. Tewa people gathered at Ka-'p-geh (Santa Clara) and at Tetsugeh they joined the fight, as did people from Walatowa (Jemez).[46]

Indian leaders ordered the Spaniards to leave and executed the priests who refused. Spanish settlers in the north learned of the revolt and made their escape to Santa Fe or Mexico. Pueblo warriors from Taos to Isleta raided and destroyed Spanish settlements and expelled the settlers.[47] Although many settlers escaped south to El Paso, many others fled to northern towns such as Santa Fe and took refuge in the capital with the colonial governor Otermín. Neighboring tribes led by Juan El Tano invaded the capital. They surrounded the Plaza and cut off water and supplies.[48] Again, Pueblo leaders told the Spaniards to leave or be killed. Choosing to fight, Otermín attacked, initially with some success, but the arrival of Pueblo reinforcements from Teotho (Taos) and We-lai (Picuris) and Keresans led by Alonzo Catití of Santo Domingo doomed his resistance.[49] An all-out Spanish charge caught the Pueblos off guard, however, allowing Otermín and his group to abandon Santa Fe and leave the territory.[50] Watching the Spanish exodus, the Pueblos gave thanks to the Great Spirit and performed such ceremonies as the Bow and Arrow Dance to honor those warriors who returned and those who did not. In many of the Pueblos today, that dance is still held.[51]

The Pueblos enjoyed slightly more than a decade of freedom from Spanish colonization. Then in 1693, the "reconquista" led by Don Diego de Vargas began. As de Vargas reoccupied New Mexico for the Spanish Crown and traveled to the new capital of Santa Fe, a group of people accompanying him asked permission to stay and settle the Middle Valley. With permission granted, they chose to settle in the area south of Sandia and Alameda Pueblos to the present Isleta Pueblo boundary. Eventually, the Middle Valley contained about forty-five estates. Alburquerque, founded in 1702, became a municipality in 1706, one of several new settlements on land that the Spaniards had abandoned during the 1680 Pueblo Revolt and had reapportioned later as land grants. On February 7, 1706, the governor of the province of New Mexico designated an elevated spot near the Rio Grande and located on the Camino Real between Mexico City and Santa Fe as Villa de Albu*r*querque in honor of the viceroy of New Spain, Fernández de la Cueva Enríques, Duke of Alburquerque.[52] By 1784, the Albu*r*querque census listed 1,784 male and 2,031 female Spaniards, 296 male and 307 female Indians, three ministers, and two ministers of the royal treasury.[53] For the Indigenous peoples surrounding Albu*r*querque, this growing municipality already symbolized Spanish dominance over their land and continuing conflict over religious beliefs and practices. The town was only one more reminder of the foreigners, and the violence that accompanied their presence. As Indigenous lands became the site of conflicts and marked by ever narrower political boundaries, this violence would continue to shape Indigenous lives and interactions.

The Mexican Revolution appeared at first glance to be a revolution for Indians as well, but the transfer of power did not return sovereignty to Indian inhabitants of the Spanish colony, even though it asserted their rights. Mexico gained its independence from Spain on September 27, 1821, and the New Mexico territory became a province of Mexico. The Mexican revolutionary forces stated that "all inhabitants of new Spain without distinction, whether Europeans, Africans, or Indians, are citizens of this Monarchy, with the right to be employed in any post according to their merit and virtues. . . . [T]he person and property of every citizen will be respected and protected by law."[54] Indigenous autonomy under the Mexican monarchy was short-lived, however. Although the revolution resulted in liberalization of Mexican landholdings, government, and trade, it also opened the region to U.S. acquisitiveness. The Santa Fe Trail was a major trade avenue, and Americans sought it for purposes of nation-building. In 1846, during the war with Mexico, U.S. General Stephen Watts Kearny took possession of Santa Fe. On February 2, 1848, the Treaty of Guadalupe Hildalgo ended the war, and Mexico ceded the areas then known as New Mexico and upper California to the United States. Although not so dramatic for Pueblo people as the first encounters with Spaniards or as Diego de Vargas's "reconquista," Kearney's quiet "possession" of Santa Fe had lasting consequences.[55]

Fig. 3 **An Indian enclave in Albuquerque, 1912.** (Courtesy of Still Picture Records Section, Special Media Archives Services Division, National Archives at College Park, MD. Record Group 95: Records of the Forest Service, 1870–2008.)

ALBUQUERQUE

For many years, La Villa de San Felipe de Alburquerque had remained small, its residents living in isolated farms and ranches scattered from Bernalillo to Isleta. Between 1846 and 1867 under the American occupation, Albuquerque's economy became dependent on the army post on the west side, or the "plaza across Main Street"—the street now known as Rio Grande Boulevard.[56] As the population grew and more Americans arrived, about sixteen small Hispanic towns formed early Albuquerque.[57] The changes from Spanish to Mexican to American colonialism had little practical effect on the Indian population. The Mexicans had not challenged the Spanish claims upon Indian land, and the U.S. government claimed that it would recognize private claims established under the Spanish and Mexican governments. Even though this may not always have held true in practice, the lack of acknowledgment of Indigenous claims demonstrates that Indians were not considered full participants and that their systems of governance were not recognized.

The nineteenth century altered the landscape of New Mexico dramatically for the Indian population, through continued colonization partnered with developing technology that increasingly compressed space and time. In the 1860s, Congress approved a charter for the Atlantic and Pacific Railroad Company, allowing the construction of a transcontinental line from Springfield, Missouri, to San Francisco, California. The news of a transcontinental line was exciting in itself, but the line's route along the 35th parallel exhilarated Albuquerque citizens. On April 5, 1880, the Atchison, Topeka, and Santa Fe railroad came to Albuquerque.[58] Its arrival brought new industry and a new vitality to Albuquerque.

The railroad, moreover, brought significant changes in the racial and political dynamics of the city. Afraid that it might hurt their mercantile enterprises, some traditional Hispano businessmen had opposed it. Newspaper columnists tried to address their qualms, and financial returns eased some of their doubts.[59] Unforeseen, however, was the railroad as a death knell for Hispanic hegemony.[60] The new influx of U.S. citizens now began to overwhelm Spanish rule and culture.

The influx of Americans created a power dynamic that continues to pervade New Mexican politics, economy, and society, and particularly that of Albuquerque. The Spanish created a political and economic hierarchy in which European (white) elites held power over the poorer Mexican (mestizo) and Indigenous populations. Maintaining *Spanish* identity became even more important with the Anglo-American incursion in order to maintain their social, economic, and political standing. According to historian John Nieto-Phillips, "at the dawn of the 20th century, Nuevomexicanos were painfully aware that their racial identity mattered[,] particularly if they wished to enjoy social and civic equality with Anglo Americans."[61]

After 1848, powerful intersections of race and class allowed the Anglo and Spanish elites to consolidate their hold on power, as wealthy Anglos married into upper-class Spanish families. United by marriage, Hispanic and Anglo elites influenced the administration of an Albuquerque that was no longer Spanish.

Class could not transcend the differences of culture, however, and the city's social geography shifted to reflect this growing reality. Anglos developed a new Albuquerque, originally called New Town, located toward the Sandia Mountains and east of the railroad tracks. The Old Town, the site of the railroad depot and the center of Spanish Alburquerque, began losing its political and social influence. Protestants established themselves in New Town, leaving Old Town to Catholicism.[62] Soon, New Albuquerque exceeded Old Town's population and significance.[63]

In line with Spanish views of Indians, many of the Albuquerque newcomers saw Hispano culture as backward and alien. The two towns eventually experienced a great divide, politically and culturally, as more the affluent Spanish businessmen made their way into Anglo society.[64] A working class also formed, mostly comprised of Pueblos, Navajos, and some Apaches, especially those associated with the tourism brought in by the railroad or with a boarding school founded near Albuquerque in 1881. These new class dynamics ultimately played a role in Albuquerque's political system and the city's relationship with Albuquerque urban Indians.

As much as the new economy affected Albuquerque, it also affected Native people. Besides trade goods, the railroad brought passengers traveling west to Arizona, Nevada, and California. As it stopped to load and unload on the Laguna Pueblo reservation, Laguna and Acoma potters sold to passengers. Thus, by producing and selling crafts, Native people began participating in a wage-based economy.

For Lagunas, the railroad furnished a unique opportunity to participate in construction and operations. In the 1880s, the Atlantic and Pacific railroads began laying track south of Albuquerque westward through the Laguna Pueblo reservation. Laguna officials first put a stop to the construction and then set a precedent by striking a "gentlemen's agreement of friendship" with the railroad company.[65] The Lagunas refused a lump sum payment as compensation for right-of-way-passage through the reservation[66] and instead, struck a verbal agreement, renewed yearly, allowing the A&P railroad, and later, the Atchison, Topeka and Santa Fe railroad, to pass unfettered through the Laguna reservation. In exchange, the railroad company employed as many Lagunas as desired to work to build and maintain the system, "so long as the governor of their Pueblo granted the workers his approval."[67] Laguna leaders also requested that the railroad provide living accommodations on railroad premises for the Laguna workers.[68]

The agreement introduced many Lagunas into the wage economy but also took them off the reservation. While many Lagunas laid track and returned home, others began moving to cities along the route, such as Gallup, New Mexico; Winslow and Holbrook, Arizona; and Barstow, Richmond, and Los Angeles, California.[69] The Atchison, Topeka and Santa Fe Railway company employed many Laguna men and women while continuing to renew their informal agreement, or, as it was termed, "watering the flower."[70] Kurt Peters's study of the Richmond, California, Laguna colony illustrates the importance of the colonies that were created.[71] The precedent of the colonies eventually reached the Albuquerque urban Indian community and informed the creation of a Laguna colony in Albuquerque.

As the railroad was infusing the Indian world with American culture through tourism and wage labor, boarding schools were doing the same. In 1878, Major B. M. Thomas, the U.S. Indian agent of the Pueblo agency at Santa Fe, proposed the establishment of a central Indian school in New Mexico. Albuquerque was chosen because its location in the "heart of Indian country" allowed easy access to Pueblos, Apaches, Utes, and Navajos.[72] Given the authority to find a site and erect a school, Thomas received an offer from the Catholic mission of twenty acres three miles from Albuquerque. The offer came with the condition that the school be administered under the immediate management of the archbishop of the New Mexico territory.[73] The federal government declined the offer because of the condition and the small size of this tract of land. Another site, a 160-acre lease on San Felipe Pueblo, also was rejected. Thomas then asked the people of Albuquerque to donate suitable land to establish an Indian training school.[74] Some Albuquerque citizens saw the potential economic benefit of an Indian school, whereas others considered Indians uncivilized and barbaric, and did not want them in town.[75]

On January 1, 1881, Reverend Sheldon Jackson established the U.S. Indian Training School, later renamed Albuquerque Indian School, in Duranes under contract with the Home Mission of Presbyterian Church. Only fifty students could be taught in this small facility.[76] By October 1882, Albuquerque citizens, mostly prosperous businessmen, including Franz Huning, F. H. Kent, E. S. Stover, and Santiago Baca, raised $4,500 to buy sixty-two acres of land to donate to the Department of Interior for the permanent con-

Fig. 4 **Pueblo tribal members visiting officials of the Albuquerque Indian School, ca. 1912.** (Courtesy of National Archives, Rocky Mountain Region, Denver CO, Record Group 75: Records of the Bureau of Indian Affairs, 1793–1999.)

struction of the Albuquerque Indian School.[77] The Presbyterians contracted with the Interior Department to open the school in the fall and operate it until the government could take over. They constructed new buildings that accommodated 150 students.[78] Most students came from the nineteen Pueblos of New Mexico, but Navajos and Mescalero Apaches also enrolled. Not all the Pueblos accepted the boarding school. Santo Domingo and Jemez refused to send students. Reports of illness and death at the school also made many parents resist sending their children to this new institution.[79]

Like many other boarding schools of the time, the Albuquerque Indian School focused on assimilation. The curriculum was designed to transform Indigenous people into American citizens and ideally, to assimilate them into white society. To do so, school officials insisted on changes to student names and physical appearances. The teachers enforced a militaristic dress code and strict hygiene involving cleanliness of the body and clothing. They compelled the children to speak only English and to receive religious education centered on Christian values and morals. As Pablo Mitchell noted in his book *Coyote Nation*, "[O]ne of the main goals of the classroom . . . was to clearly differentiate whiteness from Indian-ness. This racialization centered on the careful monitoring and reforming the bodies of Indian children."[80] As an industrial institution, the school sought to teach students to compete with whites for economic survival. The location of the school, however, was an important impediment to assimilation, because the students were close enough to their reservations to return home for two-month summer breaks.[81]

The boarding school era attempted to eradicate Indigenous cultures, to "kill the Indian in him, to save the man."[82] Some students went to school, lost their cultures, and never went back to their tribal communities. Other boarding school survivors went home and tried to erase the schooling. Still other individuals found the experience difficult but at times enjoyable and tried to find ways to utilize their education. For example, Larry Martin's mother and father attended Carlisle Indian Industrial School and Sherman Institute, respectively. According to Martin,

> [I]t really had some effect, because my father moving to a boarding school near Los Angeles made him a stronger person in that he understood the white man's way of life and he could see into the realm of what he could do back home on his reservation and learning the aspects of white culture and his culture and it made him a stronger person. But it didn't take the main aim of trying to inculcate a way to forget his ties on the reservation.[83]

As with other Indian schools around the nation, the Albuquerque Indian School focused on agricultural and industrial education. The outing system sent students to work outside the school, providing low-wage laborers to Albuquerque businesses, farms, and homes. This form of industrial education benefited both the school and the local community.

Generally, Anglo residents agreed with and approved of the policy and valued the students' labor. The practice became a convenient source of skilled and agricultural labor, as well as domestic help.[84] Industrial education taught boys farming, furniture manufacture, carpentry, blacksmithing, engineering, and shoe-making.[85] Student labor in the fields produced food for the school, and their carpentry, stone cutting, and furniture making equipped it. The oldest boys worked on the railroad or in beet fields in Colorado.[86] The outing system provoked protests by Anglo mechanics, however, who com-

Fig. 5 **Young Albuquerque Indian School girls in sewing class, ca. 1912.**
(Courtesy of National Archives, Rocky Mountain Region, Denver CO, Record Group 75:
Records of the Bureau of Indian Affairs, 1793–1999.)

plained that free education and lower wages gave students an unfair advantage in the competition for employment.[87]

Girls learned the domestic arts of Anglo cuisine, sewing, laundry, housework, and caring for the sick. They used their training to provide sewing, cooking, and laundering to the school. The outing system provided domestic labor, child care, and cooking to white families in Albuquerque. The girls earned $10 to $15 a month.[88] As a young woman, my grandmother, Elizabeth Roberts, worked for an influential white family in Albuquerque. She babysat and cleaned house, and the family paid the school directly. Elizabeth mentioned that the school kept most of her wages in savings and allowed her to keep "a little spending money," which she used for herself or to buy groceries for her parents when she went home to visit in Laguna.[89]

By 1929, the Albuquerque Indian School housed students from many tribes, including Pueblos, Navajo, Utes, Tohono O'odham (Papagos), Choctaws,

Dakota (Sioux), Muscogees (Creeks), Mojaves, Crows, Modocs, Sacs and Foxes, Chemehuevis, and Osages.[90] Some of these students remained in Albuquerque after leaving the school. Superintendent Reuben Perry wanted to improve the school's academic standards to meet those of white public schools.[91] Although Perry was unable to implement his programs that would have allowed boarding students to transfer to a public high school after graduation, some students did go on to public school.[92] Three students went on to complete public high school.[93] A few of the Indian art pupils enrolled at the University of New Mexico.[94] Larry Martin recalls moving to Albuquerque as a young child, part of the larger migration of Indian people to Albuquerque.

> This is the reason why we moved to Albuquerque. My mother was born on the Laguna Indian reservation known as Paguate and my father was from Acoma, which is a nearby reservation. . . . My father attended school in Riverside California, known as Sherman Indian Institute. He learned the basics of mechanics so consequently, when he came back [to] our land, and he took a job as a machinist for the Santa Fe railroad, . . . located in Albuquerque. Consequently, [when I was four or five], . . . all of our family moved from the reservation to Albuquerque. We attended the public schools, we were probably the first . . . Pueblo Indians to attend schools in Albuquerque. . . . [T]here weren't very many Indians going to public schools; . . . most of our relatives . . . attended boarding schools.[95]

By the 1920s, larger buildings, skyscrapers (southwest adobe-style), and hotels had appeared in Albuquerque. Paved roads brought even more tourists and residents; new trading centers and distribution points provided services for smaller, neighboring towns, farms, and ranches.[96] Fred Harvey and his son-in-law, John Frederick Huckel, hired Pueblo and Navajo weavers and jewelry makers to demonstrate their crafts by the railroad stops. The Indian Building became an exhibition space for Native artisans to show and sell their jewelry, baskets, rugs, and pottery to the travelers stopping for meals in Albuquerque.

For many tourists, that exchange was their first introduction to American

Indians and their arts.[97] The Fred Harvey Company seized the opportunity to popularize and develop markets for Indian arts. Indian artists began selling their works at the rail station platform to tourists. Eventually, the market for Native arts and culture had an enormous effect on the New Mexican economy, and in Albuquerque that led to an ongoing association between the City of Albuquerque and Indian tourism.

Mike Kirk created The First American Pageant, which exploited the American Indian as tourist spectacle by reinforcing the imagination of a mythical West and perpetuating the image of Indigenous people in a primitive past. In order to encourage tourism in Albuquerque and as a response to the Gallup Ceremonial, which had begun in 1922, The First American Pageant was marketed as an analogous event that could be combined with the Santa Fe Railway and the Harvey Company's "Indian detour." Kirk created and directed the pageant from 1928 to 1930, as a "four-day spectacle absolutely unique in the world" that focused on and reinforced the notion of Indigenous peoples as a past phenomenon.[98] Kirk stated that the theme of "The First American is the history of the Indians, re-lived and re-acted by the Indians themselves. The spectacle opens at a night performance, showing dawn in a primitive pueblo before the coming of the Spaniards."[99] As twenty thousand watched (in 1928), the history retold began with Indians, continuing to the Spanish, and then the Americans, moving from the Sunrise Call to the "the mighty flag of Spain rippling onto the scene. Then war and the clash of arms, the flight of winged arrows. Peace and fiestas, song and dance of the Indians, throbbing beat of tomtoms, quavering rise and fall of ancient chants."[100] Eventually the cowboys (Americans) make their way into the picture with a campfire, coffee brewing, and the old trail songs accompanied by a twanging guitar.[101] "Then the grand finale, the blazing spectacle of a thousand Indians from eighteen tribes dancing weird and different dances, fading from the scene, and high on the pueblo top the loosing of the Last Arrow, the final gesture of a dying race."[102] For Indians in Albuquerque, these images of Indians as tourist commodities and figures of the past persisted in the Albuquerque imagination. But in fact, it was The First American spectacle that died with the coming of the Great Depression, not the Indians.

The Great Depression slowed, but did not halt, the growth of Albuquerque. Postwar federal spending contributed much to the city's growth.

Kirtland Field, site of an Army Air Corps flying school, became Kirtland Air Force Base. The development of the atomic bomb at nearby Los Alamos created new opportunities for the city and led to the formation of the "Sandia Complex, composed of Sandia Base, Sandia Laboratory, Sandia Corporation, Kirtland and Manzano Air Force Bases, local offices of the Atomic Energy Commission, and satellite manufacturing firms and service agencies."[103] The economy and population boomed. Many new "skilled technocrats" and other employees arrived, increasing the number of Sandia Corporation employees from 3800 to 7800 in ten years.[104] From 1951 to 1961, the Sandia base was worth $55 million to the business community of Albuquerque. According to Bradford Luckingham, another product of this military and technological development was a sharp increase in the city's educational status: by 1960, the Albuquerque population had the highest percentage of doctorates of all U.S. cities.[105]

The boom did not bring equal benefits to all segments of the population. American Indians and working-class Hispanos were still excluded from upper-level jobs. As in other cities of the Southwest, such as Tucson, Phoenix, and El Paso, Hispanics and Anglos controlled access to education, capital, and political power, while exploiting cheap Mexican and Indian labor.[106] These power relations persist today in Albuquerque. They can be seen clearly in hiring practices: Hispanics and Anglos dominate most of the city's workforce, and internal hires maintain the status quo. Such power dynamics render Indian people invisible.

THREE

Indians in Albuquerque

POLITICAL, ECONOMIC, AND PHYSICAL RECOGNITION

NEW MEXICO CONSIDERS ITSELF a bilingual state focusing on Spanish and English, yet Indigenous languages spoken there receive little or no recognition.[1] Their obscurity is consistent with a political landscape that has developed over the past three hundred years: the Hispanic and Anglo-American cultures dominate the state, and political, social, and economic institutions reflect their dominance. Descendants of Spaniards glorify the state's Spanish influences in general and Oñate in particular as the first governor of New Mexico. This perspective overlooks or rejects the experience of Indigenous people, whose historical record, passed down orally, recalls the brutality of the Spanish leader, Spanish settlers, and Spanish Catholic clergy. The incompatibility of the Indigenous and the Spanish versions of history and the ongoing problems in ethnic relations of the "tri-cultural" state erupted in 1998, when New Mexico's 400th anniversary commemorated Oñate's leadership. Albuquerque artist Reynaldo "Sunny" Rivera created a monumental statue, a bronze sculpture of Oñate, for the Oñate Monument and Visitors Center north of Española. The statue cost $108,000, and together with the visitors center cost taxpayers nearly $1.2 million.[2] The monument drew much criticism not only for its insensitivity to American Indians, but also as an inappropriate use of taxpayers' money. And then, in an act of historical justice, as the state and local governments geared up for the quadracentennial celebration, someone cut off Oñate's right foot.[3]

The identity of the person or persons who altered the Oñate statue has never come to light. Soon Oñate had a new foot, and the act of mutilation initiated a discussion of historical facts, political correctness, and injustices toward American Indians. Despite that controversy, the Albuquerque Arts Board and the Albuquerque Cuarto Centenario Committee commissioned a statue of Oñate to be placed in Tiguex Park, a park dedicated to Indians. The city council approved the project, but Mayor Jim Baca (1997–2001) vetoed it.[4]

These two incidents reveal the insensitivity and political maneuvering of the commemoration and their roots in New Mexico's historical memory. Similar attitudes prevail in some quarters of contemporary political society. In September 2008, a BBC news blogger interviewed the Bernalillo County (NM) Republican Party Chairman Fernando C de Baca for a "Talking America" blog posting. Asked how New Mexicans might vote in the upcoming presidential election, Fernando C de Baca stated that Hispanics would not vote for Democratic presidential nominee Barack Obama: "The truth is that Hispanics came here as conquerors. African-Americans came here as slaves. Hispanics consider themselves above blacks. They won't vote for a black president."[5] New Mexican Republican Party leaders urged C de Baca to resign, and he later did; other Hispanic politicians also spoke out against his comments, calling them divisive.

The depth of the differences between Indigenous peoples, on the one hand, and Hispanics and Anglos, on the other, has not been mitigated by the increased economic role of Indian nations in New Mexico. They have gained a stronger social and political presence as their economies have grown, powered by gaming and resorts. Nonetheless, much tension remains between and among the "three" cultures in the state, and relations are strained between Indigenous people and the state and local governments. In this chapter, I address the lack of recognition for Indigenous peoples in Albuquerque, despite their integral role in the city and therefore in the state. I then analyze how federal Indian policies have contributed to the marginal position of urban Indians in Albuquerque and how the lack of clear jurisdiction over Indians has obstructed their access to services available to other citizens through local and state governments. Finally, I explore how Indigenous peoples have continued to negotiate the contemporary racial and political landscape of Albuquerque by forging relationships with the city to address issues of employment, land development, and political representation.

One of the major problems confronting American Indians in Albuquerque is that in the popular imagination they are not recognized as residents of the City of Albuquerque or as citizens of the state and nation. This lack of recognition hinders their formation of a substantial relationship with the city government. Popular assumptions are reflected in literary works on Indians of New Mexico, which continue to portray Indians as separate and isolated, rather than as contributing to New Mexico's history and its political and economic development.

Most city histories portray Indians as peripheral to Albuquerque—as craftsmen influencing architectural style, raiders disrupting urban dwellers, or students enrolled in the Albuquerque Indian School.[6] The citizens of New Mexico recognize American Indians living in the state on reservations, but most assume that Indians are detached from the political, economic, and social activities of everyday life. Only recently, with the economic successes of gaming, have Albuquerque residents and politicians begun to acknowledge Indians living within city boundaries. Indeed, the Museum of Albuquerque begins its historical narrative with the Native populations who inhabited the region, displaying showcases of pottery, tools, and arrowheads. When Spaniards arrived, the Indians disappeared only to materialize as raiders disrupting Spanish and American settlements and as iconic images of the Southwest in the Museum's art exhibits.

In reality, Pueblos, Apaches, and Navajos have a strong cultural, political, and economic presence in the state. Much as their labor contributed to the colonies of New Spain, their cultural labor now contributes to New Mexico's identity through the Indian arts industry, which distinguishes New Mexico with the unique lifestyles; superb artistry in jewelry, pottery, basketry, and painting, and distinctive social and religious ceremonies (dances) at various reservations.

Table 3. Albuquerque's Largest Employers, 1997 and 2009

Employers	1997			2009		
	Number of Employees	*Number of American Indian Employees*	*Percent of American Indian Employees*	*Number of Employees*	*Number of American Indian Employees*	*Percent of American Indian Employees*
University of New Mexico	7,955	291	3.7	10,606	445	4.2
Sandia National Labs	7,500	200	2.7	*	*	
Presbyterian Healthcare Services	5,698	163	2.9	7,439	230	3.1
City of Albuquerque	6,500	140	2.2	6,294	116	1.8
Albuquerque Public Schools	10,711	129	1.2	*	*	
University Hospital	3,029	105	3.5	5,814	254	4.4
State of New Mexico	N/A	N/A	—	3,864	132	3.4
Lovelace	N/A	N/A	—	3,600	162	4.5
Intel Corporation	3,372	101	3.0	*	*	
CNMC (formerly Albuquerque TV-I)	1,800	24	1.3	2,210	95	4.3
Veterans Health	N/A	N/A	—	2,199	113	5.1
Bernalillo County	1706	24	1.4	2,487	58	2.3
Rio Rancho Public Schools	N/A	N/A	—	2,464	21	.85

*not available at time of writing

Source: Theodore S. Jojola, *Urban Indians in Albuquerque, New Mexico: A Study for the Department of Family and Community Services* (Albuquerque, NM: City of Albuquerque, 1999), 27. 2009 figures obtained by author.

The state's tourism and hospitality industry ($5 billion per year statewide, $2 billion concentrated in Albuquerque) relies on Indian culture to set New Mexico apart from other states.[7] In Albuquerque, the city's Convention and Visitors Bureau has culture and heritage tourism at the top of their "Destination Master Plan."[8] The annual Santa Fe Indian Market in August is one of the largest Indian arts markets in the country, boasting over a thousand artists from more than one hundred Indigenous nations.[9] The Indian Market alone brings in millions of dollars in revenues from tourists who come from all over the United States and abroad. The feast day dances held by various Pueblos attract countless tourists to Santa Fe, Taos, and Albuquerque. In addition, some of New Mexico's best hunting, fishing, and camping, as well as important mineral resources, are located on reservation lands. Nevertheless, despite their cultural and economic contributions, Indigenous people are recognized primarily as separate—as the "other" state citizens— if acknowledged as state citizens at all. As New Mexico historian Marc Simmons points out,

> To most New Mexicans today, the Pueblo Indian is a person who peddles his handicrafts on the old plazas at Santa Fe and Albuquerque, or one who dances with feathers and rattles at appointed times of the year. He is rarely seen in any depth as a representative of a rich and honored culture that has flourished and suffered on these same deserts and mesas since before the time European crusaders marched to Jerusalem.[10]

Albuquerque, too, has gained from American Indians, especially those in close proximity to the city. Within a sixty-five mile radius of the city are Cochiti, Isleta, Jemez, Laguna, Sandia, San Felipe, Santa Ana, Santo Domingo, and Zia Pueblos (Map 3). Twenty-five miles west of Albuquerque lies a small Diné community, To'hajiilee. Annually, Indian events bring millions of dollars in tourism revenue to Albuquerque. The annual Gathering of Nations Powwow, billed as the largest powwow in the world, is held in Albuquerque on the last weekend of April. In 1989, the powwow attracted 36,000 people. By 2001, attendance had grown to about 100,000 and in 2005 the numbers increased to 3,000 registered participants (dancers, singers, and other performers) with over 100,000 people expected to attend.[11]

TABLE 4 American Indian Populations in Albuquerque, 1980, 1990, 2000, and 2005–2007 (estimates)

Year	Albuquerque Total Population	Albuquerque American Indian Population	% of Total
1980[1]	418,206	8,559	2.0
1990[2]	497,120	13,681	2.8
2000[3]	556,678	23,175	4.2
2005–2007[4]	505,578	29,629	5.9

1. Urbanized area, Albuquerque (SMSA), American Indian, Eskimo, Aleut. From 1980 U.S. Census.
2. Urbanized area, Albuquerque, American Indian, Eskimo, or Aleut. From 1990 U.S. Census.
3. Urbanized area, Albuquerque, American Indian and Alaska Native. From 2000 U.S. Census.
4. American Community Survey (ACS), *Demographic and Housing Estimates 2005–2007*, Albuquerque City, NM, American Indian and Alaska Native (Washington, DC: U.S. Census Bureau, 2007).

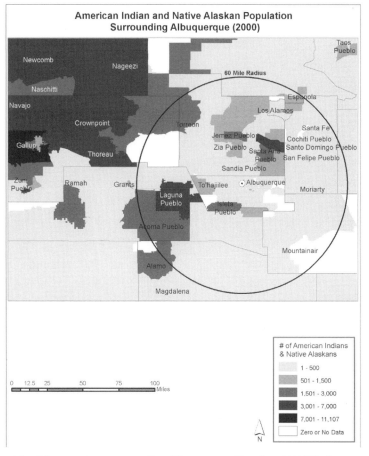

Map 3 **Reservations surrounding Albuquerque.** (Based on 2000 U.S. Census data. Courtesy of Nandhini Gulasingam, Chicago, IL, April 2010.)

The Indian National Finals Rodeo, the most prominent rodeo in Indian country, attracts approximately 40,000 people every year. A four-day event comprising a rodeo, powwow, and trade fair, it features Indian cowboys from twelve Indian rodeo regions across the United States and Canada.[12] Rodeo has long played an important role in Indian lifestyles and culture.[13] Its continued significance is evident in the large crowds who attend this event. Albuquerque hosted the Indian National Finals Rodeo for twenty years after its founding in 1975, and as of this writing negotiations were underway for the rodeo's return to the city. The deal is expected to bring in more than $1.5 million per year.[14]

With Indians comprising 4.9 percent of its total population, the city of Albuquerque ranks fourth among U.S. metropolitan areas with populations of 100,000 or more.[15] Many Indians have moved there for jobs. The increasing economic development on New Mexico reservations—gaming, manufacturing, services, agriculture, livestock, residential development, golf courses, fisheries, mining, forestry, and soccer fields[16]—still cannot employ all available workers. Therefore, many people have relocated to Albuquerque (and elsewhere) from their reservations, and many others commute to work. Besides the many Indians who have moved to Albuquerque for personal, economic, and educational purposes, many others, including Native people from outside the state, came under the federal relocation policy.

Although Indigenous people have been good for Albuquerque's economy, the city government, until recently, has rarely recognized or provided for their social or economic support. One issue relating to the lack of recognition has been the question of jurisdictional responsibility. Confusion about jurisdiction over urban Indians creates discord between Indigenous people in the city and the local, state, and federal governments under which they live. The past four hundred years of patchwork policy toward Indigenous nations has created a confusing quagmire of inclusion and exclusion for Indians at the federal, state, and municipal levels. One consequence of the confusion is an ambiguous comprehension of federal trust responsibility and state and local accountability relating to American Indians as state, county, and local citizens. As discussed in Chapter 1, urban Indigenous residents deal with multiple dilemmas based on this confusion concerning health, educational, and social welfare services.

As mentioned earlier, the confusion stems from beliefs that Indians are exclusively under the federal jurisdiction and that respective tribal nations or Pueblos are providing social and economic support. City officials have presumed that Indigenous urban residents come from or are members of nearby Indian nations, and therefore their communities will provide social service or health care needs. In 1980, 65 percent of the Indian populations represented in Albuquerque were Navajo and Pueblo; in 1990 this percentage increased to 75 percent (Table 4). Many of the urban Indians in Albuquerque, however, are from nations outside New Mexico. According to the 2000 census, respondents listed their affiliations with numerous other nations outside New Mexico, including Anchorage, Annette Island, Browning, Hopi, Hualapai, Jones Ranch, Keweenaw Bay Indian Reservation, Koyukuk, Los Angeles, Mohegan, Pearl River Indian Reservation, Red Valley, Shawnee, Sioux Falls, Stevenson, Teesto, Wind River Indian Reservation, and Yakama.[17] (See Appendix A for complete table.)

TABLE 5   Top Ten Specified Tribal Affiliations in
Albuquerque, NM, MSA, 2000

1. Pueblo	16,867
2. Navajo	13,305
3. Apache	872
4. Sioux	616
5. Cherokee	605
6. Latin American Indians	456
7. Choctaw	267
8. Chippewa	239
9. Comanche	144
10. Iroquois	136
American Indian tribes specified	35,438
American Indian or Alaska Native tribes not specified	3,238

Source: U.S. Census Bureau, Census 2000.

A misunderstanding of residential status has also affected the political recognition of permanent residents of urban Indigenous residents. Not all Albuquerque Indian residents come from nearby Indigenous nations, but

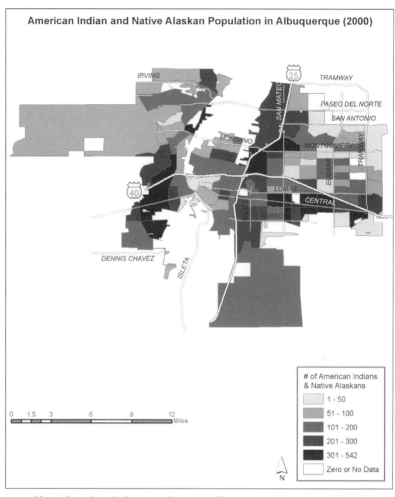

Map 4 **American Indian population in Albuquerque.** (Based on 2000 U.S. Census data. Courtesy of Nandhini Gulasingam, Chicago, IL, April 2010.)

ironically, Indigenous residents are sometimes disadvantaged by the proximity of reservation communities. Because reservations are close by, city officials wrongly assume that urban Indigenous populations are transient. It is true that between 5,000 and 10,000 of the city's Indigenous residents are mobile. They commute to their homes on nearby reservations or reside for short periods to attend Southwestern Indian Polytechnic Institute, Central New Mexico Community College (formerly Albuquerque TV-I), the Univer-

57

sity of New Mexico, Job Corp, or other vocational schools. A significantly larger proportion of Albuquerque Indians, more than 30,000, are permanent residents, however.[18] In the 1998 Study for Department of Family and Community Services questionnaire, the length of permanent residency ranged from two months to 1,500 years. If 1,500 years is discarded from the analysis, the mean length of residence for Indians in Albuquerque is ten years.[19]

One possible contributing factor to this misconception of residency is that the urban Indigenous community in Albuquerque, like most urban Indigenous communities around the country, is not limited to designated geographic neighborhoods. During the 1960s, in the wake of federal relocation programs, the Diné population tended to reside near educational centers and sites that employed large numbers of Indians—mostly the Old Town, downtown, and University of New Mexico areas.[20] Today, however, the Albuquerque Indian population is widely distributed throughout the city. The largest population cluster lies south of Lomas Boulevard between San Pedro and Wyoming Boulevards, which includes the site of the American Indian Center. Another large cluster lives between Alameda Road and Paseo del Norte Boulevard and west of the Rio Grande.[21] The dispersal of the population camouflages the size of Indigenous populations, rendering them somewhat invisible.

Community and political invisibility have caused misconceptions that confuse issues of importance to Albuquerque Indians, especially those concerning political accountability, recognition, and access. According to Geri Loretto, former liaison for Indian affairs to Mayor Martin Chavez (1993–1997):

> We tend to be kind of invisible. . . . [W]e don't make a whole lot of waves here, and we just kind of exist, hoping that we'll make it from day to day. So, I think that was one of the biggest issues . . . that we tend to be the silent community. We never make waves, we don't say anything, and we just exist, hoping that things will be okay.[22]

In the words of Emmett Francis, former liaison for Indian affairs to Mayor Jim Baca (1997–2001):

Right now, in this urban community in Albuquerque, we have always used the word "invisible," because we are not heard from at all. We don't speak at all. Historically, we have always had someone speak on our behalf, either a leader or a recognized person in the Indian community.[23]

In Phoenix, Arizona, this same political invisibility inspired the creation of the Native American Community Organizing Project (NACOP), a group focused on increasing political recognition and participation in the political process for Indigenous nonreservation residents. In discussions with state representatives and senators, NACOP members found that politicians thought everything was fine with urban Indians. That belief was based mostly on a lack of participation of and communication with the urban Indian population. If they were not expressing concerns or problems, all must be fine.[24] In an attempt to inform legislators, NACOP has organized meetings and community actions.

Education of politicians, service providers, and the general public about urban Indigenous issues will be paramount if Albuquerque Indians are to achieve the visibility, recognition, and solutions that they need. Most politicians have no idea of the vast differences between reservations and urban areas. Acknowledging that sentiment, Geri Loretto commented, "We had to do a lot of educating to let [the city] know that urban Indians, in essence, don't qualify for a lot of these [tribal] programs."[25] Carol Weahkee, former director of the Albuquerque Indian Center, remarked:

Once, when I was still on the board, the city council voted for a $50,000 cut in our employment program because they said that we had casinos, and so we should get the remainder from the casinos. So I guess part of this job [director of the American Indian Center] is public relations, and a lot of what I have to do is education, and let them know that just because Indians have casinos doesn't mean that it belongs to us. And that we have different issues as urban Indians from the reservation groups.[26]

Recently, a formal relationship has begun between the City of Albuquerque and the urban Indian population. It arises from interactions over issues facing Albuquerque Indians, such as employment, education, political visibility, and lack of social services geared toward American Indians. Although Mayor Martin Chavez (1993–1997) formalized the political relationship between the city government and Indian residents, previous mayors such as Harry Kinney (1981–1985) and Louis E. Saavedra (1989–1993) had made attempts.

In the 1960s and 1970s, an urban Indian center existed in Albuquerque. It lost funding in the 1980s, however, and the Indian community lost the social services that the center delivered, as well as a central meeting place for activities. Those who fought for the establishment of the second Indian center and other social services made an uncommon effort to educate the city on Indian affairs. They had to prove the need for an Indian center. Under Mayor Saavedra's administration, the city council set up a task force to evaluate the need for an Albuquerque Indian center. The analysis confirmed the need for a center and other programs.[27]

In July 1989, the City of Albuquerque provided a small seed grant to start an Urban Indian Center, and in 1990, a city council resolution made the Indian Center permanent.[28] Further discussion of the Indian Center can be found in the next chapter. Meanwhile, the creation of a task force and the ten-year disestablishment of the Albuquerque Indian Center illustrate the city's disregard of Indian needs, as well as a lack of strong urban Indian leadership.

A consummate politician, Mayor Chavez recognized the rising urban Indian political voice (or potential voice) and asked for a meeting between urban Indian administrators and the urban Indian public. At the "Mayor's Symposium on Indian Affairs" on June 27, 1994, urban Indians voiced their concerns about relations with city government. For the first time in Albuquerque's history, Indian people of Albuquerque and New Mexican tribes communicated directly with the mayor, the city council, the school board, various department directors, and key city contractors. Emerging leaders and others in the Indian community began speaking directly about their needs and concerns. They made recommendations for improvements that covered health, education, employment, social services, and economic development.[29]

At the meeting, local Indian leaders suggested solutions to many problems. They asked that the city take steps to hire Indians in all departments and give more attention to Indian health, homelessness, education, and social services.[30] More importantly, they suggested that a permanent political body be created to advocate for the needs of Albuquerque Indians, that is, an Indian Commission, composed of members of the Albuquerque Indian community, to keep the city informed of the status of urban Indians. They also asked for a position in the mayor's office to coordinate with the Indian community. In response, the mayor set about establishing the Albuquerque Commission on Indian Affairs. The city council followed Mayor Chavez's recommendation and established the Commission on Indian Affairs in Albuquerque in 1995 as a way to coordinate among the urban Indian community, the city council, and the mayor's office.

Once the commission was in place, it was time to create a position within the city government for a liaison person. The liaison is a city employee on loan from another department to work with the Albuquerque Commission on Indian Affairs.[31] Unfortunately, it is not a permanent position, but rather, it exists only as long as the current mayor feels the need or desire to continue that position.[32] Mayor Chavez established the position with Geri Loretto, a Navajo city planner, as the first liaison. Loretto dealt with issues that included education, the Indian Center, and the old Twelfth Street Indian school property. Loretto and Mayor Chavez met with many Indian groups, including the Laguna colony, Albuquerque Cherokees, the Indian Center, and First Nations (an organization focused on the health care needs of Albuquerque urban Indians).[33] Chavez's successor, Mayor Jim Baca, continued the position of liaison and appointed Emmett Francis, another Navajo city planner.

The National Indian Youth Council (NIYC) has maintained a close connection to Albuquerque civil rights issues and urban Indigenous issues. Beginning in the 1950s and incorporating in 1961, the NIYC began advocating for Native rights across the country (this is further discussed in Chapter 6). Norman Ration, current director of NIYC, comments that, "In the very beginning, [NIYC] did a lot of [activism around] discrimination, fishing rights, land rights, and voting rights."[34] That activism and focus on human rights violations led to numerous lawsuits in the areas of education and employment.

Currently, NIYC runs a statewide employment training program, mostly funded by the Department of Labor. However, they maintain their advocacy role for Native people by networking with other Native and non-Native organizations and service programs, such as the Network of Indian Organizations.

City employment has been a contentious issue. Allegations of racial and gender discrimination have been leveled for thirty years, and many have led to lawsuits. In June 1976, the NIYC filed an employment discrimination complaint with the city's Human Rights Board.[35] The suit alleged that the City of Albuquerque discriminated against American Indians in employment practices, as evidenced by disproportionately low numbers of Indian employees compared to the number of the city's Indian residents.[36] By 1977, a conciliation agreement articulated the city's plan to achieve a more representative workforce, and promised that 5 percent of city employees would be American Indian.[37]

Two years later, in June 1979, NIYC wrote to the Human Rights Board alleging that the city had not adhered to its agreement. The city was found to be negligent in recruitment, training, and advancement of American Indian employees.[38] The 5-percent goal established in 1977 changed with the city's adoption of its current affirmative action plan in July 1993, which sets a goal of 3.6 percent American Indian employees.[39]

Others, including African Americans and women, also have levied complaints of employment discrimination against the city as well. The Albuquerque chapter of the National Organization for Women filed a class action employment discrimination complaint with the U.S. Equal Employment Opportunity Commission in the early 1970s. They alleged that the city discriminated against women in employment practices, and particularly in supervisory and management level positions and positions for police and firefighters.[40] Further, in 1986, the Albuquerque Chapter of the National Association for the Advancement of Colored People (NAACP) sought to establish a black affirmative action council to deal with employment of blacks. They argued that the city maintained a 50 percent employment goal for Hispanics and 3 percent for blacks, although those goals were disproportionate to city population numbers. Therefore, in 1987, the NAACP filed a class action employment discrimination complaint against the city.[41] The complaint alleged that blacks had been discouraged from seeking city employment, black women had not been recruited or hired as police officers or firefighters, and blacks were underrepresented in clerical and blue collar positions. In addition, the complaint noted that the city had used the affirmative action target number as a maximum number of black employees, and city workers had retaliated against black employees involved in discrimination complaints.[42]

Because employment remains a major issue for Albuquerque Indians, the Indian commission must consider how to increase their numbers.[43] That task might not seem difficult: Albuquerque is a major employment center for Indian service organizations. The city's largest employer of Indians is the Bureau of Indian Affairs (BIA). The IHS and the Southwest Indian Polytechnic Institute are a distant second and third.[44] A number of Indian-focused organizations hire primarily American Indians. Those organizations focus on the needs of Indian people, both in the city and on nearby reservations. The City of Albuquerque, however, either lacks the commitment to improve Indian employment or has not fully recognized the employment needs of Albuquerque Indians.

When Albuquerque's human rights office reviewed the city's employment policies and procedures, a paucity of Indian workers became apparent (Table 6). One barrier is the internal advertisement of city jobs. Because few Indians work for the city government, many potential workers are not privy to internally advertised jobs. The policy review pointed out that few Indians applied for city jobs advertised in 1995. The review showed that a great majority of the jobs were going to Hispanic and white applicants. Asian Americans, American Indians, and African Americans were not applying for jobs, and therefore were not part of the city government. In 1996, only nine of 2,985 applicants for city jobs were Indians.[45]

The lack of representation within city government departments has an impact on all residents, especially Albuquerque American Indian residents. The impact concerns not only how persons will be treated, but the ways in which the city governmental system views and serves a specific population. As addressed in Chapter 1, the health care dilemma illustrates why education concerning urban Indigenous health care coverage is so important. While some procedures and social services may apply to a majority of individuals, the lack of awareness or recognition of a person's culture may im-

Table 6. City of Albuquerque, 1995 and 1996: Applicants, Applicants Interviewed, and Applicants Selected, by Race/Ethnicity

	Asian		American Indian		Black		Hispanic		White		Unknown	
	M	F	M	F	M	F	M	F	M	F	M	F
Applicants	11	1	17	2	27	20	1,692	775	241	192	1,059	714
Total	12		19		47		2,467		433		1,773	
Percent of total applicants	0.3		0.4		0.9		52.0		9.1		37.3	
Applicants interviewed	1	1	5	1	5	5	351	189	86	69	103	61
Total	2		6		10		540		155		164	
Percent of total applicants interviewed	0.2		0.7		1.0		61.5		17.6		19.0	
Applicants selected	1	1	4	1	2	3	126	60	33	42	0	0
Total	2		5		5		186		75		0	
Percent of total applicants selected	0.7		1.8		1.8		67.7		28.0		0	

Compiled from Human Rights Office, *Review of the City of Albuquerque's Employment Policies, Procedures, and Practices, As They Impact upon Equal Employment Opportunities* (Albuquerque, NM: City of Albuquerque, 1998).

pact treatment, and how one is viewed at the time of need. One place where cultural understanding is especially critical is in law enforcement and the issue of domestic violence.

In recent years, domestic violence has taken center stage in awareness and prevention efforts, and the development of resources. The issue of violence against American Indian women has been well documented in a number of studies.[46] Most notably, the Amnesty International report, *Maze of Injustice: The Failure to Protect Indigenous Women from Sexual Violence in the USA*, states that Native American and Alaska Native women are "2.5 times more likely to be raped or sexually assaulted than women in the USA in general."[47] The report focuses on the complex jurisdictional maze in Indian country that allows perpetrators to get away with crimes, the lack of survivor services and support, and the inaction or indifference of police or prosecutors.[48] The National Congress of the American Indian's "Fact Sheet on Violence Against Indian Women in Indian Country" named insufficient funding for domestic violence resources, and victim fear of apathy, judgment, or lack of sympathy by judicial, law enforcement, and medical personnel due to misperceptions of or racial prejudices toward American Indians.[49] While both reports primarily focus on the reservation environment, Native women in urban areas face similar domestic abuse statistics.

In 1996, the Department of Emergency Medicine at the University of New Mexico in Albuquerque published a study examining the impact of domestic violence on the homicide rate involving women in New Mexico.[50] Researchers found that between 1990 to 1993, almost half of female homicides involved domestic violence.[51] The large number of women's deaths due to domestic violence raised a red flag in New Mexico.

The study does not differentiate between American Indian women residing on the reservation and non-reservation urban dwellers. Yet, the study indicated that the rates of domestic violence homicide and non-domestic homicides were highest among American Indian/Alaska Native women at 4.9 per 100,000. Domestic violence homicide rates for Hispanic and non-Hispanic women were at 1.7 and 1.8 per 100,000, respectively.[52] American Indian women also have a higher average than the national average of 4.1 per 100,000.[53] As with the Amnesty International and NCAI reports, lack of access to resources is given as a partial reason for the high rate of domestic violence homicides in American Indian populations.[54] As a result, a more concerted effort to address domestic violence issues in New Mexico resulted. For American Indians in Albuquerque, it meant the development of Morning Star House.

Morning Star began in 1996 as a grassroots initiative in response to an urgent need in the Albuquerque urban Indian community.[55] Morning Star provides support and services for American Indian women and children who are victims of domestic violence in Albuquerque. Donations of clothing, appliances, food, school supplies, hygiene supplies, toys, and other everyday items provide essentials to women who are homeless or starting over because they fled an abusive environment. These are important items if a woman has to flee her home, leaving everything, including her children's school supplies and clothing.[56]

Numerous individuals and organizations have made donations to the Morning Star House. In 2005, the Construction Industries Division of the New Mexico Regulation and Licensing Department donated thirty-five cell phones to both Morning Star House and a domestic violence shelter in Shiprock, New Mexico.[57] The cell phones provide added safety to get needed help. Many women cannot afford cell phones. Gwendolyn Packard, former director of Morning Star House, stated that, "Native American women have a higher incidence of domestic violence than any other ethnic group. The silence of the Native American community leads to a vast underreporting of violence. It's hard for the women to ask for help because they've never had to do it before, and there's that fear that everyone's going to know what's going on."[58]

Addressing domestic abuse requires a multidimensional focus, and must consider the perpetrator, victim, family, and law enforcement. In 1998, the Albuquerque Police Department (APD) created a Domestic Abuse Response Team (DART). The team was trained to deal with domestic violence situations, which included police as first responders who were also trained to interpret and apply domestic violence laws.[59] Advocates would then address the victim's and/or children's needs and provide information about support resources and obtaining restraining orders.[60]

An important aspect of the DART program was training personnel to understand the intricacies of domestic violence situations. Having advocates from various domestic violence organizations also meant that, more likely than not, the advocates had training or understanding in the cultural dynamics that overlap with many domestic violence calls. A woman may call the police because she is being abused, but if alcohol or drinking is suspected, the woman also may be taken to jail for public drunkenness.[61] With so few American Indians represented in city government departments, including law enforcement, the importance of such advocates cannot be overstated. The Albuquerque Police Department worked with Resources, Inc. (which operated the APD Victims Assistance Unit) and Morning Star House to send advocates on domestic violence calls.[62] Unfortunately, the DART program was discontinued in 1998 by then–Albuquerque Police Chief Jerry Galvin.

Morning Star House has had its own share of difficulties. Early on the program experienced upheaval when two employees sued the organization.[63] Then, following rumors of improprieties, Morning Star was forced to close its doors in August 2007. Understanding the dire need for a domestic violence organization, Darlene Reid-Jojola reopened the Morning Star under a new name, the Urban Indian Advocacy Program.[64] As of this writing, Morning Star House operates as the shelter component of the Urban Indian Advocacy Program. Mayor Martin Chavez in 2001 donated an old building in need of renovation to the organization to be used as the shelter. Looking at the plans, Jojola remarked,

> This is where the women and children will live, if we could just focus on this portion. We had many interested parties, people getting caught up in the moment and they want to help. [They asked,] "How can we help?" . . . [The] Bernalillo County Sheriff's Department has indicated that they would like to help us. But there are still things that we have to do. I've got the permits. . . . But then again, I am not sure what [can be done] without an architect.
>
> One [side] will be the shelter program and [the other] side will be the administrative offices. . . . We do have to be careful that [the shelter and the advocacy program] will be known as two separate entities. We will probably be located in the same shelter on Trumbull Street once that gets up and running, but both places will have a role. The shelter will be for . . . women transitioning out, or . . . legal services, . . . mental health counseling and parenting classes. The administrative offices will be more like intake searching for dollars, to help women transition into the workforce and lobbying—getting politically active. That is . . . more or less, the umbrella for Morning Star House so that the women and children . . . are in a safe place. . . . It will hold up to 30 people.[65]

Between January and June 2008, the Urban Indian Advocacy Program served 1,450 women seeking services. Most were Navajo but others were from Pueblos and other tribes from around the country. About 10 percent of the women served were non-Native. A difficulty for the program according to Reid-Jojola was the lack of staff.

> We work with a large number of women and children, [and] average 215 up to 285 per month. We are stretched pretty thin; it is not unheard of to be here 56 hours a week. . . . We're truly back to grassroots, women helping women with little or no money. And I'm really blessed that we have volunteers.[66]

Reopening the shelter was difficult with the loss of funding and employees, but the number of women seeking Urban Indian Advocacy Program's services illustrates the need for this program. Domestic violence impacts families throughout Albuquerque, and American Indian cultural representation and awareness in law enforcement and social services play important roles in advocacy and support.

Another crucial area of cultural representation is education. In New Mexico, the education of Indians initially took place in boarding schools, mostly in Albuquerque and Santa Fe, or in out-of-state boarding schools such as Sherman Indian School in California or Carlisle Indian Industrial School in Pennsylvania. The silence of urban Indian voices has allowed the assumption that Indians are still in boarding schools instead of in Albuquerque public schools. In the past, the Albuquerque Public School (APS) district schools have incorporated very little Indigenous material, whether addressed to Indian or to non-Indian students, that specifically discusses Indian peoples and cultures, and their contributions to U.S. and New Mexico history and literature. According to the *Albuquerque Tribune* in April 2000,

> The Albuquerque Public School system has been extremely resistant to recent efforts by urban Indian parents to examine federally funded programs that target American Indian students for culturally appropriate curricula, tutoring, and other educational support activities.[67]

In Albuquerque public schools, most of the teachers are non-Indian. While state and city school systems acknowledge the value of diversity, this view is not reflected in public school curricula.

In 1974, the Indian Education Department (IED) was established as part of the Albuquerque Public School district.[68] The IED works with the district to increase graduation rates, communication with parents, and student attendance. Using funding from Johnson O'Malley, Title VII and Title VIII and state Exemplary Grants for supplemental services, the IED implements various programs that promote Native student development and empowerment.[69]

In 2005, APS served 5,614 American Indian students who come from 160 different tribes and pueblos. High truancy and dropout rates have plagued APS graduate rates. According to the "Native American Report Card" presented by the Albuquerque Metro Native American coalition, the dropout rate in 1998–1999 was 19.7 percent.[70] By 2005, graduation rates had increased and dropout rates had decreased, but as seen in Table 7, American Indian students in APS continue to have low graduation rates and high dropout rates.

The State of New Mexico Indian Education Summit Report, the Re-

Table 7. Albuquerque Public School District: Graduation and Dropout Rates, 2005

Ethnicity	Graduation Rate (%)	Dropout Rate (%)
Anglo	62.4	13.6
Asian (American)	69.2	10.3
Black	44.5	22.0
Hispanic	46.7	25.1
Native American	36.1	18.6

Source: Abby Wihl, "APS Dropout Rates Down," *Albuquerque Tribune*, July 13, 2007, 1.

sponse to the Mayor's Symposium on Indian Affairs, and Governor Bill Richardson's 2004 State of the State address, all emphasized the need for more American Indian teachers, staff, and administrators. Keith Franklin, discussing Albuquerque urban Indian education, noted that "American Indian students need role models, academic enrichment, health, and intervention programs that encourage school attendance, motivation, and academic success."[71]

Recent efforts to address the lack of Indigenous-based curricula have included a few classes on Indigenous languages and Native American studies in schools. At Painted Sky, Principal Pat Woodard has seen improvement in Navajo students' reading scores since implementing Navajo language classes. Woodard commented, "I wouldn't say the class is the only reason. But I do think it's played a big part."[72] A few schools teach Native American studies at high schools and middle schools.[73]

The Native American Community Academy (NACA), founded by Kara Bobroff, has taken a significant step in addressing the cultural disparity in the APS district. Located near Wilson Middle School, NACA teaches grades six through twelve.[74] Bobroff states, "For a long time, there [has] been a lot of discussion about the need for . . . either a magnet school or a charter school that . . . had a specific cultural focus that meets the needs of our (Native) students in the area."[75] The mission of the NACA follows:

> To engage students, educators, families, and community in creating a school that will prepare our students to grow from adolescence to adulthood and begin strengthening communities by developing strong leaders who are academically prepared, secure in their identity and healthy.[76]

NACA's mission is far-reaching, not only focused on the student in the present, but also on their future as community members, role models, and leaders.

With the aid of an Echoing Green fellowship, Bobroff took time to meet with community members, leaders, educators, and professionals on the needs of American Indian students and the school curriculum.[77] In addition, the creation of working relationships to use community knowledge and expertise is key to community involvement. American Indian (reservation and Albuquerque) community members and leaders support the school through sharing knowledge "that you do not typically find in a public school setting around culture, tradition, [language] and history," and act as positive role models for the students.[78]

Another misconception and issue separating the Albuquerque Indian community from the city government and non-Indian residents concerns the old Albuquerque Indian boarding school property on 12th Street and Menaul

Boulevard. Plans to develop the property resemble the frustrating search for the site in the 1880s. From 1966, when a new Albuquerque Indian School was planned (and never built) to 1969, Domingo Montoya, chair of the All-Indian Pueblo Council (AIPC), and S.D. Aberle worked tirelessly to get the Albuquerque Indian School land deeded for economic purposes to AIPC.[79] The chair of the APIC, Delfin Lovato, and Albuquerque BIA director Ronald Esquerra signed the agreement that made the AIPC the first tribal organization to procure director responsibility and control of a BIA school following Public Law 93–638.[80]

Deteriorating buildings, declining quality of education, and problems with students led to the closing of the Albuquerque Indian School.[81] Albuquerque Indian School transferred many of its students to the Santa Fe Indian School, and on the final day in 1981, the dormitory was intentionally set ablaze.[82] After more than a decade of abandonment, the old school had become occupied informally by some of Albuquerque's homeless population. In 1990 another fire gutted the building, and in 1992 the body of a man was found in one of the buildings. Consequently, the buildings were demolished to the joy of neighbors and the sadness of school alumni.[83]

The question of how to develop the 12th Street site has been a matter of dispute among the AIPC, residents of the North Valley and their neighborhood associations, and, at times, the city of Albuquerque.[84] Protests against Indian Pueblos Federal Development Corporation, the AIPC, and the City of Albuquerque by neighborhood associations located near the Twelfth Street property, such as the Near North Valley/Old Indian School Neighborhood Association, have delayed development.[85] Neighborhood associations have complained that the property was left unfenced, allowing access to homeless persons and that tumbleweeds were blowing from the site onto private properties.[86] A more important issue is the trust status of the land. Neighbors are afraid that, because the land is held in trust, a casino may be built there. As a result, the associations have forced the city to negotiate with the Indian Pueblos Federal Development Corporation, the development arm of the AIPC, on various questions and have filed lawsuits to stop development. Darryl Felipe, the corporation's chief executive officer, comments:

We tried to reassure them that [we are not] . . . going to put a casino there. We have nineteen Pueblos sitting on this board, . . . and they're not going to vote [for] that. But they didn't believe us, they said, "Well, put it in writing." . . . I offered to put it in writing that we weren't to put any kind of Class III gaming on that property for ten to fifteen years . . . but the only thing I need [is] for you to drop that lawsuit and any other future lawsuits [of this nature]. . . ." Then they looked at each other and said, "I think we can work something out . . ."

So, I get a call about two days later from these neighborhood associations. . . . "Mr. Felipe, I think you misunderstood us, we really didn't . . . want to agree to that, we need the other things that we spelled out in this package . . . not only the casino not being built . . ."[87]

Despite such confusion, all parties have moved toward consensus. To ease residential and commercial transitions, the plan includes pedestrian-friendly designs with walkable areas, bicycle lanes, and sidewalks.[88]

Clearly, development of the Albuquerque Indian School property has been a long time coming.[89] The AIPC has considered various plans, such as an amphitheater or a soccer field complex. The latter idea failed because its estimated water usage was considered excessive.[90] In 2001, the Council was "looking at making it to be a conference complex," says Felipe, "with a hotel, conference center, shops, and a landscape that mom and pop can walk in the evenings."[91] A museum was being planned, similar to the Heard Museum in Phoenix, that would house "artifacts" currently in the Smithsonian Museum. That idea was abandoned because the Indian Pueblo Cultural Center was already planning such a museum.

In 2004 and 2006, the Indian Pueblos Federal Development Corporation (IPFDC), the for-profit development arm of the AIPC, opened two buildings on the property, the Pete Domenici Indian Affairs Building and the Manuel Lujan Jr. Building, respectively. They house the Department of the Interior's National Indian Programs Training Center and tribal employees from various agencies.[92] Housing the training center and maintaining the BIA regional office on this property, the development importantly helped New Mexico and Albuquerque to keep federal jobs.[93]

Recent plans include a hotel, retail space, and a park. In 2007, the AIPC received a $1 million grant from the Department of Commerce, Economic Development Administration. The grant will provide infrastructure development support for the forty-seven-acre property. On the west end of the property plans include a retail center, restaurant, and bank. In 2007, a Holiday Inn Express was in the final stages of completion.[94] For Everett Chavez, chair of the AIPC, it means economic development that will impact both the city and Pueblos: "This means more employment opportunities to . . . [meet] the tourism and business industry needs of the city. We are prepared to capture these opportunities and make them work for our people. More jobs, thriving business opportunities and a stable economy—this is what we strive to accomplish."[95]

This property is one of the last undeveloped lots in metropolitan Albuquerque. Within the next few years the value of the property could bring a new level of urban-based Pueblo sovereignty and economic self-determination. This kind of development could create a bridge between reservation and urban Indian government and leadership that could strengthen the benefits, recognition, and political power base of both segments of the Indian population.

FOUR

Maintaining Our Lives

ORGANIZATIONS, MUSIC, AND PROGRAMS

LIVING IN ALBUQUERQUE is living in the middle of Indian country. If you are from one of the New Mexico Indian nations, often you can tell what reservations people are from by listening to their accents and observing how they dress, how they wear their hair, or how they acknowledge you. Few places exist in Albuquerque where you do not see Indigenous people. You see them in stores, restaurants, shopping malls, gas stations, and bus stops, or just driving down the street. You see multiple generations of Indigenous people shopping together: reservation residents in town to visit the stores or urban Indians who permanently live in town. Urban Indians in Albuquerque find or create formal or informal organizations, formulating cultural ties as Indian people, and confirming tribal connections. This chapter is about various organizations, places, and communities that help Albuquerque Indians maintain cultural identities and create a formal and informal urban Indian community. Of the many such organizations, I focus on those that maintain connections to tribal cultures in the urban environment. Therefore, I focus less on the church organizations and other pan-Indian groups that most scholars emphasize.

Albuquerque is an enigma when it comes to urban Indigenous peoples. The number of reservations around the city creates diverse relationships and interactions. The proximity does not necessarily indicate increased political activity or recognition, but it does produce a distinct notion of urban Indian community—one that is based on an understanding of Indigenous cultural differences. This notion enables community members to continue identifying with "Indianness" and, more importantly, to sustain tribal connections and identities.

The Albuquerque Indigenous population is diverse. According to the 2000 Census, the overall Indigenous population of Albuquerque was 48,239. The three largest tribal populations are Pueblo (18,001), Navajo (14,255), and Cherokee (1,721), and more than thirty-five other Indigenous nations are represented.[1] In addition to that diversity of Indigenous nationality, the Albuquerque Indian community consists of various of economic and social groups.

Donald Fixico notes class distinctions within urban Indian communities. Relocation contributed to the rise of an urban Indian middle class in which the core consists of relocatees who established homes and raised their children in the cities and whose formal education resulted in higher incomes. For Fixico, the Indian middle class specifically refers to those in the mainstream middle class who have retained their Indian identity.[2] This concept of an urban Indian middle class is relatively new because most scholarship about urban Indians has focused primarily on Indians living at a lower socioeconomic level: a community based on need.[3]

In Albuquerque, urban Indian middle class identity may reflect education, income level, or home ownership, but more importantly, the urban Indian middle class intersects more strongly with tribal or national identity than with "Indian" or "pan-Indian" identity. Some individuals have attained degrees or advanced training and have gone home. This highlights the importance of the reservations surrounding Albuquerque, since individuals can find qualified work within the city and either live on the reservation and commute to work or live in Albuquerque. Others, after earning degrees, have stayed in Albuquerque to work in their occupations. Still others with varying educational qualifications have achieved the economic standard of the middle class; many of them are employed by the Bureau of Indian Affairs (BIA) or Indian Health Service (IHS).

In many ways, these BIA or IHS federal employees' lives are similar to those of active military people, in that many have moved around the country with their families and worked at various IHS or BIA offices. Many are professionals with salaries at or above the American average, and they have access to health insurance, although they may still use the IHS hospitals. Some own homes, their children attend public schools, they may work and socialize with other Indian co-workers, and they will retire or have retired from these agencies. Because of their economic status, they have no need for the social service programs administered through the Indian center, but they may attend powwows and other Indian activities in Albuquerque. Furthermore, many may be from one or more of the New Mexico tribes.

Another socioeconomic class may include those who have been the focus of many books on urban Indians. To non-Indians, they are the most visible group. These Indigenous people may have trouble finding and keeping employment. They may have substance abuse problems, and may live in substandard housing. Their socioeconomic status, rather than ethnic identity, may determine the places they live and socialize.[4] They are the population that frequents the Albuquerque Indian Center; the Native population in the census tracts surrounding the Center is more numerous than in most other areas of the city.[5] While these people do not completely represent urban Indians living in Albuquerque, they represent a significant population subset.

As discussed in Chapter 1, the welfare reform law, or the Personal Responsibility and Work Opportunity Reconciliation Act of 1996, created a shift in the urban Indian population. Individuals who are on welfare must find work and, if programs or employment are not available on reservations, they often must move to the city to find employment. The enactment of welfare-to-work programs thus has increased this particular population of urban Indians, many of whom are single parents with little education, who are forced to take low-paying jobs.[6]

Despite the socioeconomic and national diversity represented among Albuquerque urban Indians, they share with people of other tribes the difficulties of urban life that are further exacerbated by the distance from their family. They also share certain cultural ties and ties to the land, which is their spiritual base and origin. Many urban Indians attempt to maintain some connection with their reservation homes. For some, this entails attending a ceremony once a year, and for others, it means trying to make it home two, three, or more times a month. Even with visits to the reservation, urban Indigenous people make the choice between remaining culturally isolated in the city or seeking and nurturing an Indian community for support and to maintain cultural ties.

Within an urban context, a community may entail relationships with other Indigenous people from similar or dissimilar tribal or socioeconomic backgrounds. For many individuals, it is the product of a search to find other Indigenous people with common worldviews, common experiences of surviving a colonizing environment, or common appearance and linguistic patterns. Whatever the common connections, the interactions and intersections of those commonalities of being Indigenous in an urban environment create community. The importance of the development of a community for Indigenous people in an urban environment is that it helps maintain Indigeneity. Renya Ramirez, in her book *Native Hubs: Culture, Community, and Belonging in Silicon Valley and Beyond*, discusses community building and place in terms of a "hub," a geographic and cultural concept.[7] Hubs are not "based in space, but include virtual activities such as reading tribal newspapers on the Internet and emailing. Moreover, the hub as a cultural, social, and political concept ultimately has the potential to strengthen Native identity and provide a sense of belonging, as well as to increase the political power of Native peoples."[8]

Many times within the urban context, connections to specific cultural, spiritual, linguistic, and social ties have been severed through years or generations of separation. In the urban landscape, however, the temporal landscape is not so much community based as it is based in one's place in the city's economy and political structure. To claim one's Indigenous identity on a consistent basis requires effort and appropriate infrastructure.

In Albuquerque, many of the Pueblo people are able to return home frequently and thus can maintain a much stronger tribally based identity. Many travel after work to prepare and/or take off from work to attend or participate in ceremonies. For others, maintaining a specific tribal identity is much more difficult. Distance from a cultural center is a barrier to strengthening and practicing cultural relationships and obligations. Each nation has its own origin stories, religious practices, histories, and cultures, which are critical to maintaining and reclaiming one's own specific historical and national identity. On the reservation, these practices and histories are embedded in the patterns of everyday life, a part of the landscape. Outside that landscape, their continuity is difficult, but some individuals and organizations have made great strides toward reclaiming and reconnecting with the specific nations they come from. While maintaining connections is difficult at a distance, it is not impossible, and some urban organizations, such as Toyah Band of Comanches, Cherokees of Albuquerque, and the Laguna Colony of Albuquerque have developed for such a purpose. They are building those important bridges home.

Integral to the development and maintenance of Indian community, both pan-Indian and tribally specific, has been the emergence in Albuquerque of Indian organizations that address the needs of urban Indians and stage pan-Indian events. The 1970s to the present have witnessed the establishment of the Gathering of Nations Powwow, the Albuquerque Indian Center, the All Pueblo Indian Council, the Indian Pueblo Cultural Center, and the local Native radio shows. In some cases, the proximity of the Pueblos to Albuquerque has detracted from efforts to create centralized services for the city's urban Indians. In this section, I discuss how organizations and events contribute to the process of maintaining Indigeneity and community.

THE GATHERING OF NATIONS

Powwow is a fever in Indian country—one of the few fevers not passed on by Europeans—that infects every Indian nation without devastation. People "do" the powwow circuit, spending most of the summer on the road, dancing at powwows all over the country. Although it is a tradition that derived from some but not all nations, it has become a tradition that brings Indians together. It is a place where Native people of any nation can gather, as well as a safe place where those who do not know their traditions can participate. As a pan-Indian event, the powwow attracts people to participate, watch, or just enjoy the music and food.

Powwows have become popular in the Southwest, although they are not a Southwestern tradition. In Albuquerque, the annual Gathering of Nations Powwow connects the Indigenous urban population with Indians from throughout the United States and Canada. A number of powwow drum groups from southwestern tribes participate, such as the Cathedral Lake singers and the Rio Grande singers, both having Diné and Pueblo members. The Gathering is held at the University of New Mexico's basketball arena, fondly nicknamed "The Pit." It has grown so large in recent years that the venue has been reaching maximum capacity, and the floor cannot hold all the dancers at grand entry. Although organizers of the powwow might disagree, common sense suggests that a larger site will have to be found. This annual event began in 1983 as the University of Albuquerque Powwow, attended mostly by residents of Albuquerque. The next year, The Gathering introduced the Miss Indian World pageant and crowned Ms. Codi High the first of many winners.[9] Within a matter of years, The Pit was filling consistently, and The Gathering swelled to 3,000 dancers, 60 drums, and an overall assembly of 100,000 people.[10]

The Gathering is a place where Indigenous people are the majority; and where Indigenous language, culture, and laughter are not marginalized, but celebrated. It is a time when Indian people from all over the country meet, fall in love, and go home. In the parking lot are cars from all over the United States and Canada, many with bumper stickers proclaiming "Indian power," "Frybread power," or "America is Indian land." During these events, the presence and acknowledgment of Indians intensify what Indians in Albuquerque already feel.

ALBUQUERQUE INDIAN CENTER

In many cities, such as Los Angeles, Minneapolis, and Chicago, Indian centers constitute the core of a city's urban Indian community. The center is both a central meeting place and a source of socioeconomic support. The Albuquerque Indian Center serves similar purposes: it furnishes needed assistance for urban Indians having difficulty surviving in the urban environment. Its stated mission is "to empower the Native American community of Albuquerque through the provision of services and programs designed to promote . . . wellness, healing, self-sufficiency and traditions."[11] It also seeks to educate and inform the public, city, and state about the unique status of Indian people and to promote interethnic and political relations among Indians of various tribes. Here, people can meet, interact, and continue cultural ties through language classes, sweats, or talking circles. They can avail themselves of services that relate to matters of wellness, substance abuse, domestic violence, employment, and housing.[12]

The first Albuquerque Indian Center was a creature of urban Indian circumstances of the 1970s. The 1970 Census records Albuquerque's Indian population at 3,350, but public school figures in 1974 for Indian enrollment indicated an Indian population of 17,500, representing at least thirty different tribes.[13] These figures demonstrated the existence of a significant Indian population that would use the services of an Indian Center. Because funds were scarce, Albuquerque Indian organizations and individuals needed to be creative with little or no funding. Sam English recalls that "some of our first initiative(s) with City Hall with Mayor [Harry] Kinney were very receptive. But they never had any money. . . . So what happened was we were able to start a hot meal program on top of our weekend church. It became the Indian Center mid-town meal center."[14]

In 1974, Governor Bruce King (1971–1974, 1979–1983, 1991–1995) approved the proposal for the first Albuquerque Indian center. With a $99,282 grant from the regional office of Department of Health, Education, and Welfare in Dallas, Texas, Albuquerque Indian organizations organized a board of directors and planned their mission. Leaders of fourteen of the twenty-nine Albuquerque Indian organizations comprised the board of directors. Together, the organizations envisioned the center as a place where Indian people who encountered difficulties could go for job assistance, overnight lodging, food, and other "catch-all" services.[15] Thus, the Indian center would provide much-needed services and a central location from which to administer them. Under executive director Nate Parker, the Albuquerque Urban Indian Center (AUIC) had a twenty-two person staff in its central office at Albuquerque Tower Plaza. It later moved to a new headquarters at the former Harwood School at 7th Street and Mountain.[16] The Department of Health, Education, and Welfare funded them year to year, not for direct services (provided to clients) but for administrative functions and office space to provide social services.

On weekdays from 11 a.m. to 1 p.m., the Albuquerque Urban Indian Center (AUIC), in cooperation with the City of Albuquerque, sponsored a lunch program for elderly Indians. The Southwest Indian Polytechnical Institute (SIPI) prepared and served the meals in return for AUIC donations for SIPI programs. The Elderly Nutrition program furnished balanced meals to elderly urban residents at the AUIC in the Harwood School. About twenty-five elderly people, both singles and couples, received meals regularly through this program. It also provided a regular space for Indian senior citizens to converse and visit with other Indian elders and to participate in activities such as ceramics, beadwork, bingo, crochet, and knitting.[17]

In the early 1980s, however, the federal government slashed funding for social services programs, including funding for the Department of Health, Education, and Welfare. The Albuquerque Urban Indian Center lost its funding and closed. No one stepped forward to establish another Indian center. In 1989, Sam English, Melton Compton, and Henrietta Stockel began advocating for urban Indians. They demanded the reestablishment of an Albuquerque Indian center to serve the needs of Albuquerque Indian residents.[18] At the time, city officials did not understand such needs. Louis Saavedra, mayor of Albuquerque (1989–1993), assigned Geri Loretto to look into the needs of urban Indians. Advocates acknowledged that IHS and other reservation programs existed, but that urban Indians did not have access to them. Policymakers had to be educated in the realities of urban Indians' circumstances. Loretto recalled the following:

> [T]he city of Albuquerque had not stepped forward with the initiative [for the Indian center] to actively say, yes, we are going to help you because it is our responsibility. It was through the advocacy of city residents approaching the city government with [the push for the Albuquerque Indian center] and then they [the city] finally stepped forward.[19]

The city of Albuquerque was convinced that the IHS, AIPC, and the surrounding tribal communities furnished urban Indians with the necessary services. Only Indian advocacy acquainted civic officials with the issues specific to urban Indians.

In 1989, the city council finally responded by forming an American Indian task force to research and report on the need for an Indian center in Albuquerque. By this time, the Albuquerque urban Indian population had been

Fig. 6 **Albuquerque Indian Center.** (Photo by Myla Vicenti Carpio.)

without certain services for more than ten years. More tribally focused organizations, such as AIPC and Two Worlds, targeted Indians in the nearby
Pueblos but designated no resources for urban Indians.[20]

The task force study found a definite need for an Albuquerque urban Indian center and its services. The city council subsequently allocated
$40,000, which was used to start another Indian center. After using the initial
funds, the Indian Center received money through donations and grants. Although by no means the front-runner in providing Indian-oriented services,
the city under Mayor Louis Saavedra recognized its responsibilities to urban
Indian residents and provided funding for the Indian Center.[21] As of this writing, the Indian Center was primarily funded through the city and receives additional grants from the state and the Office of Indian Affairs.[22]

The Albuquerque Indian Center tries to address many issues of the Indian community, including homelessness, recovery, health, and the need for a
community center. Carol Weahkee, former director of the Albuquerque Indian Center, commented about short-term emergency needs:

I've always been an advocate for native people, but then it . . . slaps you in the face because you see the people coming in drunk or the desperation about "where can I stay tonight?" The people who come into the city because they have someone sick in the hospital and they don't know where to stay so they're staying in the waiting room or in their trucks. . . . There's some really heavy-duty issues with the people that I'm working with now. The number of people—relatives, aunts, uncles, cousins—who live in one small apartment. . . . [If Native people living in severe overcrowding conditions were included among the homeless,] the homeless population would go up even higher than it is now . . .[23]

In addition to emergency services, the Albuquerque Indian Center also advocates for health, education, and employment. It arranges and supplies computer classes, GED classes, resume-preparation training, job training, and job placement. In addition, it provides a telephone for general use, which is especially important for the many Indian people who cannot afford phones. The Indian Center takes messages and also provides faxing services. Because of the high degree of mobility among urban Indians, some also use the Indian center as their permanent address. "We're like a mini post office," says Weahkee, "People can come in, get their mail and messages."[24]

The Center also involves itself in community social activities. Weahkee emphasized that the center is a place where people can interact, and that she envisions the Center as contributing to a vibrant Indian community.

There's a lady that came in yesterday and said, "I wanna make frybread." I guess she doesn't have a place to cook. She said, "I'll make all of you frybread if you let me use your kitchen." So she comes in, and she makes frybread and gives it out. . . . I'd like to build more on that part of this community. We have another group of people who are really involved in the sweat ceremonies, and . . . they put on a powwow. . . . [T]he Indian center sponsors with the City of Albuquerque five powwows.[25]

The Center cooperates with groups that organize powwows in Albuquerque. The Albuquerque Indian Center's powwow committee also provides food for a powwow honoring high school graduates. Just as importantly, the Center provides a central space for planning powwows, and the Spirit committee organizes about five powwows a year.[26] The Center also hosts community meals at "Thanksgiving" and Christmas.

The Albuquerque Indian Center also envisions language instruction as a major goal, which is highly linked to traditional culture and religion. According to former board member Larry Martin (1987–1989),

[Language] is one of our main objectives . . . even [for] the older ones of our organization, to get back in the fold, learning our language. [An elder] teaches us many of the culture and traditional religion aspects of our Indian way of life. You have to remember that our religion transcends all else. Really it is the core of our existence. . . . I dwelt off the reservation for many years, and going back to the oral tradition is quite helpful, meaningful, because we learn from these people the basic philosophy of our ways of life.[27]

The Indian Center's main issues have been recovery and healing. Meetings there on Thursday nights have typically attracted forty to sixty people. Two sweat lodges, one for men and one for women, that helped provide spiritual healing were located behind the building for many years. The Center sponsors an "Indians in Sobriety Camp-out" once a year and provides facilities for the group that plans a Red Road convention.[28] Addiction prevention is another of the Center's main goals: if you encourage a kid to learn tribal traditions and a spiritual way, he or she is less likely to use addictive substances. Therefore, the powwows and sweat lodges provide places for kids to go and opportunities for high school students to help plan cultural activities.[29]

A photo of the Albuquerque Indian Center (Figure 7) shows red slats on a fence concealing the sweat lodges. The space to the left between the fence and the white buildings is also Albuquerque Indian Center property. The white buildings are an old dilapidated motel complex that, circa 2001, the Center had planned to buy and expand into a new, improved facility.[30]

Various programs furnish services similar to those of the Indian Center. As in other cities, health care is an important issue. The First Nations Community Health Source, IHS, and Albuquerque Area Indian Health Board de-

Fig. 7 **Albuquerque Indian Center (rear).** (Photo by Myla Vicenti Carpio.)

liver many of those services. First Nations was established in 1985 to contribute improved health services to Albuquerque urban Indians and other
underserved populations, although approximately 80 percent of its clientele
are urban Indians. It is a non-profit agency, whose certified nurses and doc-
tors on staff provide primary care; behavioral health; the Women, Infants,
and Children program (WIC); and HIV testing and prevention. Fees are
based on a sliding scale.[31] Funding sources include the IHS and other federal health programs; state health, children, and family programs; and the City
of Albuquerque.

The IHS gives direct patient care to urban Indians who are enrolled
members of tribes. Special contract health care is available to Indians living
on Sandia, Santa Ana, Zia, Jemez, or Isleta Pueblos, and the Alamo Navajo
Chapter. Services include treatment for mental health, substance abuse, and
diabetes; and HIV testing and treatment. However, as funding decreases,
IHS provisions have become increasingly limited.

The Indian Center collects these service providers at a central location
where Indians in Albuquerque can create a community space. Not all Indians
in Albuquerque use these services or get involved in the community around
the center. Nevertheless, it is a definite site in which community is created.

Other organizations located elsewhere also contribute to Indian commu-

nity and identity in Albuquerque. The Indian Pueblo Cultural Center, for example, asserts a strong Pueblo presence and identity within the city, reflect-
ing the influence of reservations surrounding Albuquerque. This Pueblo influence both informs the strong Indian identity of the city and helps many
Indians in Albuquerque maintain a tribal identity.

ALL PUEBLO COUNCIL

In 1922, Pueblo leaders formally created the All Pueblo Council, but according to noted Jemez historian and writer Joe Sando, the council existed informally long before its title was in place.[32] The Pueblos understood the need
for a united front, first against Navajos and Apaches, then Spaniards, then
Mexicans, and finally Americans. Although they spoke a variety of languages
and dialects and lived separately, their problems were similar and affected
one another. Leaders of the various Pueblos would meet to deal with fac-
tionalism and land problems. Pueblo leaders realized that they needed a formal united front, the All Pueblo Council, to confront the Bursum Bill, which
threatened Pueblo lands contested by non-Indian people. A general meeting
of Pueblo leaders was called on November 5, 1922, to oppose the bill, setting
a precedent for the All Pueblo Council.[33] The Council is an administrative
body of the nineteen Pueblo nations of New Mexico. As administrative
heads, the governors represent their people in the assembly, electing a chairman for political affairs who is not a Pueblo governor.[34]

On February 13, 1964, Domingo Montoya of Sandia Pueblo became
chairman of the All Pueblo Council and immediately had to deal with insufficient funds and facilities. He oversaw the moving of the All Pueblo Council
to the administration building of the old Albuquerque Indian School and
centralized their offices in Albuquerque. The Council created two programs,
the Talent Search program and the Pueblo Indian Scholarship Program.[35]

The All Indian Pueblo Council was then, and remains, a political entity
engaged in strategies to ensure the protection and self-preservation of
Pueblo Indian tribal culture, religion, and ways of life. Their mission is to (1)
provide an organization for the nineteen Pueblo Tribes of New Mexico
through which the Pueblos can centralize their efforts to advance the educational, economic, and social position of all Pueblo Indians; (2) develop and

Fig. 8 **Indian Pueblo Cultural Center Travel Center and Smoke Shop, 2010.**
(Photo by Myla Vicenti Carpio.)

promote educational, business, job training, environmental, health, and social service programs for the benefit and advancement of Indians and the protection and preservation of tribal lands; and (3) support programs and employees of AIPC, Inc., who provide valuable services and foster cooperative relations with Pueblo communities through their dedicated and professional work and the Council's resources.[36]

AIPC programs focus mostly on reservation populations. The Pueblo Office of Environmental Protection (POEP) runs radon testing and air quality control. Two Worlds focuses on the emotional, mental, physical, and spiritual well-being of Albuquerque urban Indians.[37] AIPC's HIV prevention and testing services with substance abuse counseling and rehabilitation assistance serve about thirty-six people a month. The Johnson O'Malley program serves Pueblo Indian students in the Albuquerque public schools. Home/school coordinators monitor grades and attendance and provide tutors, and a parent committee and board of directors oversee the program. The Johnson O'Malley program serves more than 90 percent of Indian students living in the city.[38] Helping Indian Children of Albuquerque (HICOA) provides assistance to Albuquerque Native parents of children with mental, physical, and economic disabilities. It guides families by offering training in parenting skills and identifies a support system for them. HICOA serves approximately thirty-four clients per month.[39]

While the AIPC provides little in terms of urban Indian services, it is important because it provides a united front and a strong Pueblo presence in the state and within the city. Although it often gives the inaccurate impression that AIPC is taking care of Albuquerque urban Indians, it does provide jobs for many Indians living in the city and nearby reservations. Many of those jobs are through the AIPC's Indian Pueblo Cultural Center (IPCC).

INDIAN PUEBLO CULTURAL CENTER

On August 22, 2008, the IPCC inaugurated its new 18,443-square-foot addition. The addition created more dining room space, a new entrance rotunda, and a south entrance with gallery spaces.[40] The State of New Mexico recognizes the importance of the IPCC, with the state legislature providing funding for both the Pueblo House and expansion and improvements. The expansion of the main building also means an expansion of events, activities, and partnerships held by and with the IPCC. For instance, on October 15, 2008, the IPCC organized a luncheon, "Women Inspiring Women," to celebrate the roles of American Indian women in work and communities.[41] Moreover, IPCC has partnered with the Robert Wood Johnson Foundation Center for Health Policy to form the Center for Native American Health Policy. The Center is located at the IPCC and the University of New Mexico. It will "provide a forum and expertise dedicated to health policy analysis, health literacy and community engagement to a degree that we have not seen before in our state."[42] Another partnership was developed with the National Indian Council on Aging, Inc. to form teaching/learning teams with IPCC staff while employing Native seniors.[43] The expansion provides a larger relationship with the city, state, and Pueblo peoples, while maintaining its location as a central meeting place.

The IPCC provides a variety of services for New Mexico, Albuquerque, and surrounding Indian communities. It houses a restaurant, a museum, an auditorium, a "plaza" for dances and other outdoor events, an art gallery and

Fig. 9 **Indian Pueblo Cultural Center entrance, 2010.**
(Photo by Myla Vicenti Carpio.)

gift shop, and offices for meetings and personnel. The museum presents Pueblo cultural history from a perspective controlled by the Pueblos. Such a focus on the Pueblos is rare, despite their importance in New Mexico's history. The Museum of Albuquerque, for example, reflects little of the Native influence in the city's development and barely mentions the existence of the Pueblo people in Albuquerque.

The expansion of the Indian Pueblo Cultural Center and Pueblo Harvest Café provided much more dining and patio space, as well as two private dining rooms and a patio on the new second level.[44] Along with the larger main dining room, the Café now has a covered dining patio. The Pueblo Harvest Café serves Native-fusion cuisine, American foods, and Pueblo standards such as Pueblo oven bread, red chile, green chile, blue corn enchiladas, frybread, and Indian tacos.[45] Food is such an important tie to culture that Indians appreciate this source of foods specific to their home lives.

The Café is a place for Indians to get a taste of home and to hold meetings with other Native people. The restaurant also serves as a social gathering place for many Indian people. Coming into town, many Native people stop in to eat before shopping or going home. Indian officials from around

Fig. 10 **Indian Pueblo Cultural Center east entrance and restaurant area, 2010.**
(Photo by Myla Vicenti Carpio.)

the city frequently stop in. Local Indian groups have breakfast or lunch meetings in the restaurant. The National Indian Youth Council meets there for breakfast the first Tuesday of every month. It is also a common place for informal meetings. People whom I approached for information while working on the book often would suggest that we meet at the Cultural Center.

The Cultural Center also runs the Pueblo House Children's Museum, a hands-on learning facility that introduces students and visitors to Pueblo history and culture. In 2007, the Pueblo House expanded to 1,000 square feet with a classroom, kitchen, and restroom. Visitors work with artists learning pottery making, beadwork, weaving, and cooking.[46] The IPCC guides students through the museum tours, the mini-theater, the Pueblo House Children's Museum, and, sometimes, the restaurant. Tourists have an opportunity to learn about Pueblos from Pueblo sources in a "cultural exchange setting in which the Indian . . . speaks and presents his world."[47] Moreover, the Pueblo House provides a summer camp for children ages ten to twelve to learn about traditional Pueblo agriculture and foodways.[48] These expansion projects apply to the Center's mission: "To preserve and perpetuate Pueblo culture and to advance understanding by presenting with dignity and respect, the accomplishments and evolving history of the Pueblo people of New Mexico."[49]

NATIVE RADIO

Urban Indians usually have little access to broadcast music from their cultures. That lack of access is important, because music functions within a culture to help tie a person to his or her community. Music not only helps people maintain ties to their cultures and reservations, but also connects reservations with urban areas.[50] For over twenty-five years, Albuquerque residents have enjoyed The Singing Wire program, which airs on radio station KUNM every Sunday from noon to 4:00 p.m. The program plays contemporary rock, country-and-western, powwow, and folk music, as well as traditional Pueblo, Diné, and Apache music. Albuquerque Indians can hear music of the Taos Round Dance, San Juan Turtle Dance, Diné Two-Step, and more. The Indigenous languages, sacred content, and emotional stimuli heard in this music connect Native city dwellers to their reservations.

The Board of Regents of the University of New Mexico owns the radio station's license. Two of the first DJs were Francis Montoya of Isleta Pueblo and Conroy Chino of Acoma Pueblo, a former anchor on KOB-TV in Albuquerque and investigative reporter on KOAT-TV in Albuquerque.[51]

Another way The Singing Wire connects people with home is through Native news, requests, and dedications. The program carries announcements of the many ceremonies and feast days that take place throughout the year at the nineteen Pueblos. Listening to the requests and dedications, one hears names of relatives from home or dedications such as a happy birthday from your aunt and uncle in Santa Ana Pueblo. This creates a direct bridge between the reservations and the city, between relatives' homes and residents of Albuquerque and other cities. According to Darrell "Lawrence" Felipe, longtime KUNM volunteer,

> The reservation is tuning in. . . . [T]here are no other choices, basically . . . unless you live in the Navajo area, in Dulce, who [have] their own radio stations. . . . [W]e are more of a variety, we play everything from traditional, modern or . . . contemporary music. Since we are in the middle of

a major city we have the opportunity to interview . . . artists who come through town, performing here . . .[52]

Another Indian radio program is Native America Calling, hosted by Harlan McKosato. Like The Singing Wire, this program originates from Albuquerque and KUNM. Called the "electronic talking circle," the program covers numerous topics from Alcatraz to water rights. As a national call-in program, it also ties in the local community with national Native issues, politics, culture(s), and other Indian nations.

THE TOYAH BAND OF COMANCHES AND THE CHEROKEES OF NEW MEXICO

The Albuquerque Indian community has a number of cultural groups tied to reservations. Three such groups—the Comanches, the Cherokees, and Laguna Pueblo—have organizations that are recognized by their tribal governments and communities. The Toyah Band of Comanches is recognized by the Comanche Nation. La Donna Harris, a founding member of that group, recalls,

> From Oklahoma, most of the Indian people that came in this area were . . . trained professionals, so now that we are kind of middle class or retired, a lot of us . . . feel we want to do more with our tribe, society. So we organized ourselves and we call ourselves the Comanche band, or Toyah band, which is the mountain band. Then we sent a letter to our chairman, you know, our government, and told them we'd like to organize.[53]

Harris said that some thirty to fifty members participate consistently in Toyah Band activities. The band meets at Santa Ana Pueblo. Sometimes they have covered-dish lunches or dinners at the Americans for Indian Opportunity house in Santa Ana, to which they invite the Comanche students from Southwestern Indian Polytechnic Institute in Albuquerque. They meet weekly to learn or practice their language.[54]

Harris estimated that at least three hundred Comanches were living in the Albuquerque and Santa Fe area in 2001. "The Comanches have been migrating to Albuquerque since the early forties," said Harris. In the 1940s and 1950s, Comanches moved to Albuquerque and Santa Fe for jobs with the BIA or the IHS or to teach in schools. Harris's sister worked for the IHS, so her sister and her husband moved to Albuquerque. Her sisters, mother, and aunt would visit them and eventually moved to the area themselves. Harris's family is typical of the many Comanches who moved to the area, as they already had strong familial or community ties in Albuquerque.[55]

The Toyah Band of Comanches keeps their connections to the Comanche people in various ways. They meet once a week for Comanche language classes. The group is also close to the Comanche Language and Cultural Preservation Committee based in Elgin, Oklahoma. The committee sponsors trips to places significant to Comanches, and the Toyah Band joins them. When, for example, the committee sponsored a trip to Palo Duro, Texas, near Amarillo, the Toyah Band drove there to meet them.[56] When the committee visited the Paiutes, who speak a Uto-Aztecan language related to Comanche, members of the Toyah Band joined them.[57]

The Toyah Band and their Oklahoma tribespeople provide mutual assistance and camaraderie. "When they come visiting, we always fix a meal for them," says Harris. Band members return to Oklahoma to attend tribal events.[58]

Toyah Band members work together when returning to their reservation. "Sometimes we just load up and go back for the Comanche Fair in September." The Toyah Band has participated in the parade at Comanche Fair. But despite this degree of involvement in the life of the tribe, the Toyah Band is not a voting precinct for the Comanche Nation and would like to become one. Because there are so many members in the Santa Fe and Albuquerque area, it only seems appropriate.[59]

In some ways, the Cherokees of New Mexico are similar to the Toyah Band of Comanches. Unlike the Toyah Band, however, the Cherokees of New Mexico are recognized by the Cherokee Nation and included in the Nation's constitution.[60] The group teaches the Cherokee language (both spoken and written) and Cherokee history. The organization is open to anyone who has an interest in the Cherokee Nation. The by-laws state, however, that office holders must be enrolled Cherokees. Sometimes Choctaws and members of other non–New Mexico tribes that do not have local organizations will attend this group's meetings.[61] Originally a single group, the Cherokees of New Mexico has splintered into two.

Community in Albuquerque derives from many aspects of an individual's life. People remain Indian in the urban setting partially because of the associations that exist in their lives, the music they hear, the restaurants where they eat, the people with whom they associate, and the organizations in which they participate. As Indians, they associate with other Indians, but another aspect of identity exists: tribal identities. Those identities are maintained in a variety of ways, such as spending time with individuals from the same tribe at the Indian center, or by going home to the reservations to visit or for ceremonies; or, as in the case of the Toyah Band of Comanches and the Cherokees of New Mexico, creating organizations that reflect tribal unity and community.

Members of the Laguna Colony of Albuquerque are tied closely to their home reservation. As with the Comanche and Cherokee groups, the Laguna Colony is recognized by the tribe. The history the Laguna Colony of Albuquerque is unique, however. By looking at the Laguna Colony, we can further understand the desire for and importance of building bridges between the reservations and urban Indian communities.

FIVE

"Let Them Know We Still Exist"

THE ALBUQUERQUE LAGUNA COLONY

THE FEDERAL GOVERNMENT'S RELOCATION PROGRAM, coupled with the termination policy, attempted to usurp Indigenous lands and dissolve Indigenous cultures. Beginning in the 1950s, relocation and termination provided a way for the government to withdraw "legally" from its federal trust responsibility and impose a policy of assimilation on Indigenous peoples. Terminating trust responsibilities, altering borders, and disparaging "Indianness" sent a clear message that the federal government intended for American Indians to cease to exist as cultural and self-determined peoples. The federal government's formula was to get Indians off the reservation; if no one lived on the reservation, then no one needed funds or the land. The relocation program would send Indigenous people off reservations, and provide vocational training, a place to live and a job, all toward the desired goal of absorbing Indigenous peoples into mainstream society. As with other policies of earlier eras, Indigenous people and U.S. officials had different ideas about the goals of relocation.

Relocation created a variety of opportunities for and diverse views among Indigenous people. A wide range of factors influenced journeys from reservations to cities. The appeal of department stores, movie theaters, or adventure sparked imaginings of city life. Some potential relocatees believed the government's relocation literature, which stated, "If you are not able to find work near home to support yourself and your family and to buy the things you need and want, relocation to the cities where jobs can be obtained may be the answer to your problem."[1] For most, such promises proved to be simply propaganda, and the abject poverty and lack of economic opportunities on many reservations continued in the cities.

Regardless of the reasons for moving, relocation with or without assistance from the federal relocation program failed to assimilate Indigenous people completely into American society. The myriad experiences of migration to the cities or staying on reservations created dynamic relationships between urban and reservation Indigenous identities.

Unfortunately, early studies of relocated Indians characterized assimilation simplistically in terms of success or failure, staying or returning.[2] These terms created another simplistically characterized dichotomy related to that of traditionalism versus progressivism. The reservation versus urban split utilized colonial labels of progress, positing the "good" Indian against the "bad" Indian. Those who stayed in the city were "successful" despite unmeasured living conditions and situations; the only important criterion by federal standards was that they stayed. Failure meant leaving the city and returning to the reservation. Consequently, "the urban Indian" was seen as the assimilated Indian no matter what his or her socioeconomic and cultural status.

As a result, for many people—including historians, policymakers, and even Indians themselves—the rez/urban dichotomy denotes an urban Indian experience completely distinct from, and less authentic than, reservation life. The reservation is believed to generate the "authentic Indian," one who knows the traditional culture, practices the traditional religion, and speaks the tribal language while always challenging the colonial policies of the federal government. By contrast, the dichotomy posits urban identity as separate from the reservation: creating a home in the city represents a changed identity farther from the reservation, either assimilated, a generic pan-Indian, or "Indian" with no tribal distinction. As these polarized identities become internalized, the process of American colonization further obscures, divides, and devalues Indigenous people's lived realities. According to Lisa Poupart's analysis of internalized colonization, "As Western constructions of abject difference are both forced upon and accepted by American Indians, we define ourselves through these constructions and subsequently participate in the reproduction of these codes . . . the very codes that created, reflected, and reproduced our oppression."[3] In this case, the internalization of this dichotomy further isolates and devalues Indigenous people living in urban centers.

The generic "Indian" and/or pan-Indian identity may be a reality for some. However, this chapter argues that the concept of pan-Indian identity limits our understanding of the lived reality of urban Indigenousness. Instead of concentrating on the division between the reservation and the urban, I focus on the intersection where urban Indian organizations develop community while maintaining and nurturing connections with reservation life and culture. The history of the Laguna colonies, particularly the Laguna Colony of Albuquerque, illustrates the intersections of urban and reservation life and the dual landscapes where Indigenous peoples counter colonization. Instead of assimilating the dichotomy of "reservation" and "urban Indians," members of the Laguna colonies live outside their reservation home while maintaining their cultural connections through the colonies.

Moving to the city does not necessarily end a personal or spiritual connection to the reservation. Nevertheless, although home communities may seem a short distance away, distance is a significant obstacle to maintaining religious, cultural, and language ties. To overcome that problem, as discussed in the previous chapter, Indigenous urban people have formed associations and relationships to build bridges to home and to a specific culture or a specific people. Some make connections with others informally at pow-wows, churches, Indian centers, and bars where diverse Indigenous people gather.[4] Others gravitate toward individuals of their own nation or cultural background, as the Comanches in Albuquerque formed the Toyah Band and the Cherokees formed the Cherokees of Albuquerque. These organizations gather, share meals, and sponsor classes in the history, culture, and language of their particular tribes, and thus maintain a tribal identity despite the distance of miles. Elected officials or candidates from the reservation travel to attend those meetings to solicit votes.[5]

Another such group is a community of Albuquerque residents from Laguna Pueblo. The Laguna Colony, as they are known, furnishes a social support system while also offering a way to maintain many cultural obligations, language, and connect Laguna tribal members living in Albuquerque with Laguna Pueblo. Laguna has a unique history of extending formal recognition to off-reservation tribal members by according them the status of a colony. This process began when the railroad reached Laguna in 1880. The railroad changed the lives of the Laguna people permanently. The Pueblo of Laguna saw the railroad as a unique opportunity to involve Laguna people economically in construction and operations. In the 1880s, the Atlantic and Pacific Railroad Company (later the Atchison, Topeka and Santa Fe Railway) began laying track south of Albuquerque. In time, they reached the Laguna Pueblo reservation lands.

The Lagunas stopped the construction to negotiate a precedent-setting handshake agreement or "gentlemen's agreement of friendship" between Laguna officials and the railroad company. The company employed many Laguna men and women while continuing to renew their agreement called "watering the flower."[6] As part of this agreement, the company offered the Lagunas a lump-sum payment as compensation for right-of-way passage through the reservation.[7] Instead of this payment, Laguna leaders and the railroad company fashioned a renewable annual verbal agreement to exchange right-of-way for employment. In exchange for passage through the Laguna reservation, the company agreed to employ any Laguna who wanted to work at building and maintaining the railroad system. Workers had jobs "so long as the governor of their pueblo granted the workers his approval."[8] The agreement introduced Lagunas into the wage-earning economy, but it also took them off the reservation. While many Lagunas laid track and then returned home, others stayed with the company to work in construction, and as mechanics, clerks, and conductors.

Laguna leaders anticipated the emigrants' need for a home away from home, so they included a provision in the agreement obligating the company to provide housing off the reservation and along the route from New Mexico through Arizona and into California: Gallup, Winslow, Holbrook, Barstow, Richmond, and Los Angeles.[9] In this way, the Pueblo maintained a formal connection with the workers. The railroad company's idea of adequate housing did not consist of houses. Instead, the railroad put aside box-cars on railroad property, which became homes for many Laguna and Acoma railroad workers and their families.[10] The Acomas and the Lagunas stayed near one another, partly to re-create their proximity at home, and partly because of a linguistic kinship, for both spoke dialects of the Keresan language. In order to create a home away from home, the Lagunas decorated and fashioned the boxcars into residences for their families. Their homes represented life away from the Pueblo without forgetting their origins. The railroad communities consequently became cultural communities that sustained Laguna language, culture, and ceremonies.

The railroad communities of Laguna people asked that the Pueblo of Laguna formally recognize them as colonies of the Pueblo. Laguna formally recognized the colonies in Gallup, New Mexico; Winslow, Arizona; Barstow, California; and Richmond, California. This recognition of the Laguna railroad workers' communities served as the basis for a more structured community.[11] Formal recognition allowed for both an actual and a psychological connection to home. The colonies continued social dances in a meeting hall that was, of course, a converted boxcar. Colony members used this same meeting hall to host deer dinners, meetings, and feasts.[12] The hall must have echoed from the drumbeats of the deer and corn dance songs, beats that bounced off the floors and ceilings to be absorbed by those in attendance. Residents even built Indian ovens to make Pueblo oven bread, supplying the smells and foods of home. In fact, many members of these original colonies eventually became members of the Albuquerque colony.

Katherine Augustine, a member of the Laguna Colony of Albuquerque, spent her summer vacations from the Albuquerque Indian School as a youth in the Laguna Colony of Gallup where her parents worked.[13] A small front deck led to the entrances of each family's two-room boxcar. Inside, homes had wood stoves for cooking and for heat. Outside were wood piles, clothes lines that stretched from the box cars to barbed wire fences, and the occasional horno, or bee-hive oven, to bake bread. Families shared men's and women's community bathrooms, which were equipped with bathtubs, showers, and toilets. Homes had electricity, but people obtained water at a spigot next to the bathhouse.[14]

Fathers worked at the railroad, and most women took care of the homes and children. Augustine remembered, "Sometimes they made sandwiches for the hobos who got off the freight trains."[15] Some of the children went to boarding schools in Albuquerque or Santa Fe, and others went to public or Catholic schools in Gallup. The children sought entertainment in Gallup at dances at the Catholic Indian Center or at the Sunday afternoon movies at the Chief or the El Morro Theaters where they would have a cherry coke before going home.[16] These boxcar communities were home to many Lagunas and some Acomas, providing a community established partly through work, yet held together more substantially by common culture, language, and spiritual beliefs.

Whereas other Laguna colonies began as Laguna railroad communities away from the Pueblo, the Laguna Colony of Albuquerque originated in urban community-building with the priority of maintaining Laguna culture and language. In some ways, therefore, the Laguna Colony is quite different from the other five colonies. For people in the railroad colonies, work was the means to live together and support one another away from home. In Albuquerque, however, jobs did not bring Lagunas together geographically. They were spread out across the city and came from a variety of educational and employment backgrounds.

Despite basic differences, the roots of the Laguna Colony of Albuquerque are similar to those of the Laguna railroad colonies. Both types of colony represent the reciprocal relationship between members off and on the Pueblo and their connection to Pueblo community and culture. For many, economic circumstances were such that there was no choice but to leave the reservation. For instance, a larger number of Lagunas lived in Albuquerque than in the other colonies because of the limited availability of railroad jobs. In addition, students from Albuquerque Indian School stayed in the city after they graduated. Female students stayed to become nurses and teachers or to work in homes of wealthy families, and men stayed to work for the railroad or in mechanics, retail, or agriculture. Others returned to the reservation or worked for the Bureau of Indian Affairs or the Indian Health Service.

With increasing numbers of Lagunas living in Albuquerque, many Laguna people felt the need for unity and interconnectedness in Albuquerque.[17] The distance from the Pueblo contributed to that feeling. Laguna Pueblo is only forty miles west of Albuquerque, but that distance is immense separation when away from one's culture, language, and relations. The Laguna urbanites exercised their right to seek recognition as stated in Article III, Section 5, of the Laguna Constitution, which discerned "populations" of adult Pueblo members located outside the boundaries of Laguna Pueblo.[18] The Pueblo recognized the Laguna Colony of Albuquerque in 1955.

The discovery of uranium on Laguna land was one factor in the Pueblo's decision to grant recognition. In the late 1940s and early 1950s, the Cold War spurred the federal government's search for domestic uranium deposits. In New Mexico, uranium was located near Grants and then, eventually, on the Laguna reservation near the village of Paguate. The discovery of uranium brought needed economic opportunities to the Pueblo. In the early 1950s, the Anaconda mining company contracted with the Pueblo of Laguna to extract the uranium. This agreement provided royalties to Laguna Pueblo and, soon after, the Laguna people wanted the royalties distributed.[19] Before uranium, the tribe had experienced little economic development and had garnered little surplus funds. As a consequence, the Laguna Pueblo Constitution stated that the tribe would never distribute tribal funds. To change that restriction, the Pueblo needed to revise their constitution.[20]

Elders on the council called in a number of Laguna individuals living outside the Laguna reservation to help the tribal council revise the constitution. Ulysses Paisano, one of those members, recalls:

There were two guys from Winslow, Arizona, one from Santa Fe; and the main thing was to try to help the council. How to get the job done, to distribute the money. So we had to hire a lawyer, and the government lawyer also helped us a lot. So the first thing we [had] to do was to revise the old Constitution, it was outdated. . . . Of course, up to that time the tribe had little money. So, revising the Constitution . . . took a lot of work, [and] it took . . . about five years. Finally, we [had] to set up a tribal roll in addition to the Constitution revision.[21]

The old constitution had specified several colonies—Gallup, Winslow,

Barstow, and Richmond—but not Albuquerque. Therefore, Ulysses Paisano asked the council and then Laguna governor Tom Daily about the possibility of setting up a colony in Albuquerque. At first, the tribe did not see the feasibility of such a request. They thought that Albuquerque was close enough for Pueblo members to drive home for community obligations. With some persuasion, Pueblo officials approved the colony on December 31, 1955.[22]

> We weren't organized at all, and so the councilmen kind of objected because they [thought] we were too close [to Laguna Pueblo]. [They] said, "you can come to meetings, village meetings." But we argued with them that it was too costly to run out there. So they finally agreed to let us set up a new colony in Albuquerque.[23]

Authorized to set up a colony, they notified all the Lagunas in Albuquerque. Ulysses worked for the Albuquerque Indian School, and the superintendent let them hold their first meeting on February 15, 1956, in the Albuquerque Indian School gymnasium. John Paisano, Sr., the 1956 governor of the Pueblo of Laguna, also attended.[24] According to Ulysses Paisano,

> there was about eighty-five people who showed up. That's how many Lagunas were here then. And we established the Colony right then and there and elected the officers. They elected me as chairman, and so I served as chairman after that, I guess about four times. So that's how we got started.[25]

According to the by-laws of the Laguna Colony of Albuquerque, the purpose of the organization "is to establish the principal line of communication between the Pueblo government and the Colony members."[26] To keep up that communication, the tribal council and village officials regularly send the minutes of their meetings to the colonies. Moreover, colony members must adhere to the Laguna Pueblo Constitution, ordinances, customs, traditions, and other applicable regulations, meaning that they still must meet tribal obligations. More importantly, the colony serves to promote and provide educational, cultural, and charitable services to its members while "preserving the culture of the Pueblo in an urban setting."[27]

The colony takes seriously its mission to maintain Pueblo customs and beliefs away from the reservation. The committees and activities within the Colony illustrate one venue through which cultural continuity is maintained. The colony relates and adheres to the Pueblo of Laguna through community or communal customs of shared responsibilities. In the Pueblo, community work was and continues to be valued as important. For instance, during early spring, before planting crops and gardens, on one mutually chosen day, all the men in each village come together to clean the irrigation ditches. As in all desert areas, water is a treasure. Since agriculture (along with hunting) was the main form of subsistence for the Pueblos, the uninhibited flow of irrigation water to crops was the lifeline of the people. Therefore, cleaning the irrigation ditches was not only important for physical survival, but it also brought the community together.

Now that many Lagunas live or work away from the Pueblo, wage work has affected performance of community obligations. Traditionally, men have cleaned the plaza where many ceremonies take place, dug graves for funerals, and attended village meetings. The men digging the graves receive recognition for their work through gifts of food, drink, and cigarettes while they work. Each man in the village assumes these responsibilities, with some exceptions for age and handicaps. A man who does not participate in these activities must pay fifteen dollars to the Pueblo. Posted signs along the road announce the next village meeting. Men are obligated to attend village meetings, but women are not, although women do take part. Missing village meetings incurs a fine. Tribal officials collect these dues at the time of per capita distribution.[28] Although some men who work outside the Pueblo return to fulfill their obligations, others elect to pay the fines.

One intersection of the Albuquerque Laguna Colony's dual landscapes concerns the interactions between the Colony and Pueblo officials. Recently, the mayordomo at the village of Paguate asked the former chairman of the Colony, David Melton, to send the attendance records of the Colony's meetings. He assured the chairman that attendance at Colony meetings will count toward attendance at the Paguate Village meeting.[29] Perhaps the other villages will eventually follow this precedent to validate the Colony's meetings. Melton hopes that Pueblo officials will recognize the political potential of Laguna Colony members as voters and as representing other educational and political assets.[30] This communication and recognition strengthens, nurtures, and maintains connections between Lagunas living on and off the Pueblo.

The Colony strives to maintain connections and communications with the Pueblo through many avenues. In 2001, Melton envisioned more communication between Colony and Pueblo, a two-way conversation, in which the Pueblo recognizes the strengths of the colony members and how to use them. At that time, he wanted office space to house the Colony's documents permanently.[31] Melton believed that office space could benefit the tribal officials who come to Albuquerque on business; instead of renting expensive office spaces in town, they could use the Colony's space.[32] This, in turn, would create a closer, more personal relationship between on- and off-reservation officials.

Colony membership incorporates and appreciates all inhabitants of the Albuquerque Laguna community. Membership consists of enrolled members of the Pueblo of Laguna residing in Albuquerque, associate members, and a board of directors. The Colony acknowledges non-Laguna spouses and children of members with associate membership.[33] The associates play an invaluable role in the colony, especially with the cultural and state fair committees.[34] Both members and associate members have voting privileges.[35]

The board of directors is the governing power of the Laguna colony. The members include a chairman, a vice-chairman, a secretary, a treasurer, and a member elected at large by the membership.[36] The board is the decision-making body that conducts meetings, appoints committees, develops the annual budget and presents it to the membership for approval, as well as creating the financial management plan for investments and disbursement of the Colony's funds. Most actions need approval by colony membership.[37] Members of the board of directors are colony members, and, therefore, also members of the Pueblo of Laguna.

In December of each year, all colony members, including associate members, elect the board of directors to one-year terms. The chairman is the principal contact among the Colony, the Laguna governor, and the tribal council, and travels to the Pueblo to meet with the governor and council. The chairman manages affairs for the Colony from matters as small as products to sell at the state fair to arranging formal communications with the Pueblo. The vice-chairman fulfills the duties delegated by the chairman and keeps an inventory of colony equipment, such as a sound system, file cabinet, and so on. The chairman and vice-chairman work together on meeting agendas, decide who will receive and read the council and village minutes at the meetings, and deal with the projects and decisions that arise. The secretary, of course, takes the minutes of the meetings, maintains a permanent file of minutes and colony membership information, and keeps the tribal office informed of the Colony's administrative changes and events.[38] Money matters, such as deposits, record keeping, disbursements, and reports, are the responsibility of the treasurer. The board of directors appoints two sergeants-at-arms to prepare and clean up the meeting area while upholding the peace and order of meetings. The board member-at-large serves as liaison between colony members and the board of directors.[39]

During the past twenty years, a change in leadership has taken place within the colony that has also influenced tribal politics at Laguna Pueblo. Until the early 1990s, men held the positions of chairman and vice-chairman. Then in 1992, the Albuquerque Laguna Colony elected its first woman chair, Cheryl Paisano, daughter of the first chairman, Ulysses Paisano.[40] Her election was and still is regarded by Lagunas as a major feat, for traditionally, Laguna leadership is comprised of men only. Cheryl Paisano comments:

Daddy and I were just talking, saying how he was the first chairman, and years later I was the first woman chairman. . . . [U]ntil then the Colony didn't have [a woman chairman]. We had women officers, but we didn't have a woman chairman, and I've been secretary, and . . . vice-chairman for several years. And so I was selected and it was really interesting because back then when the news got out at the Pueblo that the Colony had a woman chairman, . . . they said, "How come we don't have women officers?" And so a lot of things have evolved since then.[41]

Cheryl Paisano was elected chair in the early 1990s. In 1996, Emily Cheromiah of the village of Paguate became the first woman to run for elected office at Laguna Pueblo. This became a point of contention since men have traditionally held political offices, and men are also the religious leaders, appointed for life.[42] In 1908, Laguna became the first Pueblo to write and approve a constitution. After the Indian Reorganization Act of 1934, Laguna adopted another written constitution, and the political authority of Laguna moved from the religious leaders to elected politicians. This meant only men could hold a leadership position or office. Yet Emily Cheromiah was nominated for the office of treasurer (an elected position), and the twenty-one–member tribal council declined her nomination. This led to a referendum vote to decide whether to allow women to hold office.[43]

Cheromiah understood the ramifications of her attempt to get on the election ballot. She also understood that she was not impinging on religious traditions. Language in the constitution focused on "traditional standards" and used the male pronoun "he" when describing the office and elections. Laguna voters eventually approved women's eligibility to run for the offices of tribal secretary, treasurer, interpreter, and tribal council representatives.[44] Women still do not hold governing positions, as they do in the Laguna Colony, but the Colony appears to have at least influenced the Pueblo's political consciousness.

The structure of the Laguna Colony of Albuquerque is designed to emphasize Laguna cultural and social cohesiveness within the colony and its connectedness with the Pueblo. Colony committees—Sunshine, Social, Arts and Crafts, Recreation, Education, Cultural, and State Fair—provide a space where members maintain customs of shared responsibilities to each other and to Laguna culture. Each committee, in its own way, plays an important role in building a cohesive community to foster and maintain Laguna culture. For example, the Sunshine Committee, consisting of only one person, keeps track of Colony members who are sick at home or in the hospital and of deaths within the colony or the Pueblo. That person sends flowers to those colony members and provides a small amount of money to the family of a deceased colony member to cover burial costs. Through the Sunshine Committee, the Colony supports members in their times of need.

The Social Committee, with some help from the State Fair Committee, puts together the governor's dinner and the Christmas dinner. Every year, the Colony pays respect to elected tribal officials by hosting the governor's dinner. The Colony's leaders invite Laguna Pueblo officials and council members and their families. This dinner is an opportunity for members of the Laguna Colony and tribal officials and their relatives to meet one another and feast together. The governor of the Pueblo gives a brief update on tribal business and concerns, and Colony members can ask questions. When the governor cannot attend, he sends the lieutenant governor or another official of the Pueblo in his behalf. In his talk, the governor usually gives words of encouragement to members of the Colony and reminders of their political power as Lagunas in the city.[45] As with other social functions, the Governor's dinner reinforces the bonds between the Colony and Pueblo leadership.

The Christmas dinner affords an opportunity for Colony members and friends to maintain relations with one another.[46] Colony members have contributed door prizes such as Pauline Acoya's favorite cookies and Marie Aragon's beadwork. Dan Atsye has led Christmas carols and played Santa for the kids.[47] These dinners provide important opportunities for family and friends of all generations to come together, even giving young people a place to meet and fall in love. Cheryl Paisano remembers that "Roland Johnson's son and Dan Atsye's son were best friends, and they married sisters, a family that lived at Isleta but were part Laguna came to the functions. . . . So the guys met the sisters at one of the Christmas parties. And they ended up dating."[48]

The Cultural Committee organizes a program to teach the Laguna language and culture. Many of the Laguna Colony members grew up in Albuquerque outside the reservation and either never learned the Keresan language or know only "bits and pieces." Even for someone whose first language was Laguna, the language is lost if not spoken every day. Language classes provide an opportunity to use the Native language and a place where other members can learn or improve their skills. Before Roland Johnson returned to Laguna to serve as governor, he taught the language and culture class. Recently, Dan Atsye supplemented the language class by emphasizing Laguna origin stories, clans, and family structures.[49] With a grant from the University of New Mexico, the committee created a curriculum for the language, placing fluent speakers with non-fluent speakers for weekly classes to teach the language and culture. Dan Atsye has also made audio tapes for some members of the Colony.

The Education Committee deals with education, contributing to members' postsecondary education through a small scholarship fund. Committee members review scholarship applications, which require the applicant to be in attendance at six meetings and be a Laguna Colony member. The colony also helps its members with scholarships for work-related meetings and courses, especially those that encourage the use and persistence of Laguna language and culture. Scholarships have been funded by the money made at the state fair concession booth and totaled $550 per semester.

The Arts and Crafts Committee gives Colony members the opportunity to learn or teach crafts. In order to offer specific classes, the committee considered paying class fees for members who attended classes and then returned to teach the class at the Colony. The classes provide a social environment for learning such skills as quilting, weaving, beading or moccasin making.[50] In addition, members learn to make tamales, Easter pudding, and other traditional foodstuffs. Cheryl Paisano remembers,

> I taught beadwork. And then, Grace Andrews let us meet at her house, and we had an embroidery class . . . and cross-stitch. Bruce Paisano . . . taught us how to do weaving, and Grace's husband made the looms for us. I think they really need to get the people more involved, like we did with the cross-stitch. Initially it was [a] learning experience, and after that it got to be a social thing like a quilting bee or something. People would just look forward to [meeting], the women especially, getting out at night. And too, they would tell stories, they would tell of things that happened before. A lot of it was cultural[ly] related, and those kinds of things are really neat. We grew a lot. I miss some of those ladies; they aren't with us anymore.[51]

While the committees and groups contribute to social and cultural camaraderie, no other project unites or embodies the Laguna Colony of Albuquerque as much as its concession stand at the state fair. Fund raising by the State Fair Committee is the single greatest source of financial support for the Colony. At its founding, the Colony had little money to manage its affairs. As Ulysses Paisano recalls, in the Colony's first mass mailing, its leaders had "to ask everyone to chip in for postage and stationery."[52] To raise funds, the Laguna Colony looked toward the New Mexico State Fair, held in Albuquerque, as a possible economic avenue, since the Fair included a Spanish Village and an Indian Village with concession and merchant booths. With Ruth Paisano's hard work, the Colony set up a concession booth and began to sell food about a year after the Colony's creation.[53] Profits from the fair would cover costs of sending out meeting announcements and a newsletter, and educational scholarships to encourage and support Colony members at post-secondary institutions.

In 1881, the New Mexico State Fair began as the New Mexico Territory Fair. Albuquerque businessmen thought a fair might do well, and sheep raisers and cattle ranchers wanted a venue to show off prize sheep and cattle. The first territorial fair easily displaced a similar event, the "función or patronal feast," known as a "Jamaica," at the San Felipe church in Old Town. The feast involved musicians, jugglers, needlework, and horse racing, among other events. Then a morning Mass was sung followed by another series of events. An evening service and a dance concluded the Jamaica.[54] Thus, in its attempt to proclaim the territory as "civilized," the organizers of the first state fair adopted the theme, "The Civilization of the 19th Century Contrasted with the Civilization of Prehistoric Times." The exhibits positioned Albuquerque's gentility against Indian dances, Indian athleticism, and collections of Indian pottery advertised as "relics from the ruined cities of the Montezuma."[55]

Along with "the civilization of prehistoric times," the present civilization displayed horse racing and exhibits of horses, sheep, and livestock. The next year, at the second fair, the big attraction was the City of Albuquerque balloon, which foreshadowed Albuquerque's present claim as (hot air) "balloon capital of the world."[56] To encourage attendance at the fair, the railroad offered reduced rates for fair attendees on all railroads and advertised that Albuquerque had hotel accommodations for fifty thousand people.[57] By 1882, the city had officially organized the annual territorial fair.[58]

Although it began with depictions of "the uncivilized Indians," the New Mexico State Fair has become increasingly and legitimately multicultural. Recently, the tri-cultural designation has expanded to include the African-American pavilion, which displays the history and contributions of African Americans to New Mexico history. The State Fair also oversees the Spanish and Indian Villages, with both areas offering ethnic foods, music, and dances. Walking into the Spanish village, fair goers are met immediately with a large selection of New Mexican and Mexican food booths, in addition to enchiladas, tacos, rice, and burritos. Vendors also surround the square to sell items from Mexico and northern New Mexico. Throughout the day and evening, programs of dance and music illustrate the colorful Hispanic culture. Similarly, the Indian Village is the site of numerous food booths selling Laguna, Jemez, and Navajo foods, booths of art vendors from various Indian nations. Indian frybread, music, and dances are also popular attractions. Every day, dance groups from Laguna, Mescalero Apache, Zuni, and Hopi perform, as do contemporary bands. During the weekend, a small powwow takes place in the recently renovated performance and audience areas.

During the early years of the state fair's Indian Village, it had few or no buildings in which to sell foods or crafts. Later, the Laguna Colony, the Council of American Indians, and the Navajo Club built the first booths there. In the Colony's early years, however, the men would build ramadas from which the Colony would sell food. Remembering those days, Cheryl Paisano said:

> The men would do a ramada-type of thing where they cut the poles, and the booth was covered with branches, and the side is where they fried the bread. . . . They had a tarp out there, and . . . gas stoves. . . . I was in high school then, and I remember going out there to help. Sometimes it would be raining, and that rain would hit the pots, and hot oil would just splatter. . . . Eventually, [it was] enclosed, and then the fairgrounds helped a little more, and they included electricity.[59]

In those early days of the Laguna Colony Fair booth, people of all ages and both genders cooperated. Running the concession booth involved preparing the booth, and preparing the food and selling it. All Colony members consulted about the booth for this study commented about the amount of work involved, but more importantly, they all spoke of the fun and cohesion it produced within the Colony. Most of the work was done by hand, men and women working together. Cooking green chile stew for thousands of orders meant bushels of green chile had to be prepared. The men roasted the

Hatch green chile, and the women peeled and bagged them. According to Cheryl Paisano,

> There were times that's what we did all day. The men would roast all the chile, and the women would peel it, cut [it] up, and bag it. People would take X amount home and put it in their freezers, and as . . . needed . . . they would bring [it] in. And I remember one night, I swear we did twenty bags . . . of chile. We didn't have a whole lot of help. We started out about eight in the morning, and we were usually done by maybe four or five, and then they would have a steak fry. But that time we were there until 10'clock at night, and there was chile everywhere. So people ended up taking sacks home to peel at home, then we had to try to round it all back up. But I remember people turned on their car headlights toward the booth so that . . . we could see what we were doing.[60]

In this process, even children helped by rolling spoons and forks in napkins to be passed out with orders of stew and Indian tacos.

The next largest endeavor was the fry bread. Making fry bread is a relatively simple process: just mix flour, salt, and baking powder with milk or water to make a dough, flatten a piece of dough, and fry it. It is a relatively simple process, that is, until you need enough dough to yield three hundred or more pieces of fry bread. That much fry bread requires twenty-five pounds of flour, handfuls of baking powder and salt, and considerable water. The ingredients must be mixed thoroughly, rolled out, and then placed in the hot oil. Grace Andrews remembers:

> We used to have these big tubs where people would mix . . . [the] dough for the fry bread. There would be ten to twelve people all lined [up] . . . rolling out the dough, because sometimes people would order five or six fry bread at one time. That's our biggest seller actually, . . . the fry bread. And, of course, now Laguna tacos is another big one.[61]

Rolling the dough is hard work, and everyone must work together. Even with such a high volume of dough to work, Colony members and friends maintained camaraderie. Cheryl Paisano remembers,

We would have to roll those things out by hand, and they would mix by hand. It was a lot of work. I mean, everybody pulled together, and we would be laughing. In fact, I had a friend of mine volunteer, and she came and helped. She was rolling her bread, and you know you have to flip it and do all these other things to roll it. And her [dough] kept shrinking, and so she worked on hers for about five minutes, so finally one of the ladies said, "Wouldn't you rather serve the drinks?"[62]

Eventually, the Colony invested in an industrial-sized mixer and two rollers. The mixer took the place of the big tubs and a few people struggling to combine the ingredients. People must still roll out and flap the dough (from hand to hand), but the rollers took out an initial step, making the work easier for subsequent rolling.[63]

In those early days, many of the Colony members who volunteered at the concession stand would take their annual vacations from their jobs so that they would be free to work the fair. This annual project promoted community cohesion and cultural expression through foods and arts, and garnered funds for the Colony's needs. Most importantly perhaps, the Laguna Colony members had to draw on one another, working together as Laguna people to run a busy seventeen-day business.

In recent years, volunteerism has given way to paid participation. Many members of the Colony work or go to school and cannot make time for volunteer work in the concession stand. The work is divided into two shifts: the day shift works from 8:00 a.m. to 4:00 p.m., and the night shift works 4:00 to 9:00 p.m. on weekdays and 4:00 to 10:00 p.m. on weekends.

While the Laguna Colony constantly adjusts to the many forces that bring change, they have remained cohesive and ardent in keeping their ties to Laguna Pueblo and flourishing as a community. Colony numbers recently totaled thirty to forty members, although the estimated Laguna population in Albuquerque is 828.

The Laguna railroad colonies were created as a way for off-reservation community members to maintain cultural and political connections while away from the Pueblo. These Lagunas remained bound to the Pueblo, thereby perpetuating Laguna culture, history, and language. Likewise, the Laguna Colony of Albuquerque has kept its cultural and political connections to the

Laguna Pueblo. These ties are especially visible at the meetings. All generations participated, from elders to grandchildren. The Colony's leaders have
made a serious attempt to keep the group together so that all voices can be
heard. In lively discussions, participants always show respect for those who
speak up.

The Colony encourages ties to the Pueblo through communication, activities, or participation in feast day dances. It seeks to "make a good showing for the Colony to demonstrate the importance of the Pueblo world in our
daily lives."[64] Minutes of meetings at Laguna villages inform Albuquerque
Lagunas of events at the Pueblo. Furthermore, Chairman David Melton
pushed for a two-way communication between Pueblo and Colony, in addition to the usual one-way communication in which minutes are read at the
Laguna Colony meeting. "Let them know we still exist" is the idea behind
creating such two-way communication.[65]

Through these connections, the Laguna Colony asserts its role as a part
of the reservation. Many still return home to Laguna to participate in the ceremonies. Their participation keeps them connected, along with the Colony.
Few are fluent in the language; the older members who do speak fluently,
were raised on the reservation. As Cheryl Paisano explained, "Once people
get away, then there is really no one to converse with."[66] Her children do not
speak the language.

The Laguna colonies are communities with governments patterned after
that of the Pueblo. The government of the Pueblo of Laguna officially recognizes these colonies as extensions of the Pueblo, as does the Bureau of Indian Affairs.[67] The Colony receives minutes of meetings at the Pueblo to
keep Albuquerque Lagunas informed. That the Albuquerque colony was created for an urban community illustrates certain aspects of urban Indian life.
It wants to "make a good showing for the Colony to demonstrate the importance of the Pueblo world in our daily lives."[68]

Initially, most of the members were born and raised in one of the villages
of Laguna. The members continued to practice and participate in the ceremonies at home. Most were fluent in their language. Many left the reservation for railroad and other jobs, or to study at the Albuquerque Indian School,
the Santa Fe Indian School, or an Indian school outside New Mexico.

Signs of cultural apathy within the Colony, however, illustrate issues in the general urban Indian population. Over time, meeting attendance by young people has declined. The few young people who attend come from families with a longtime history in the Laguna Colony. Others, for various reasons, do not see the Colony as a viable tie to the reservation community. Many of the younger generations view the link to the reservation differently from their parents and grandparents. The language is spoken less and less; this loss of language is both a symptom and a cause of Lagunas' separation from their culture. Throughout Native America, increased urbanization brings decreased fluency in tribal languages and decreased participation in religious ceremonies. Moreover, many Native people living on their reservations are increasingly apathetic about their traditional cultures. Nonetheless, this does not necessarily mean a decline in tribal identity. The Colony, like other communities, is trying to teach the language and the culture. As with urban Indians generally, the Colony's increased efforts targeting cultural revitalization makes use of skills learned in the urban setting.

The relationship between Laguna Colony and the Pueblo has demonstrated a strikingly different use of the colony as a means of cultural preservation. Imperial colonies facilitated political and economic expansion as a "new political organization created by invasion," exploiting and subjugating Indigenous peoples.[69] Colonies, as hegemonic structures, "became imperialism's outpost, the fort and the port of imperial outreach."[70] In America, European powers used exploitative and settlement colonies toward the economic exploitation of Indigenous resources and the utilization of cheap land and labor.[71] Spanish, Mexican, and American colonization arrived through European colonial structures that invaded Indigenous lands. In the Southwest, the many Indigenous nations understood the destructive capacity of colonial settlement. When the Pueblo of Laguna used colonial structures, however, it did so not for hegemonic expansion, but, rather, to counter white America's continuing colonial pressures on Laguna land and culture.

The history and lived experiences of the members of the Laguna Colony of Albuquerque illustrate the dynamic intersections of reservation and urban life. Within these intersections, members of the Colony maintain and nurture cultural connections with the mother Pueblo and oppose destructive dichotomous identities that divide and isolate many Indigenous peoples. Throughout North America, even Indians who have not lived on a reservation for years continue to travel home and maintain communications with tribal entities. The examples of the Cherokees of Albuquerque, the Toyah Band of Comanches, and the Laguna Colony of Albuquerque can contribute to a new conceptual framework for viewing urban Indians. Those groups suggest a new and different dynamic in which to examine American Indian history. In brief, Indians in the city further the history of survival and persistence of American Indians generally.

SIX

Decolonizing Albuquerque

LBUQUERQUE'S IMAGINING of and relations with American Indians today is a product of the city's history of colonial relations with Indigenous peoples. The colonial relationship continues in the city's exploitation of tribal images at the same time as it displays indifference to the interests of its Indian residents. In both cases, the colonial relationship manifests as an "absent presence" of Indigenous cultures within the city. An "absent" or deliberate exclusion of the "other's" history is used to sustain a dominant narrative. In Albuquerque, Indigenous history and worldviews have been erased from the city's consciousness and historical memory. In their place is an abundance of commercialized and romanticized images of American Indians.[1]

This absent presence of urban Indians can also be found in scholarship, which until recently has viewed urban Indians through the dichotomy of urban versus reservation, concluding that Indians cannot survive culturally and do not belong in urban environments. Early literature on urban Indians illuminated issues of cultural deterioration or loss of tribal identity, emphasizing a "pan-Indian" urban culture and identity and portraying urban Indian communities with no—or few—ties to reservation communities. Such a narrow focus overlooks essential aspects of urban Indigenous life and culture. In this book, I have sought to provide a wider view of Indigenous peoples in the city and in developing communities.

Furthermore, few scholarly works delve far into the problems of Indians living in the urban environment. A move to the city from a tribal community creates complexities for the relocated tribal member. I have examined some crucial ones, especially the problematic relationships of urban Indians with federal, state, and local governments. Scholarship on urban Indians tells us much about adjustment or lack of adjustment but little about urban Indians' access to health care, education, and housing. The latter kind of knowledge must come from the narratives that only experience, and not just observation, can produce.

Scholarship must also examine the complex problem of Indigenous cultural perseverance. The survival of American Indian cultures and governments is by no means assured. The dehumanizing processes of colonization continue to afflict Indigenous peoples. Many of the social problems attributed to reservation life or Indigenous existence result from the legacy of conquest and colonization. "[C]ontemporary American Indian communities struggle with devastating social ills," writes Anishinaabe scholar Lisa Poupart, "including alcoholism, family violence, incest, sexual assault, fetal-alcohol syndrome, homicide, and suicide at startling rates similar to and sometimes exceeding those of white society." She notes that those social pathologies were "virtually nonexistent in traditional tribal communities prior to European invasion."[2] Such problems threaten the political sovereignty of tribes and the survival of their ancient cultures, and tribal people are responding to those threats with urgent programs of decolonizing action.

Decolonization refers to a discourse and action used to disturb and disrupt the continuing processes and impacts of colonization's narratives and paradigms of oppression. These impacts manifest themselves as physical and psychological transformation or destruction of persons, places, and beliefs, such as in bulldozing over sacred sites, Indian children posing in military uniforms, and smallpox blankets. The retelling and reclaiming of our Indigenous histories and images constitutes a critical step toward a scholarship that places decolonization at the center of its analysis and purpose. This book, for example, addresses the experiences of urban Indians in Albuquerque and institutions that have been developed to address the unique needs of this community, and makes an argument for the histories and experiences of urban Indians to be valued and documented. Asserting Indigenous historical realities can transform Indigenous lives, restore health and self-esteem, and empower Indigenous individuals and governments. With more than 50 percent of American Indians living in urban areas today, urban Indian communities have to be part of the decolonizing process.

DECOLONIZING ALBUQUERQUE: BEYOND TRIBAL IDENTITY

Because of the many reservation communities that surround Albuquerque, the interethnic dynamic there is unique in the experience of Indian urbanization. The relationship among the city government, urban Indians, and the reservation communities and their governments involves strong connections between city-dwelling Indians and their tribal communities; these connections contribute to the culture of the city and condition the ways in which Albuquerque Indians view themselves. Confronted with prejudicial attitudes and social structures of inequality, some Indians in Albuquerque have developed organizations dedicated to advocacy on Indigenous issues.

Before the emergence of social movements hailed by scholars as the beginning of American Indian mobilization, American Indian students in the city of Albuquerque founded one such organization, a multitribal group whose goal was the empowerment of American Indian youth to transform their own histories, claim their rights, and embrace their cultures. The American Indian Youth Council began as a local effort and grew into a national movement. The support of Pueblo leaders was a key factor in its founding.

INTERTRIBAL ACTIVISM

The significance of Albuquerque, New Mexico as a site for intertribal organizing is evident in the emergence of what would become known as the National Indian Youth Council (NIYC). In 1952, American Indian undergraduate students at the University of New Mexico (UNM) founded the Kiva Club. NIYC director and former Kiva Club member Herb Blatchford later observed that UNM was "the campus where the youth conferences as we know them were born."[3] Within a year, the club had nearly forty members, and, under the leadership of president Joe Herrera of Cochiti, began raising scholarship funds for Indian youth.[4] To raise money, the Kiva Club put on the Nizhoni Days, a celebration of American Indian culture with UNM students, staff, faculty, and the general public, which now includes a powwow, guest speakers, films, and food. In 1955, the new club president Herb Blatchford chaired a meeting at St. Francis Auditorium in Santa Fe. At the meeting, Pueblo leaders offered to support the club's efforts by sending dancers to the second annual Nizhoni Dances. This meeting is regarded as the first meeting of the Indian Youth Council.[5]

At the meeting, the Kiva Club encouraged other schools to send delegates to the next year's meeting. The second Indian Youth Council in 1956 attracted greater numbers, including students from the Santa Fe Indian School and other schools. Again, Pueblo leaders attended and praised the speakers and the program, which addressed "juvenile delinquency, sanitation, welfare, adjustment to college . . . adjustment to prejudice and competition," and other topics relevant to Indian student life.[6] By 1957, the Indian Youth Council was established as a statewide organization in New Mexico, and inspired chapters in the other Four Corners states and Oklahoma. These Indian Youth Councils became the Southwest Regional Indian Youth Council as other regional councils took shape in the Great Lakes region, the Great Plains, and the Northwest. Thus, what began as a local college club in Albuquerque inspired the organization of Indian students across the western United States and Canada.[7]

The Indian Youth Councils took the first steps toward forming a national organization at the American Indian Chicago Conference (AICC) in 1961. During the AICC, members of the regional youth councils were among a group of young, mostly college-aged, leadership-minded men and women who met separately as the Youth Caucus.[8] Mel Thom, a Northern Paiute, recalled, "Just out of college, we were very young. So we looked on. We saw the 'Uncle Tomahawks' fumbling around, passing resolutions and putting headdresses on people. But as for taking a strong stand, they just weren't doing it."[9] Another historical account of the NIYC notes that this Chicago meeting "pointed out the absurdity of Non-Native scholars trying to solve Native Indian problems" and "pointed out the need for a national Indian organization to define problems and offer solutions consistent with Native Culture and Tradition."[10] This caucus produced its own statement of purpose, much of which was adopted into the conference's statement, "which included the right to identify and survive on their own tribal terms."[11]

After the Chicago Conference, Youth Caucus members wanted to continue the exchange of ideas concerning Indian issues that they had begun in Chicago.[12] In written correspondence, they talked about the importance of maintaining their unity and encouraging each other's developing leadership. In letter to Thom, Blatchford wrote:

> While in college, Indian students do try their hand at organization, and they have made many accomplishments, which are to be commended. But what happens after a person graduates from college? Where can he go to further his training before attempting to hold a leading position? Can we, in some small way, fill this need? . . . We were born at a time when changes occur more rapidly than before. Can we, in our humble way, find ways to keep up these changes, thus give a lending hand to other national organizations to maintain their positions?[13]

To address these questions, Blatchford, Thom, Shirley Hill Witt, Robert E. Dominic, Larry Martin, and others formed the National Indian Youth Council. The first meeting was in Gallup, New Mexico, on August 10 and 11, 1961, during the Annual Inter-Tribal Indian Ceremonial. They met at the Gallup Indian Community Center and slept in Manuelito Hall, the BIA dormitory used by students attending Gallup Public High School. Their agenda was to determine the administrative needs to set up the organization base, set goals and decide how to meet them, adopt rules and policy, and discuss membership and projects.[14] In 1964 and over the next two years, the NIYC would become a moving force in the fish-ins that inspired a wave of Indian activism that eventually produced the occupation of Alcatraz Island, the occupation of the BIA building in Washington, DC, and the siege of Wounded Knee village.[15] As already mentioned in Chapter 3, the NIYC also promoted educational efforts and participated in lawsuits against school districts alleging discrimination and calling for attention to the needs of American Indian students.

Thus, a local intertribal campus group in Albuquerque had grown into a broad-based Indian activist organization. In turn, this activist organization, with its emphasis on building "A Greater Indian America," contributed to actions that claimed Native leadership over Native issues and sought to end assimilationist policies before a national audience.[16] The role of the Kiva Club in the creation of the NIYC reflects not only a particular moment in U.S. history among disenfranchised communities, but also the important role of urban Indians—and the role of cultural institutions such as the Annual Inter-Tribal Indian Ceremonial as a gathering site for political organization—in the development of national intertribal organization and awareness.

COALITION BUILDING OUTSIDE NATIVE AMERICA

Indians in Albuquerque, then, must be seen as members of tribes with continuing ties to their tribal communities and as members of pan-tribal urban communities who pursue their interests in common with people of other Indigenous ethnicities. Increasingly, Albuquerque Indians also are learning to form coalitions with non-Indian groups to build an effective political power base in pursuit of common goals of social justice. Groups such as unions, environmental groups, community interest groups, and disadvantaged demographic groups are natural allies of Indian groups who see common interests in a variety of local issues. Such coalition building does not require the rejection of tribal identities, but it does require a vision that extends beyond Native America. One example of coalition organizing that transcends national and cultural differences is the SAGE Council, a political alliance formed to protect a large area of petroglyphs on the west side of Albuquerque from a destructive plan by city officials and developers.

The petroglyphs are sacred to several Indian nations, but to city officials and developers, they are obstacles to development and economic growth. Although relations had warmed between the city government and Indian residents in the 1990s, the fourteen-year battle over the petroglyphs revealed the city's underlying disposition for ongoing colonization and appropriation. It also revealed new possibilities for decolonization through coalition building.

The ancestors of Indigenous peoples etched or drew the petroglyphs on the lava rocks that lie on Albuquerque's west side. The drawings are involved in religious ceremonies, they mark relations with sacred spaces, and they serve as reminders of spiritual obligations. Just as ancestors revered this place, contemporary Indigenous people remain connected through oral traditions, history, and continued religious practices. Contemporary Pueblo leaders state that the petroglyphs "are a part of our living culture . . . to remind us of who we are and where we came from as Indian people. We need to return to them to teach our sons and daughters. Sacred ceremonies have been going on [here] for centuries, before the time of Spanish conquistadores and the white man."[17] While the National Park Service has claimed this site and treats it as a tourist attraction, many Indigenous people of the Southwest continue to view the space as a sacred site for pilgrimages, prayers, and offerings.[18] The petroglyphs remain a fundamental memorial marking cultural pasts that strengthen the cultural present and future.

The petroglyph area encompasses five volcanoes aligned north to south forming an escarpment of lava beds that Indigenous spiritual leaders have described as a spine or backbone of the earth.[19] Indigenous people consider this a living memorial to their communities' relationship with the Earth. Moreover, the Earth's crust is so thin in this area that in the wintertime, visitors and park rangers see steam rising from the Earth; they see the Earth breathing.

Western ideologists, anthropologists, and city officials have renamed and reconceptualized the petroglyph area. The Petroglyph National Monument was established within the National Park Service in 1990 with Public Law 101–313. The Monument stretches seventeen miles, or 7,236 acres, along Albuquerque's West Mesa and is cooperatively "owned" and managed by the National Park Service and the City of Albuquerque with the purpose of preserving, protecting, and interpreting the petroglyphs and their setting.[20] The National Park Service describes and reconceptualizes the Petroglyph National Monument as a "volcanic basalt escarpment that dominates the city's western horizon," and protects "a variety of cultural and natural resources including five volcanic cones, hundreds of archeological sites and an estimated 25,000 images carved by native peoples and early Spanish settlers."[21]

The City of Albuquerque supported the establishment of the Petroglyph National Monument, initially perceiving the petroglyphs as a tourist attraction. As the west side, including Rio Rancho, experienced a rapid expansion, housing developments, shopping centers, schools, and roads spread over the area above Coors Road. An editorial in 2004 questioned urban sprawl:

> The PGS [Planned Growth Strategy] land use assumptions project hous-
> ing units in Bernalillo County to increase from 239,074 in 2000 to about
> 328,000 in 2025, an increase of almost 90,000 units. According to
> MRCOG [Mid-Region Council of Governments], housing for the entire
> metropolitan region is expected to increase by over 162,000 units for the
> same time period. How is our community going to deal with 6,500 new
> housing units a year for the next 25 years? The PGS assumptions state ap-
> proximately 1,000 housing units per year can be achieved through infill
> and redevelopment. The other 5,500 homes are certainly going to have to
> go somewhere.[22]

The speed of development, combined with poor urban planning, created congested streets during morning and evening commutes. With increased growth, the only bridge large enough for the growing numbers of commuters to Rio Rancho took them fifteen miles or more out of their way. The city de-cided to relieve traffic congestion on the west side by building a new bridge across the Rio Grande. Many residents of the Corrales and Bosque areas op-posed the bridge. Nevertheless, in 1988 the city finished the Paseo del Norte Bridge, which gave new access to the west side and moved the conflict to an-other area: developers and their friends on the city council began to view the petroglyphs as a barrier to westward development.

Various city council members, city developers, and west side residents wanted a road directly through the petroglyph monument to alleviate traffic congestion, although merely widening existing roads would have served the same purpose. In 1992, city council member Alan Armijo announced the proposed extension of Paseo del Norte directly through the petroglyphs. Mayor Jim Baca did not approve the Paseo del Norte extension and sidelined the plan, but the election of Martin Chavez in 2001 rekindled the battle. To facilitate the road extension, Senator Pete Domenici introduced the Petro-glyph National Monument Boundary Adjustment Act, Congress passed it, and President Bill Clinton signed it in 1997. The act modified the monu-

Fig. 11 **Development near Petroglyph National Monument.**
(Photo by Myla Vicenti Carpio.)

ment's boundary to exclude approximately 8.5 acres.[23] With the 8.5 acres re-
moved from the protection of National Monument status, Mayor Chavez
and advocates on the city council proposed to cut through the newly available area to create a 300-foot wide, quarter-mile long roadway, destroying
two to twelve petroglyphs.[24] Supporters of the plan dismissed the idea of
widening existing roads as an alternative to creating this new one.[25] To many
city residents, developers and politicians, this road represented development and progress; to many Indigenous people, it was wanton destruction.

Some Pueblo leaders responded to the proposal by asking Bill Weahkee,
then executive director of the Five Sandoval Indian Pueblos, to see what he
could do to stop the road from being built through the petroglyphs.[26] Weahkee created the Petroglyph Monument Protection Coalition, as a number of
other groups opposed the boundary adjustment and road extension, including Petroglyph National Monument staff, environmentalists, and other Indigenous communities. While these interests viewed the situation and the
petroglyphs differently, their desire to protect a cultural and sacred site, to
protect national parks from developers' incursions, and to curb reckless

Fig. 12 **The 8.5 acres excluded.** (Courtesy of The National Park Service,
Petroglyph National Monument, Division of Resource
Protection and Management, March 2004.)

urban sprawl had enough in common to form the Coalition.[27]

In spring 2000, the Petroglyph Monument Protection Coalition restruc-
tured itself into the Sacred Alliance for Grassroots Equality (SAGE) Council.
Executive director Laurie Weahkee explained:

We came together formally in 1996. We were formerly the Petroglyph Monument Protection Coalition, and that was . . . a real coalition since we had the Sierra Club, Friends of the Albuquerque Petroglyphs, Southwest Organizing Project, Tonatzin Land Institutes. So there were about seven to eight different organizations and that's the beginning of the story. But we also decided that because the fight . . . [was] also . . . real hot, then real cold, up and down, . . . we needed to organize ourselves for the long haul. Even if . . . we won the Petroglyph fight today, there would be fifty more fights on some basic issues of equality. And so . . . we organized [the] SAGE Council.[28]

The Council continued the fight with city councilors, the mayor, and developers. In September 2002, without city councilors' knowledge or public input and notification, Mayor Martin Chavez authorized a private land developer to build a 1.7-mile road near the petroglyphs with private funds.[29] A construction company began preparing a narrow dirt road that connected Ventana Ranch to Unser Boulevard for asphalt application. Protestors blocked the road, stopping bulldozers and eighteen trucks carrying asphalt as a peaceful act of civil disobedience to stop the road. The police showed up in full riot gear and arrested seven protestors.[30]

Later that year, a proposition to approve the building of the extension road was placed on the ballot for a 2003 election. The road extension project was hidden within the proposition as projected monies for road improvement on the west side. The SAGE Council fought the proposition, which failed for various reasons including the petroglyph issue. The next year, the city again hid the road extension within another proposition for recreation improvement, and this time it passed.

Besides making deals behind closed doors and hiding ballot propositions, supporters of the extension road even stooped to the outright disparaging of Indigenous spirituality in the attempt to delegitimize Indigenous claims to the petroglyphs. Some Christian religious leaders in Albuquerque stated, "Tear down their church not mine."[31] Senator Domenici, in evident disgust, criticized Pueblo political leaders for listening too much to Pueblo religious leaders.[32]

Some allies did step forth in support of Indigenous spirituality and the petroglyphs as sacred space. At a city council meeting, Sister Agnes Calmarron, a Catholic nun, spoke about the need to respect the spiritual beliefs of Native peoples. "The land has a sacred meaning to the Native people of America. Do we really understand what holy and sacred mean to the land? What motivates us to change the landscape to fit our agenda about growth and traffic? We need to value this sacred area in a more honorable and respectful way."[33]

In 2005, the SAGE Council, along with 1000 Friends of Albuquerque, National Trust for Historic Preservation, Sierra Club, Southwest Organizing Project, Southwest Network for Environmental and Economic Justice, and others opposing the extension road, petitioned the Second Judicial District of New Mexico District Court for an injunction against the city of Albuquerque to stop building the extension road.[34] The petition claimed that the city had not complied with the state's Prehistoric and Historic Sites Preservation Act.

In October 2005, State District Court Judge Linda Vanzi ruled in favor of the road through the monument. She stated that the city had followed prescribed procedures in determining whether the road extension was the best option for handling future traffic demands.[35] However, Vanzi found that the city had not met all conditions needed to minimize harm to the area. "The way in which the record has been presented," she wrote, "leads the Court to believe there has been little action on the part of the City to substantively reach out to the Pueblos as sovereign governments, resulting in the appearance of insensitivity to the people who hold the land most sacred."[36] After Vanzi's decision, a meeting was held with the State Cultural Properties Review Committee, which cleared the city to move the sacred petroglyphs in the planned extension. The clearance stipulated that the city consult with the Jicarilla Apache Nation and Picuris Pueblo on the significance of the petroglyphs for their communities.[37]

After the Jicarilla Apaches and Picuris visited the site, the city moved the petroglyphs a few hundred feet from their present locations. Once moved, they were to be rearranged in a way that matched their "original orientation."[38] Lorene Willis, director of the Jicarilla Apache Cultural Affairs Office, commented,

When they talk about trying to put them in the same alignment, it doesn't mean anything to us. It's just their own way of justifying what they're trying to do. It doesn't make sense to us if they're going to move them. It has no more significance to us. They've destroyed something that would be sacred to our people.[39]

The movement of the petroglyphs parallels the forced removal of numerous Indigenous nations from their homelands. Be it a hundred feet or a thousand miles, the petroglyphs were located in a particular place for spiritual purposes and their removal is, once again, motivated by Western expansion.

For Indigenous peoples, then, these struggles continue, not only trying in the battle to make their histories/existence known and visible, but also in the fight for sacred sites across the country. European and now American invaders have continued to displace Indigenous peoples from lands and sacred spaces. Since the petroglyphs are objects of reverence and demarcate a sacred space, Pueblo leaders recognize the petroglyph destruction as being "tantamount to the destruction of their culture and religion."[40] Thus, the fight for this monument is grounded in religious and cultural beliefs. According to Amadeo Shije, chairman of the All Indian Pueblo Council:

Sacred areas such as the petroglyphs are as important to some [people] as churches, temples, and synagogues are to others. Members of our Native communities share the same basic rights to religious liberty, personal privacy, and cultural respect as any other citizen.[41]

Therefore, a shift in perspectives is needed, one that humanizes, reclaims, and strengthens Indigenous peoples, and their histories and cultures. Unfortunately, the City of Albuquerque built the Paseo del Norte extension and opened it to traffic on June 20, 2007.[42]

CLOSING

Where ethnic identities collide, each party's narratives of the past compete to be heard. The narratives of the conquerors often silence all others, and in the process of silencing, they erase the evidence of their own violence. Take, for example, the National Museum of the American Indian in Washington, DC, in which the destruction of Native peoples becomes naturalized and agentless.[43]

As historians, educators, or makers of historical memory, we must question and become aware of whose narratives we privilege. In the foregoing discussion, I have examined the ethnic relations and competing histories behind the imagining of Indigenous peoples in Albuquerque, especially in matters of politics, culture, and economic development. Power in Albuquerque has long privileged Spanish and Anglo-American narratives over the many local Indigenous narratives of the past, but we need not continue following that example.

With this study, I have tried to provide a step toward a decolonizing narrative of urban Indians in Albuquerque by recontextualizing "urban" Indians in a way that attempts to disrupt the divisive paradigm of urban versus reservation. Significantly, this dichotomy has been used to construct divisions among Indians based on geographic location and degrees of cultural assimilation. This division, when imposed, places greater value upon those perceived as "less Indian." These categories, divisions, and fragmentations, when internalized, manifest themselves as social and political polarizations. These disjunctions limit political and social cooperation and engagement between both the reservation community and their urban members, and between organizational entities.

When we view or define positions of identity, physical location, and membership in opposition to one another, it limits our potential to create and develop relationships for political and social organizing and interactions.[44] Bridging that division, we can see that important cultural, social, and political relationships are strengthened when reservation and urban communities—such as the Toyah Band of Comanches and Laguna Colony of Albuquerque—communicate, or when the Gila River Indian Community members and former Japanese American internees share their stories of discrimination, oppression, and community during World War II.[45] As we disturb and reject the prescribed categories that define our relationships with one another, our cultural and political vision can transcend imposed geopolitical and psychological boundaries.

Appendix

Tribes Tallied for Albuquerque, NM MSA, 2000 Census	
Total tribes tallied	40,697
American Indian tribes, specified	35,438
Apache*	872
Blackfeet	78
Cherokee	605
Cheyenne	81
Chickasaw	73
Chippewa	239
Choctaw	267
Colville	15
Comanche	144
Cree	20
Creek	126
Crow	67
Delaware	54
Houma	0
Iroquois	136

Appendix Tribes Tallied for Albuquerque, NM MSA, 2000 Census *(cont.)*

Kiowa	95
Latin American Indians	456
Lumbee	16
Menominee	7
Navajo**	13,305
Osage	47
Ottawa	17
Paiute	16
Pima	53
Potawatomi	46
Pueblotop 3 or 5	16,867
Puget Sound Salish	10
Seminole	59
Shoshone	52
Sioux	616
Tohono O'Odham	29
Ute	125
Yakama	9
Yaqui	43
Yuman	60
All other tribes	733
American Indian tribes, not specified	1,870
Alaska Native tribes, specified	114
Alaskan Athabascan	28
Aleut	22
Eskimo	35
Tlingit-Haida	24
All other tribes	5
Alaska Native tribes, not specified	37
American Indian or Alaska Native tribes, not specified	3,238

Source: U.S. Census Bureau, American Indian and Alaska Native Alone with one or more tribes reported for Selected Tribes. Census 2000 Summary File 1, 100 percent data.
* Includes Apaches from all nations.
** Includes all Navajo bands and chapters from four states.

Notes

PLAINSWORD

1. Daniel Gibson, "Reclaiming Our Place," *Native Peoples Magazine*, November/December 2004, www.nativepeoples.com/site/np_nov _dec04/nd04-on_the_wind/nd04-on_the_wind_article.html (accessed on July 23, 2010).
2. Nora Naranjo-Morse (Santa Clara Pueblo), *Numbe Whageh (Our Center Place)*, 2005, www.nativenetworks.si/edu/eng/orange/numbe_whageh.htm (accessed July 16, 2010).
3. Diane Reyna (Taos Pueblo), telephone interview by P. Jane Hafen, August 2, 2010.
4. Kathy Friese, "The Creative Terrain of *Numbe Whageh*: Creating Memory, Leading to Center," *American Indian Culture and Research Journal* 31:3 (2007): 81–98.

INTRODUCTION

1. James E. Officer, "American Indian and Federal Policy," in *The American Indian in Urban Society*, eds. Jack O. Waddell and O. Michael Watson (Boston: Little, Brown and Company, 1971), 5.
2. Donald L. Fixico, *The Urban Indian Experience in America* (Albuquerque: University of New Mexico Press, 2000), ix.
3. Jack Forbes, "The Urban Tradition among Native Americans," *American Indian Culture and Research Journal* 22:4 (1998): 15, 21, 35.

4. Ibid., 18, 21, 38.

5. Melvin L. Fowler, "Mound 72 and Early Mississippian at Cahokia," in *New Perspectives on Cahokia: Views from the Periphery*, ed. James B. Stoltman (Madison, WI: Prehistory Press, 1991), 1, 3.

6. Biloine Whiting Young and Melvin L. Fowler, *Cahokia: The Great Native American Metropolis* (Urbana: University of Illinois Press, 2000), 310–311, 316, 323. Just as pre-Contact population numbers have been disputed, so are these numbers.

7. Mark D. Varien, "Communities and the Chacoan Regional System," in *Great House Communities across the Chacoan Landscape*, Anthropological Papers of the University of Arizona, No. 64, eds. John Kantner and Nancy M. Mahoney (Tucson: University of Arizona Press, 2000), 150.

8. Douglas Anderson, Barbara Anderson, and Southwest Parks and Monuments Association, *Chaco Canyon: Center of a Culture* (Globe, AZ: Southwest Parks and Monuments Association, 1981), 10, 95. No population estimate is available for Mesa Verde, but the Mesa Verdean culture produced thousands of Anasazi sites.

9. John Kantner and Nancy M. Mahoney, eds., *Great House Communities across the Chacoan Landscape*, Anthropological Papers of the University of Arizona, No. 64 (Tucson: University of Arizona Press, 2000), 3–4. However, through Pueblo oral tradition, contemporary Pueblo peoples can inform scholars about their ancestors who lived in these communities.

10. Forbes, "The Urban Tradition," 10.

11. Brenda Norrell, "Urban Indian Summit Mirrors Population Shift," *Indian Country Today*, February 11, 2005.

12. Jack O. Waddell and O. Michael Watson, eds., *The American Indian in Urban Society* (Boston: Little, Brown and Company, 1971), 1–5.

13. Lynn C. White and Bruce A. Chadwick, "Urban Residence, Assimilation, and Identity of the Spokane Indian," in *Native Americans Today: Sociological Perspectives*, eds. Howard M. Bahr, Bruce A. Chadwick, and Robert C. Day (New York: Harper & Row, 1972), 240–248; Alan L. Sorkin, *The Urban Indian* (Lexington, MA: Lexington Books, 1978), 126–130; and W. T. Stanbury, *Success and Failure: Indians in Urban Society* (Vancouver: University of British Columbia Press, 1970), 222–229. Stanbury discusses urban Indians in British Columbia, but his statement could be applied to the experiences of most urban Indians.

14. Robert S. Weppner, "Urban Economic Opportunities: The Example of Denver," in Waddell and Watson, eds., *The American Indian in Urban Society*, 270–271.

15. Letter from Phoenix Area Office to Commissioner of Indian Affairs, Washington, DC, May 8, 1952. Walter J. Knodel, Phoenix Area Placement Officer, "Narrative Report for April, 1952," Folder 9, Reports Narrative FY 1952, Phoenix FY 1952, Series: Narrative Reports 1952–1954, 1957–1960, Employment Assistance FY 1952, RG 75, Records of the Bureau of Indian Affairs, Field Placement and Relocation Office, Employment Assistance Records, National Archives, Washington, DC.

16. In fact, surely among the most distinguishing features of social science research in the second half of the 1960s was that once again, as in the first third of the twentieth century, the American city became a focal point. "As such origins suggest," reflects Kathleen Neils Conzen, "much of this urban history was empirical and problem oriented; studies proliferated of individual city growth and of pathological aspects of urban life—social tensions, inadequate services, minority discrimination, political corruption." Kathleen Neils Conzen, "Quantification and the New Urban History," *Journal of Interdisciplinary History*, 13:4 (Spring 1983): 655. The historiography of urban history sees that social science research on urban areas focused on empirical and "problem-oriented" studies of pathological aspects of urban life-social tensions, inadequate services, minority discrimination, political corruption. Just as urban history focused on empirical studies of "pathological" aspects of urban life, so the study of urban Indigenous peoples pursued such a research focus.

17. Weppner, "Urban Economic Opportunities," 213.

18. Information on Relocation Services, Bureau of Indian Affairs, Denver Field Relocation Office. Record Group 75, Rocky Mountain Region of National Archives, Denver, CO.

19. Alan L. Sorkin, *The Urban American Indian* (Lexington, MA: Lexington Books, 1978), 126; Waddell and Watson, eds., *The American Indian in Urban Society*, 34; and White and Chadwick, "Urban Residence," 240–241.

20. Joan Weibel-Orlando, *Indian Country, L.A.: Maintaining Ethnic Community in Complex Society*, rev. ed. (Urbana: University of Illinois Press, 1999).

21. Elizabeth Cook-Lynn, Tom Holm, John Redhorse, and James Riding In, "First Panel: Reclaiming American Indian Studies," *Wicazo Sa Review* 20:1 (Spring 2005): 171.

22. As a result, community histories from relocation destinations like Chicago, Oakland, San Francisco, and Detroit have begun to collect oral histories from their communities. Two such works are Intertribal Friendship House

(Oakland, CA) and coordinating editor, Susan Lobo, *Urban Voices: The Bay Area American Indian Community* (Tucson: University of Arizona Press, 2002); and Terry Straus and Grant Arndt, *Native Chicago* (Chicago: McNaughton and Gunn, 1998).

23. I use the spelling of Alburquerque with an "r" to denote the Spanish spelling and context of the city of Albuquerque.

24. Duane Champagne, "From Sovereignty to Minority, As American as Apple Pie," *Wicazo Sa Review* 20:2 (Fall 2005): 23.

CHAPTER 1

1. U.S. Census Bureau, "The American Indian and Alaska Native Population: 2000," Economics and Statistics Administration (Washington, DC: U.S. Census Bureau, 2002), 6.

2. The concept of generations in immigration was popularized by Margaret Mead in the 1940s, but has been used recently by Judy Yung, Jon Gjerde, and Gabriela Arredondo. See Margaret Mead, *And Keep Your Powder Dry: An Anthropologist Looks at America* (New York: W. Morrow and Co., 1942); Judy Yung, *Unbound Feet: A Social History of Chinese Women in San Francisco* (Berkeley: University of California Press, 1995); Jon Gjerde, *The Minds of the West: Ethnocultural Evolution in the Rural Middle West, 1830–1917* (Chapel Hill: University of North Carolina Press, 1997); and Gabriela F. Arredondo, *Mexican Chicago: Race, Identity, and Nation 1916–1939* (Chicago: University of Illinois Press, 2008).

3. Most studies on Indian urbanization either discuss broadly the relocation period within its policy timeline or examine a certain time or place of relocation. For the most part, relocation has been looked at from the 1948 to the 1970s, and not viewed in periods or waves nor as a continuing process.

4. A majority of the scholarly work on relocation focuses on or includes this wave of migration.

5. James Bell and Nicole Lim, "Young Once, Indian Forever: Youth Gangs in Indian Country," *American Indian Quarterly* 29:3–4 (Spring and Fall 2005): 627–628.

6. Troy L. Armstrong, Philmer Bluehouse, Alfred Dennison, Harmon Mason, Barbara Mendenhall, Daniel Wall, James W. Zion, eds., "Finding and Knowing the Gang—Nayee, Field-Initiated Gang Research Project, The Judicial Branch of the Navajo Nation" (Washington, DC: U.S. Department of Justice, Office of Juvenile Justice and Delinquency Prevention, 1995), 27.

7. Ibid.

8. Bell and Lim, "Young Once, Indian Forever," 628.

9. *Cherokee Nation v. Georgia*, 30 U.S. (5 Pet.) 1, 15 (1831).

10. Ibid.

11. Brookings Institution, Institute for Government Research, Hubert Work, and Lewis Meriam, *The Problem of Indian Administration*, Report of a Survey Made at the Request of Hubert Work, Secretary of the Interior, and Submitted to Him, February 21, 1928 (Baltimore, Md.: The Johns Hopkins University Press, 1928), 736, 737. [Hereafter cited as the Meriam Report.]

12. Meriam Report, 736, 737.

13. Ibid., 737.

14. Ibid.

15. Donald Fixico, *Termination and Relocation: Federal Indian Policy, 1945–1960* (Albuquerque: University of New Mexico Press, 1986), 134–135.

16. Ibid.

17. Kenneth R. Philip, "Dillon S. Meyer and the Advent of Termination: 1950–1953," *Western Historical Quarterly* 19:1 (January 1988): 38–39.

18. Peter Iverson, *"We are Still Here": American Indians in the Twentieth Century* (Wheeling, IL: Harlan Davidson, Inc., 1998), 120–121.

19. Ibid.

20. Dillon S. Myer, "Address by Commissioner of Indian Affairs Dillon S. Myer, Before the Western Governor's Conference at Phoenix, Arizona" (December 9, 1952), University of New Mexico, Center for Southwest Research, MSS 509, BL Box 6, Folder 1.

21. Letter to members of the Utah Paiute Tribes from John O. Crow, Superintendent of Unitah and Ouray Agency, Folder 1, Relocation Service Memoranda 1961, Box 1, Series: Internal Memoranda, 1957–1961, RG 75, Records of the Bureau of Indian Affairs, Branch of Relocation Services, National Archives, Washington, DC.

22. Memorandum to All Field Relocation Officers from Chief Walter J. Knodel, Branch of Relocation Services. Folder 8 Report of Relocation and Vocational training of Utah Paiutes. Box 2. Series: Vocational Training on Terminal Tribes and Apprenticeship Policy Material, 1954–1958. RG 75 Records of the Bureau of Indian Affairs, Branch of Relocation Services. Employment Assistance Records. National Archives, Washington, DC.

23. Fixico, *Termination and Relocation*, 64, 135.

24. Ibid., 136–139.

25. Ibid., 137.

26. La Verne Madigan, "The American Indians Relocation Program," The Association on American Indian Affairs, Inc. (December 1956), 3, 5, MSS 509 BC,

Sophie D. Aberle Papers, Box 27, Folder 123, Center for Southwest Research, University Libraries, University of New Mexico, Albuquerque, NM.

27. Fixico, *Termination and Relocation*, 138.

28. Madigan, "The American Indians Relocation Program," 1, 5.

29. Fixico, *Termination and Relocation*, 138.

30. Ibid.

31. Grant P. Arndt, "Relocation's Imagined Landscape," in *Native Chicago*, eds. Terry Strauss and Grant P. Arndt (Chicago: McNaughton and Gunn Inc., 1998), 118.

32. Ibid., 118–119.

33. Fixico, *Termination and Relocation*, 143.

34. Arndt, "Relocation's Imagined Landscape," 114.

35. Fixico, *Termination and Relocation*, 139.

36. Louise Pino, pers. comm., May 4, 2001.

37. Arndt, "Relocation's Imagined Landscape," 121.

38. American Indian Policy Review Commission, Task Force Eight, Urban and Rural Non-Reservation Indians, *Report on Urban and Rural Non-Reservation Indians: Final Report to the American Indian Policy Review Commission* (Washington, DC: U.S. Government Printing Office, 1976), 34. [Hereafter cited as Task Force Eight.]

39. Mary Vicenti, pers. comm., June 5, 2001; and Pino, pers. comm.

40. Task Force Eight, 35.

41. Madigan, "The American Indians Relocation Program," 12.

42. George M. Felshaw, "Bi-weekly reports to BIA, Los Angeles Field Relocation Office, Employment Trends and Forecast" (June 27, 1958), Number 12, Folder 2, 721.8, Bi-weekly Reports, 1958, Laguna-Niguel Region of National Archives, San Pedro, CA.

43. Madigan, "The American Indians Relocation Program," 15.

44. Most books and articles on American Indians deal with tribal sovereignty and the federal trust relationship. A sampling follows: Vine Deloria, Jr., *The Nations Within: The Past and Future of American Indian Sovereignty* (Austin: University of Texas Press, 1998); Vine Deloria, Jr., and David E. Wilkins, *Tribes, Treaties and Constitutional tribulations* (Austin: University of Texas Press, 1999); Joanne Barker, ed., *Sovereignty Matters: Locations of Contestation and Possibility in Indigenous Struggles for Self-Determination* (Lincoln: University of Nebraska Press, 2005); and Edward Valandra, *Not Without Our Consent: Lakota Resistance to Termination, 1950–59* (Chicago: University of Illinois Press, 2006).

45. *Joint Resolution to Provide for the Establishment of the American Indian Policy Review Commission*, Public Law 93–580, *United States Statutes at Large*, 88 (1975): 1910.
46. Ibid.
47. Task Force Eight, 1.
48. Ibid., 2–3.
49. Ibid., 3–8.
50. Ibid., 3.
51. Ibid., 7.
52. Ibid., 2–3.
53. Indian Health Service, "An Overview: Indian Health Service," a presentation for Native American Community Organizing Project, Rep. Deb Gullett (District 18), and Urban Health Project, May 22, 2001; Myla Carpio, "Lost Generation: The Involuntary Sterilization of American Indian Women" (master's thesis, Arizona State University, 1995), 13, 14, 20, 21.
54. Indian Health Service, "Overview of the Phoenix Indian Medical Center" (Phoenix, AZ: Indian Health Service, Phoenix Indian Medical Center, 2001).
55. Ibid.
56. The contract care areas cover entire states in Alaska, Nevada, and Oklahoma. Indian Health Service, "Health Care Services Are Not Always Available to Native Americans," U.S. Government Accountability Office, Report to the Committee on Indian Affairs, U.S. Senate, August 2005, 11.
57. Eddie Brown, Stephen Cornell, Miriam Jorgensen, et al., "Welfare, Work, and American Indians: The Impact of Welfare Reform," report to National Congress of American Indians (St. Louis: Kathryn Buder Center for American Indian Studies, Washington University; Tucson: Native Nations Institute for Leadership, Management, and Policy, University of Arizona, 2001), 33.
58. Office of Civil Rights Evaluation, *A Quiet Crisis: Federal Funding and Unmet Needs in Indian Country*, U.S. Commission on Civil Rights, July 2003, 11.
59. *Indian Self-Determination and Educational Assistance Act*, Public Law 93–638, *United States Statutes at Large*, 88 (1975): 2203–2214.
60. Author's attendance at NACOP meeting with Indian Health Service personnel, March 4, 2001.
61. Emmett Francis, interview by author, Albuquerque, NM, March 13, 2001; "Metro Watch," *Albuquerque Journal*, October 17, 1995, C2.
62. Kim Krisberg, "Budget Cuts for Urban Indian Programs a Danger to Health," *Nations Health*, 36:5 (June/July 2006): 1.
63. Norman Ration, director of National Indian Youth Council, interview by author, Albuquerque, NM, August 5, 2008.

64. Ibid.

65. Larry Martin and Edward LaCroix, "Education and Employment in Albuquerque: A Response to the Mayor's Symposium on Indian Affairs" (Albuquerque, NM: City of Albuquerque, Task Force on Education, 1995), 12.

66. Julie Davis, "American Indian Movement Survival Schools in Minneapolis and St. Paul, 1968–2002" (PhD diss., Arizona State University, 2004), 75–87, 127–132.

67. Felicia Fonseca, "New Mexico Charter School Caters to Urban Indians," *Albuquerque Journal*, August 19, 2006, State and Regional Section.

68. Ibid.

69. *Personal Responsibility and Work Opportunity Reconciliation Act of 1996.* Public Law 104–193. *United States Statutes at Large* 110 (1996): 2105, especially Title I: Block Grants for Temporary Assistance for Needy Families.

70. Ibid.

71. U.S. Government Accountability Office, "Welfare Reform: Tribal TANF Allows Flexibility to Tailor Programs, but Conditions on Reservations Make It Difficult to Move Recipients into Jobs" (Washington, DC: GAO, July 2002), 1, 4.

72. Welfare Information Network, "Resources for Welfare Decisions: Tribal TANF and Welfare-to-Work Programs," *Welfare Information Network Issue Notes*, 3:5 (September 1999): 1.

73. Ibid.

74. U.S. Government Accountability Office, "Welfare Reform," 18.

75. Ibid.; Welfare Information Network. *Resources for Welfare Decisions*, 1; Brown, et al., "Welfare, Work, and American Indians," 40, 41; and Wakina Scott, "Welfare Reform and American Indians: Critical Issues for Reauthorization," *National Health Policy Forum*, no. 778 (June 17, 2002), 5.

76. Emmett Francis, interview by author, Albuquerque, NM, March 13, 2001. In 1990, six years before this act, a task force reported that most people moving into Albuquerque were Indian women under age thirty-five, including many single parents.

77. Bob Jackson, "Minorities Miss Census: Colorado May Lose Millions in Aid If 2000 Tally Again Undercounts Population," *Rocky Mountain News*, October 11, 1999.

78. Andrew Webb, "Indians Fear Census Undercount," *Albuquerque Journal*, February 10, 2001, E1; and Theodore S. Jojola, *Profiling the Native American Community in Albuquerque: Assessing the Impacts of Census Undercounts and Adjustments* (Suitland, MD: U.S. Census Monitoring Board, 2001), 2.

79. Bob Jackson, "Minorities Miss Census—Colorado May Lose Millions in Aid If 2000 Tally Again Undercounts Population," *Rocky Mountain News*, October 11, 1999.

80. Webb, "Indians Fear Census Undercount"; and Suzanne Zerger, *Health Care for Homeless Native Americans* (Nashville, TN: National Health Care for the Homeless Council, Inc., February 2004), 1.

CHAPTER 2

1. As noted in the introduction, I use the spelling of Alburquerque with an "r" to denote the Spanish spelling and Spanish context of the city of Albuquerque.

2. The Hopi town of Oraibi may contest Acoma's claim to the status of oldest inhabited city.

3. See Melissa Dyea, "One Step Forward, Two Steps Back? An Examination of Economic Development at Laguna Pueblo" (Master's thesis, Arizona State University, 1995); and Doug Brugge, Timothy Benally, and Esther Yazzie-Lewis, *The Navajo People and Uranium Mining* (Albuquerque: University of New Mexico Press, 2006).

4. Joe Sando, *Pueblo Nations: Eight Centuries of Pueblo Indian History* (Santa Fe, NM: Clear Light Publishers, 1992), 22.

5. Laura Bayer with Floyd Montoya and the Pueblo of Santa Ana, *Santa Ana: The People, the Pueblo, and the History of Tamaya* (Albuquerque: University of New Mexico Press, 1994), 1. This book not only provides great insight into the origins of the Tamayame, but also is a wonderful example of a tribal history using oral tradition and a tribal perspective. Modern Tamaya is located north and west of Albuquerque, and west of Bernalillo.

6. Bayer, *Santa Ana*, 2–3.

7. Sando, *Pueblo Nations*, 22.

8. Paguate is one of six villages that make up Laguna Pueblo.

9. Bayer, *Santa Ana*, 10.

10. Ibid., 11.

11. Curtis F. Schaafsma, "The Tiguex Province Revisited: The Rio Medio Survey," in *Secrets of a City: Papers on Albuquerque Area Archeology In honor of Richard A. Bice*, eds. Anne V. Poore and John Montgomery (Sante Fe, NM: Ancient City Press, Inc., 1987), 6.

12. Marc Simmons, *Albuquerque: A Narrative History* (Albuquerque: University of New Mexico Press, 1982), 29.

13. Peter Iverson, *The Navajo Nation* (Albuquerque: University of New Mexico

Press, 1981), xxvii-xxix. I have included here an extremely abridged version of the creation story.

14. C.L. Sonnischsen, *The Mescalero Apaches* (Norman: University of Oklahoma Press, 1972), 18, 19; Morris E. Opler, "Mescalero Apache" in *Smithsonian Handbook of Indians of North America*, Vol. 10, ed. Alfonso Ortiz (Washington, DC: Smithsonian Institute, 1978), 419.

15. Sonnischsen, *The Mescalero Apaches*, 19.

16. Veronica E. Velarde Tiller, *The Jicarilla Apache Tribe: A History*, 2nd ed.(Lincoln: University of Nebraska Press, 1992), 4.

17. Ibid., 5, 6; author's personal experience.

18. Simmons, *Albuquerque*, 29.

19. Sando, *Pueblo Nations*, 47–48.

20. Ibid., 47–49.

21. Ibid., 49; Carroll L. Riley, *Rio del Norte: People of the Upper Rio Grande from Earliest Times to the Pueblo Revolt* (Salt Lake City: University of Utah Press, 1995), 153.

22. Sando, *Pueblo Nations*, 50.

23. Ibid.

24. Riley, *Rio del Norte,* 161–164.

25. Simmons, *Albuquerque*, 29.

26. Sando, *Pueblo Nations*, 49; Simmons, *Albuquerque*, 33.

27. Simmons, *Albuquerque*, 33; Riley, *Rio del Norte*, 174–175.

28. Simmons, *Albuquerque*, 34; Riley, *Rio del Norte*, 181.

29. Joe Sando, *Pueblo Profiles: Cultural Identity Through Centuries of Change* (Santa Fe, NM: Clear Light Publishers, 1998), 7.

30. John M. Nieto-Phillips, *The Language of Blood: the Making of Spanish-American Identity in New Mexico, 1880s–1930s* (University of New Mexico Press, 2004), 24–25.

31. Simmons, *Albuquerque*, 55.

32. Riley, *Rio del Norte*, 240.

33. Simmons, *Albuquerque*, 56.

34. Nieto-Phillips, *The Language of Blood*, 16–17.

35. Riley, *Rio del Norte*, 251.

36. Ibid.

37. Sando, *Pueblo Profiles*, 11–14. Sando's discussion and creation of the meetings leading up to the revolt brings to life the encounters the Pueblo patriots may have experienced. Further, Sando illustrates the importance of oral tradition in Native cultures and how it can enhance written history.

38. Sando, *Pueblo Profiles*, 10–13; Riley, *Rio del Norte*, 265–268.

39. Ibid., 5–7.

40. Ibid.

41. Ibid., 12–15; Riley, *Rio del Norte*, 267.

42. Sando, *Pueblo Profiles*, 16.

43. Ibid., 14–16.

44. Simmons, *Albuquerque*, 69.

45. Sando, *Pueblo Profiles*, 17.

46. Ibid.

47. Ibid., 19; Riley, *Rio del Norte*, 267.

48. Sando, *Pueblo Profiles*, 20.

49. Ibid., 21.

50. Ibid.

51. Ibid., 22.

52. Byron Johnson, *Old Town, Albuquerque, New Mexico: A Guide to Its History and Architecture* (Albuquerque: City of Albuquerque, 1980), 7.

53. F. Stanley, *The Duke City, The Story of Albuquerque, New Mexico: 1706–1956* (Pampa, TX: Pampa Print Shop, 1963), 16.

54. Sando, *Pueblo Nations*, 253.

55. Stanley, *The Duke City*, 16–17.

56. Byron Johnson and Robert Dauner, *Early Albuquerque: A Photographic History, 1870–1918* (Albuquerque, NM: Albuquerque Journal and Albuquerque Museum, 1981), 7.

57. Ibid., 9.

58. Simmons, *Albuquerque*, 212.

59. Ibid., 218.

60. Ibid., 219–220.

61. Nieto-Phillips, *The Language of Blood*, 16.

62. Penny Ann Quintana, "The Early Years of the Albuquerque Indian School, 1879–1928" (master's thesis, Arizona State University, 1992), 53.

63. Bradford Luckingham, *The Urban Southwest: A Profile History of Albuquerque, El Paso, Phoenix, and Tucson* (El Paso: Texas Western Press, 1982), 18.

64. Simmons, *Albuquerque*, 234–235.

65. Kurt Peters, "Continuing Identity: Laguna Pueblo Railroaders in Richmond, California," *American Indian Culture and Research Journal* 22:4 (1998), 188. Also see Kurt Peters, "Watering the Flower: Laguna Pueblo and the Santa Fe Railroad, 1889–1943," in *Native Americans and Wage Labor: Ethnohistorical Perspectives*, eds. Alice Littlefield and Martha C. Knack (Norman: University of Oklahoma Press, 1996).

66. Ralph Paisano, "Laguna Colony's Role in Albuquerque," *Laguna Colony Info Page* (Pamphlet) (June 20, 1997), 1.

67. Peters, "Continuing Identity," 188.

68. Paisano, "Laguna Colony's Role in Albuquerque," 1.

69. Peters, "Continuing Identity," 189.

70. Peters, "Watering the Flower," 178.

71. Peters, "Continuing Identity," 189.

72. Lillie G. McKinney, "History of the Albuquerque Indian School" (master's thesis, University of New Mexico, 1934), 5.

73. McKinney, "History of the Albuquerque Indian School," 1.

74. Ibid., 2.

75. Quintana, "The Early Years of the Albuquerque Indian School," 8, 53.

76. Ibid., 55, 57.

77. Theodore S. Jojola, *Urban Indians in Albuquerque, New Mexico: A Study for the Department of Family and Community Services* (Albuquerque, NM: City of Albuquerque, 1999), 1–3; Simmons, *Albuquerque*, 309; McKinney, "History of the Albuquerque Indian School," 3; Quintana, "The Early Years," 58. The name on the deed was Elias Clark, and on June 7, 1882, Clark conveyed the tract of land for the Indian School to the United States.

78. McKinney, "History of the Albuquerque Indian School," 3, 7, 9.

79. Ibid., 14; Quintana, "The Early Years," 62, 132. The Jicarilla Apaches had fought for a boarding school on their newly established reservation. They did not want to send their children so far away to boarding school in Santa Fe.

80. Pablo Mitchell, *Coyote Nation: Sexuality, Race, and Conquest in Modernizing New Mexico, 1880–1920* (Chicago: University of Chicago Press, 2005), 34.

81. Quintana, "The Early Years," 65.

82. Official Report of the Nineteenth Annual Conference of Charities and Correction (1892), 46–59, reprinted in Richard H. Pratt, *"The Advantages of Mingling Indians with Whites," Americanizing the American Indians: Writings by the "Friends of the Indian" 1880–1900* (Cambridge, MA: Harvard University Press, 1973), 260–271.

83. Larry Martin, interview by author, Albuquerque, NM, January 3, 2001.

84. Quintana, "The Early Years," 102, 116.

85. McKinney, "History of the Albuquerque Indian School," 55; Quintana, "The Early Years," 65.

86. McKinney, "History of the Albuquerque Indian School," 36–37.

87. Quintana, "The Early Years," 75–76.

88. McKinney, "History of the Albuquerque Indian School," 55–56.

89. Elizabeth Roberts, pers. comm., February 11, 1994. Roberts took care of the Hebenstreet children. One of the girls she cared for eventually married Governor Bill Richardson.

90. McKinney, "History of the Albuquerque Indian School," 97.

91. Quintana, "The Early Years," 116.

92. Ibid.

93. Ibid., 117.

94. McKinney, "History of the Albuquerque Indian School," 100.

95. Larry Martin, interview by author, Albuquerque, NM, January 3, 2001.

96. Luckingham, *The Urban Southwest*, 56.

97. Simmons, *Albuquerque*, 330.

98. Pamphlet, "The First American: A Dramatic Pageant of Indian Life, 1929."

99. Ibid.

100. Ibid.

101. Ibid.

102. Ibid.

103. Luckingham, *The Urban Southwest*, 76.

104. Ibid.

105. Ibid., 77.

106. Ibid., 48.

CHAPTER 3

1. Keith Franklin, "The Tribes' Turn: Urban Indians' Lament," *Albuquerque Tribune*, April 5, 2000.

2. Nancy Plevin and Ben Neary, "Oñate's Foot Cut Off," *The Santa Fe New Mexican*, January 8, 1998.

3. Ibid.; Ian Hoffman, "A Man of His Times," *Albuquerque Journal*, January 18, 1998, 1.

4. Jason Gibbs, "Groups Want Probe, Boycott of Oñate Statue," *Albuquerque Tribune*, July 28, 1999; Ollie Reed, Jr., "Oñate Statue Artist Told to Regroup, Try Again," *Albuquerque Tribune*, March 13, 1998; Scott Smallwood, "Memorial Supporter Hopes for Baca Veto," *Albuquerque Journal*, March 3, 1999.

5. "County GOP Chair Urged to Resign over Comments," KOAT-TV News broadcast, Albuquerque, New Mexico, September 23, 2008, transcript, www.koat.com/news/17536179/detail.html (accessed on September 23, 2008); Jeff Jones, "Under the Gun; GOP Official's Comments Ignite Calls for His Removal," *Albuquerque Journal*, September 23, 2008; and Leslie

Linthicum, "C de Baca Voices Unspoken Issue," *Albuquerque Journal*, September 25, 2008.

6. See Marc Simmons, *Hispanic Albuquerque, 1706–1846.* (Albuquerque: University of New Mexico Press, 2003); V.B. Price, *Albuquerque: A City at the End of the World* (Albuquerque: University of New Mexico Press, 2003); Howard Bryan, *Albuquerque Remembered* (Albuquerque: University of New Mexico Press, 2006); and Debra Hughes, *Albuquerque in Our Time: 30 Voices, 300 Years* (Santa Fe: Museum of New Mexico Press, 2006).

7. Ronald J. Solimon, "A Letter from IPCC CEO and President," *Pueblo Horizons: Indian Pueblo Cultural Center Newsletter* (Winter 2008/2009): 1, www.indianpueblo.org/images/pdfs/pueblo_horizons_win08.pdf.

8. Ibid.

9. Southwest Association for Indian Arts, "Santa Fe Indian Market" (April 1, 2002), www.swaia.org/market.php (accessed July 18, 2008).

10. Marc Simmons, *Albuquerque: A Narrative History* (Albuquerque: University of New Mexico Press, 1982), 45.

11. "Annual 'Gathering of Nations' Powwow to Draw More than 100,000 People," Associated Press State & Local Wire, April 5, 2001; and "Thousands Attend Gathering of Nations," Associated Press State & Local Wire, April 30, 2005.

12. Indian National Finals Rodeo, www.infr.org.

13. Peter Iverson, *When Indians Became Cowboys: Native Peoples and Cattle Ranching in the American West* (Norman: University of Oklahoma Press, 1994).

14. Geraldine M. Loretto and Milton Ospina, "Final Report and Recommendations of Indian Center Task Force," Indian Center Task Force, Albuquerque, March 1990, 8; "Albuquerque Hispano Chamber Announces Rodeo Deal," *New Mexico Business Weekly*, June 21, 2004.

15. U.S. Census Bureau, "The American Indian Alaska Native Population: 2000," February 2002, 8, 9.

16. Veronica E. Velarde Tiller, ed., *Tiller's Guide to Indian Country: Economic Profiles of American Indian Reservations* (Albuquerque, NM: Bow and Arrow Publishing Company, 1996), 438–443, 446–448, 455–456, 459–462, 462–465, 468–469.

17. Theodore S. Jojola, *Urban Indians in Albuquerque, New Mexico: A Study for the Department of Family and Community Services* (Albuquerque, NM: City of Albuquerque, 1999), 30–31.

18. *Mayor's Symposium on Indian Affairs: Final Report* (Albuquerque, NM: City of Albuquerque, June 27, 1994), 7.

19. Jojola, *Urban Indians in Albuquerque*, 31.

20. Ibid., 5, 10, 13; William H. Hodge, *The Albuquerque Navajos* (Tucson: Univer-

sity of Arizona Press, 1969), 25.

21. Jojola, *Urban Indians in Albuquerque*, 5, 10, 13; Hodge, *The Albuquerque Navajos*, 23.

22. Geri Loretto, interview by author, Albuquerque, NM, March 8, 2001.

23. Emmett Francis, interview by author, Albuquerque, NM, March 13, 2001.

24. NACOP meeting with Representative Deb Gullet (District 18), February 2001.

25. Loretto, interview.

26. Carol Weahkee, former director of Albuquerque Indian Center, interview by author, Albuquerque, NM, March 8, 2001.

27. Loretto, interview.

28. *Mayor's Symposium on Indian Affairs*, 7.

29. Ibid., 1.

30. Ibid., 8–11.

31. Loretto, interview.

32. Francis, interview.

33. Loretto, interview.

34. Norman Ration, interview by author, Albuquerque, NM, August 5, 2008.

35. Loretto, interview; Human Rights Office, *Review of the City of Albuquerque's Employment Policies, Procedures, and Practices as They Impact upon Equal Employment Opportunities* (Albuquerque, NM: Human Rights Office, City of Albuquerque, 1998), 5.

36. Human Rights Office, *Review*, 5.

37. Ibid.

38. Ibid.

39. Ibid.

40. Ibid., 7.

41. Ibid., 6.

42. Ibid.

43. Loretto, interview.

44. Jojola, *Urban Indians in Albuquerque*, 29.

45. Human Rights Office, *Review*, attachments 59–61.

46. Amnesty International, *Maze of Injustice: The Failure to Protect Indigenous Women from Sexual Violence in the USA* (April 2007) www.amnesty.org/en/library/info/AMR51/035/2007 (accessed August 3, 2009); and National Congress of the American Indian, "Fact Sheet: Violence Against Women in Indian Country," (undated) www.ncai.org/ncai/advocacy/hr/docs/dv-fact_sheet.pdf (accessed August 3, 2009).

47. Amnesty International, *Maze of Injustice*, 1.
48. Ibid., 1–3.
49. National Congress of the American Indian, "Fact Sheet," 1, 2.
50. Justin Arbuckle, Lenora Olsone, Mike Howard, Judith Brillman, Carolyn Anctil, and David Sklar, "Safe at Home? Domestic Violence and Other Homicides among Women in New Mexico," *Annals of Emergency Medicine*, 27:2 (February 1996): 210.
51. Ibid., 212.
52. Ibid., 211.
53. Ibid., 212.
54. Ibid., 213.
55. Pamphlet, "Urban Indian Advocacy Program" (Albuquerque, NM: Morning Star House, 2007).
56. Darlene Reid-Jojola, Urban Indian Advocacy Program, interview by author, Albuquerque, NM, July 24, 2008.
57. Leann Holt, "Cell Phones Donated to Violence Shelters," *Albuquerque Journal*, December 25, 2005.
58. Ibid.
59. Susan Steiger, "Fractured Lives," *Albuquerque Journal*, April 2, 2000, 11.
60. Katie Buford, "Finding Solutions to the Violence," *Albuquerque Journal*, November 26, 2002.
61. Reid-Jojola, interview.
62. Steiger, "Fractured Lives," 11.
63. Cindy Glover, "Gift to Women's Shelter on Hold," *Albuquerque Journal*, June 4, 1997.
64. Reid-Jojola, interview.
65. Ibid.
66. Ibid.
67. Franklin, "The Tribes' Turn."
68. "Indian Education Department," pamphlet (Albuquerque, NM: Albuquerque Public Schools), undated, www.aps.edu/APS/IndianEd/ied%20FOLD%20WEB.htm (accessed June 24, 2008).
69. Ibid.
70. Albuquerque Metro Native American Coalition, "APS 2000, 80 day Native American Report Card. Why Are the APS Native American Students Being Left Behind?" (Albuquerque, NM: Author, February 2001), 3.
71. M. George, F. Ortega, and M. Martinez, "Tribal-State Indian Education Summit Report, Developing Relationships and Partnerships Between Tribes and

the State to Ensure Equitable Resources and Quality Education for Native American Students" (Santa Fe: New Mexico Higher Education Department, December 19, 2005), 12.

72. Amy Miller, "Bridging the Gap: APS Sees Cultural, Language Programs as a Way to Help Indian Students," *Albuquerque Journal*, April 9, 2006.

73. *Storyteller*, Albuquerque Public Schools Indian Education Newsletter, March 2007, 3.

74. Amy Miller, "Charters Facing a Math Problem; Coming Up with Building Funds for Both Charter and Traditional Schools Is a Challenge," *Albuquerque Journal*, November 12, 2006; and Native American Community Academy website, www.nacaschool.org (accessed August 16, 2010).

75. Echoing Green, "2005 Fellows: Kara Bobroff, Native American Community Academy," (www.echoinggreen.org/fellows/kara-bobroff (accessed on July 26, 2008).

76. Native American Community Academy website www.nacaschool.org /careers.html (accessed July 19, 2008).

77. Echoing Green, "2005 Fellows"; Miller, "Bridging the Gap."

78. Echoing Green, "2005 Fellows."

79. S.D. Aberle, "All Indian Pueblo Council and the Albuquerque Indian School Land," October 20, 1969, University of New Mexico, Center for Southwest Research, MSS 509 BC, Box 8, Folder 28; "Summary of the Development Agreement Between the Indian Pueblo Federal Development Corporation and the City of Albuquerque" (Albuquerque, NM: IPFDC, February 25, 2005), 1.

80. James Riding In, "The Contracting of Albuquerque Indian School," *The Indian Historian*, 11:4 (January 12, 1979): 21.

81. Ibid., 24.

82. Toby Smith, "Indian School Brings Sadness, Joy for Alum," *Albuquerque Journal*, November 29, 1996.

83. Ibid.

84. "Metro Watch," *Albuquerque Journal*, October 17, 1995.

85. Ibid.

86. Michael Hartranft, "Indian School Site Faces Snags," *Albuquerque Journal*, October 15, 1995.

87. Darrel "Lawrence" Felipe, volunteer for DJ of "The Singing Wire" program, KUNM, interview by author, Albuquerque, NM, March 9, 2001.

88. Juan-Carlos Rodriguez, "Hub of Activity, Indian Pueblo Cultural Center and Area Undergoing Renovations," *Albuquerque Journal*, May 23, 2008.

89. Felipe, interview.

90. Ibid.

91. Ibid.

92. Leslie Linthicum, "BIA Inaugurates New Training Center: State of the Art Complex Opens on Former Site of Albuquerque Indian School," *Albuquerque Journal*, April 28, 2006.

93. Kathi Schroeder, "Pueblos Help Save NM Federal Jobs," *New Mexico Business Weekly*, April 2, 2004, 1.

94. Carolyn Carlson, "Pueblo Council Awarded Grant; Group Given $1M for Development," *Albuquerque Journal*, July 21, 2007.

95. Ibid.

CHAPTER 4

1. U.S. Bureau of the Census, "American Indian and Alaska Native Alone or in Combination with One or More Other Races and with One or More Tribes Reported for Selected Tribes," Data Set: Census 2000 Summary File 1 (SF 1) 100-Percent Data (Washington, DC: U.S. Census Bureau, 2002).

2. Donald Fixico, *The Urban Indian Experience in America* (Albuquerque: University of New Mexico Press, 2000), 166.

3. Joan Weibel-Orlando, *Indian Country L.A.: Maintaining Ethnic Community in Complex Society* (Urbana: University of Illinois Press, 1991), 20. Just as some African-American and Mexican-American communities have hotly debated middle-class status among their populations, similar discussions undoubtedly occur among American Indian scholars.

4. Theodore Jojola, interview by author, Albuquerque, NM, March 3, 2001.

5. Ibid.

6. Geraldine M. Loretto and Milton Ospina, "Final Report and Recommendations of Indian Center Task Force" (Albuquerque, NM: Albuquerque Indian Center Task Force, March 1990), 5.

7. Reyna Ramirez, *Native Hubs: Culture, Community, and Belonging in Silicon Valley and Beyond* (Durham, NC and London: Duke University Press, 2007), 3.

8. Ibid.

9. See the Gathering of Nations web site at www.gatheringofnations.com. It is filled with photos of participants and spectators, illustrating how Indian fashions have and have not changed.

10. Ollie Reed, Jr., "Passion for Tradition," *Albuquerque Tribune*, April 28, 2001.

11. "Albuquerque Indian Center," pamphlet (Albuquerque, NM: American Indian Center, 2000).

12. Ibid.

13. *Albuquerque Journal*, June 13, 1974.

14. Sam English, interview by author, Albuquerque, NM, March 26, 2006.

15. *Albuquerque Journal*, June 13, 1974.

16. "Albuquerque Indian Center Focal Point for Urban Indians," *Pueblo News*, February 1978.

17. Ibid.; and "Urban Indian Center Meal Program Serving Nutrition Needs of Elders," *Pueblo News*, May 1978."

18. Geri Loretto, former liaison for Indian affairs to Albuquerque Mayor Martin Chavez (1993–1997), interview by author, Albuquerque, NM, March 8, 2001.

19. Ibid.

20. Ibid.

21. Ibid.

22. Carol Weahkee, former director of Albuquerque Indian Center, interview by author, Albuquerque, NM, March 8, 2001.

23. Ibid.

24. Ibid.

25. Ibid.

26. Ibid.

27. Larry Martin, former board member of Albuquerque Indian Center, interview by author, Albuquerque, NM, January 3, 2001.

28. Weahkee, interview.

29. Ibid.

30. Martin, interview.

31. Theodore S. Jojola, *Urban Indians in Albuquerque, New Mexico: A Study for the Department of Family and Community Services* (Albuquerque, NM: City of Albuquerque, NM, 1999), a-94.

32. Joe Sando, *Albuquerque Tribune*, February 17, 1994.

33. Ibid.

34. James Riding In, "The Contracting of Albuquerque Indian School," *The Indian Historian*, 11:4 (January 12, 1979): 21.

35. Joe Sando, *Pueblo Profiles: Cultural Identity through Centuries of Change* (Santa Fe, NM: Clear Light Publishers, 1998), 85.

36. All Indian Pueblo Council, Mission Statement and History, www.aipcinc.com (accessed January 4, 2006).

37. Ibid.

38. Jojola, *Urban Indians in Albuquerque*, a-98.

39. Ibid.

40. Ronald J. Solimon, "A Letter from IPCC CEO and President," *Pueblo Horizons*, Indian Pueblo Cultural Center newsletter (Winter 2008/2009), 1.

41. "Center for Native American Health Policy and the Indian Pueblo Cultural Center," *Pueblo Horizons*, (Winter 2008/2009), 6.

42. Katherine Augustine, "From Field to Feast: An Initiative of New Mexico Community Foundation," *Pueblo Horizons* (Winter 2008/2009), 1, www.indianpueblo.org/images/pdfs/pueblo_horizons_win08.pdf (accessed July 29, 2008).

43. "National Indian Council on Aging and the Indian Pueblo Cultural Center," *Pueblo Horizons*, (Winter 2008/2009), 6, www.indianpueblo.org/images/pdfs/pueblo_horizons_win08.pdf (accessed July 29, 2008).

44. "Harvest Café," Indian Pueblo Cultural Center website (www.indianpueblo.org/visit/cafe.html, accessed April 5, 2009).

45. Ibid.

46. "Pueblo House," Indian Pueblo Cultural Center website, www.indianpueblo.org/museum/pueblohouse.html (accessed April 5, 2009).

47. "Indian Pueblo Cultural Center Story," pamphlet (Albuquerque, NM: Indian Pueblo Cultural Center, n.d.), author's archive.

48. Indian Pueblo Cultural Center, "Pueblo House Re-Opens to a New Face and Expanded Educational Programming," press release, April 16, 2007, www.itsatrip.org/media/press-releases/detail.aspx?ReleaseID=30 (accessed January 10, 2008).

49. Indian Pueblo Cultural Center website, available at www.indianpueblo.org/index.html (accessed on April 5, 2009).

50. American Indian musical forms are very different from mainstream American music. Traditional Indian songs use Native languages. Many have religious significance. The songs can remind you of Pueblo feast days or other ceremonies. Contemporary Native music incorporates American Indian issues and history, sometimes subtly, as in the songs of the Native blues band Indigenous, and sometimes more directly, as in works by Annie Humphrey, Joy Harjo, and Ulali.

51. Felipe, interview.

52. Ibid.

53. Telephone conversation with La Donna Harris, founding member of the Toyah Band of Comanches, Albuquerque, NM, March 5, 2001.

54. Ibid.

55. Ibid.
56. Ibid.
57. Ibid.
58. Ibid.
59. Ibid.
60. Once a single group, it has split in two. The Cherokees of New Mexico, with the aid of Wilma Mankiller, are recognized by the Cherokee Nation and included in their constitution.
61. Telephone interview with Cheryl Paisano, Albuquerque, NM, March 9, 2001.

CHAPTER 5

1. Bureau of Indian Affairs, United Pueblos Agency, "What Relocation Means" (undated), Sophie D. Aberle Papers, MSS 509 BC, Box 22, Folder 18, Center for Southwest Research, University Libraries, University of New Mexico, Albuquerque, NM.
2. Alan L. Sorkin, *The Urban American Indian* (Lexington, MA: Lexington Books, 1978); Jack O. Waddell and O. Michael Watson, eds., *American Indian Urbanization*, Institute Monograph Series, No. 4. (Lafayette, IN: Institute for the Study of Social Change, Purdue University, 1973); Jack O. Waddell and O. Michael Watson, eds., *The American Indian in Urban Society*, The Little, Brown Series in Anthropology (Boston: Little Brown, 1971).
3. Lisa M. Poupart, "The Familiar Face of Genocide: Internalized Oppression among American Indians," *Hypatia*, 18:2 (Spring 2003): 86–87.
4. Recent works discussing organizations created in urban environments include Donald Fixico, *The Urban Indian Experience in America* (Albuquerque: University of New Mexico Press, 2000); Terry Strauss and Grant Arndt P., eds., *Native Chicago* (Chicago: McNaughton and Gunn Inc., 1998); Joan Weibel-Orlando, *Indian Country L.A.: Maintaining Ethnic Community in Complex Society* (Urbana: University of Illinois Press, 1991); Intertribal Friendship House and Susan Lobo, coordinating editor, *Urban Voices: The Bay Area American Indian community* (Tucson: University of Arizona Press, 2002).
5. La Donna Harris, founding member of the Toyah Band of Comanches, interview by author, Albuquerque, NM, March 5, 2001; and Cheryl Paisano, former chair of Laguna Colony, interview by author, Albuquerque, NM, March 9, 2001.
6. Kurt Peters, "Continuing Identity: Laguna Pueblo Railroaders in Richmond,

California," *American Indian Culture and Research Journal*, 22:4 (1998): 188, 190. Peters' work provides a fascinating look into the Richmond Colony in California.

7. Ralph Paisano, "Laguna Colony's Role in Albuquerque," *Laguna Colony Info Page*, June 20, 1997, 1.
8. Peters, "Continuing Identity," 188.
9. Paisano, "Laguna Colony's Role in Albuquerque," 1; and Peters, "Continuing Identity," 189, 190. In addition, many Acoma Pueblo members participated in the employment opportunities and lived in the Laguna colonies.
10. Peters, "Continuing Identity," 189, 190.
11. Ibid., 190, 192–193.
12. Ibid., 192.
13. Katherine Augustine, member of Laguna Colony, interview by author, Albuquerque, NM, March 12, 2001.
14. Katherine Augustine, "Gallup Round House," *Storyteller*, Laguna Colony of Albuquerque newsletter (1st quarter, 1996), 1.
15. Augustine, "Gallup Round House," 2.
16. Ibid., 2.
17. Pueblo of Laguna, *Constitution of the Pueblo of Laguna, New Mexico*, 1984.
18. Ibid.
19. Ulysses Paisano, interview by author, former chairman of Laguna Colony, Albuquerque, NM, March 9, 2001.
20. Ibid.
21. Ibid.
22. Ibid.; and Augustine, "Gallup Round House," 2.
23. Ulysses Paisano, interview.
24. Augustine, "Gallup Round House," 2.
25. Ulysses Paisano, interview.
26. Laguna Colony of Albuquerque, By-Laws, 1992, 1.
27. Ibid.
28. David Melton, former chairman of Laguna Colony of Albuquerque, interview by author, Albuquerque, NM, March 12, 2001; Cheryl Paisano, interview; and Grace Andrews, member of Laguna Colony of Albuquerque, interview by author, Albuquerque, NM, March 12, 2001.
29. Melton, interview.
30. Ibid.
31. Ibid.
32. Ibid.

33. Laguna Colony of Albuquerque, By-Laws, 1992, 1.
34. Cheryl Paisano, interview.
35. Laguna Colony of Albuquerque, By-Laws, 1992, 1.
36. Ibid., 3.
37. Ibid.
38. Ibid.
39. Ibid.
40. Cheryl Paisano, interview.
41. Ibid.
42. Leslie Linthicum, "Laguna Pueblo to Let Women Run for Office," *Albuquerque Journal*, January 4, 1997.
43. Ibid.
44. Ibid.
45. Cheryl Paisano, interview.
46. Given the legacy of Christianity among Indigenous peoples, Christmas may or may not be celebrated by members as a Christian holiday. However, the holiday affords an opportunity for a social gathering.
47. *StoryTeller*, News from Laguna Colony of Albuquerque, 2:1 (Winter 1994): 1.
48. Cheryl Paisano, interview.
49. Ibid.; *StoryTeller*, News from Laguna Colony of Albuquerque, 2:2 (Spring/Summer 1994): 4.
50. Cheryl Paisano, interview; *StoryTeller*, (Winter 1994): 4.
51. Cheryl Paisano, interview.
52. Ulysses Paisano, former chairman of Laguna Colony of Albuquerque, interview by author, Albuquerque, NM, March 9, 2001.
53. *StoryTeller*, (Winter 1994): 4.
54. F. Stanley, *The Duke City, the Story of Albuquerque, New Mexico: 1706–1956* (Pampa, TX: Pampa Print Shop, 1963), 175–177.
55. Ibid., 176–177.
56. Ibid.
57. Ibid.
58. Ibid., 176.
59. Cheryl Paisano, interview.
60. Ibid.
61. Andrews, interview.
62. Cheryl Paisano, interview.
63. Ibid.; Interview with Andrews.
64. *Laguna Colony of Albuquerque Newsletter*, March 7, 2000.

65. Author's attendance at Laguna Colony Meeting, March 2001.

66. Cheryl Paisano, interview.

67. Pueblo of Laguna, *Constitution of the Pueblo of Laguna, New Mexico*, Article III, Section 5 (effective June 6, 1984).

68. Author's attendance at Laguna Colony meeting; and Melton, interview.

69. Jürgen Osterhammel, *Colonialism: A Theoretical Overview*, trans. Shelley L. Frisch (Princeton, NJ: Markus Wiener Publishers, 1997), 10.

70. Linda Tuhiwai Smith, *Decolonizing Methodologies: Research and Indigenous Peoples* (New York: Zed Books Ltd., 1999), 23.

71. Osterhammel, *Colonialism*, 10–11.

CHAPTER 6

1. Caroline Chung Simpson, *An Absent Presence: Japanese Americans in Postwar American Culture, 1945–1960* (Durham, NC: Duke University Press, 2001), 4.

2. Lisa Poupart, "A Familiar Face of Genocide: Internalized Oppression among American Indians," *Hypatia*, 18:2 (2003): 88.

3. "Chronology of the National Indian Youth Council and the Indian Youth Councils Which Preceded It," 32 pages, 1, MSS 703, National Indian Youth Council Records, Box 1, Folder 31, Center for Southwest Research Collection, University Libraries, University of New Mexico, Albuquerque, NM. [Hereafter, CSRC.]

4. Ibid.

5. Ibid.

6. Ibid.

7. Ibid., 2.

8. Ibid., 3.

9. Ibid., 4.

10. "National Indian Youth Council," n.d., 2 pp, 1, MSS 703, National Indian Youth Council Records, Box 1, Folder 2, CSRC.

11. "National Indian Youth Council, Inc. 1961–1975," unsigned and undated typed manuscript, 15 pp, 2, MSS 703, National Indian Youth Council Records, Box 1, Folder 11, CSRC.

12. Shirley Hill Witt to Mel Thom, June 21, 1961, and Herb Blatchford to Mel Thom, June 28, 1961, MSS 703, National Indian Youth Council Records, Box 1, Folder 11, CSRC.

13. Blatchford to Thom, June 28, 1961.

14. Ibid.; Herb Blatchford, Correspondence for Chicago Conference Youth Group, July 23, 1961; and Herb Blatchford, Correspondence for Chicago Conference Youth Group to Tentative Charter Membership, July 17, 1961, MSS 703, National Indian Youth Council Records, Box 1, Folder 11, CSRC.

15. Joanne Nagel, *American Indian Ethnic Renewal: Red Power and the Resurgence of Identity and Culture* (New York: Oxford University Press, 1996), 129. As a story about NIYC in *Green Letter* described, "In 1961, ten young Indian people from across the country gathered in the back room of the dilapidated Gallup Indian Center in New Mexico and formed the National Indian Youth Council (NIYC). In the 1960s, NIYC was basically a civil rights organization. While Blacks were doing 'sit-ins' in the South, NIYC was doing 'fish-ins' in the Northwest." From "National Indian Council," clipping from *Green Letter*, Berkeley, CA, 1987, 2 pages, 1, MSS 703, National Indian Youth Council Records Box 1, Folder 16., CSRC.

16. "National Indian Youth Council," 1.

17. Valerie Taliman, "Protection of Sacred Pueblo Petroglyphs Gains Support," *Indian Country Today*, September 30, 1996.

18. Brenda Norrell, "Petroglyph Lawsuit Filed against City of Albuquerque," *Indian Country Today*, March 5, 2005.

19. Conversation with Sonny Weahkee, son of William Weahkee, and co-founder of the Sacred Alliance for Grassroots Equality (SAGE) Council, during tour of petroglyphs, July 16, 2003.

20. Public Law 101–313, Establishment of Petroglyph National Monument, 1990; Senate Report 105–176, Petroglyph National Monument Boundary Adjustment Act, 1998.

21. National Park Service, Petroglyph National Monument, New Mexico, www.nps.gov/petr (accessed March 23, 2003).

22. John Kaltenbach, "Developers, Builders Fulfill Housing Need," *Albuquerque Journal*, August 30, 2004.

23. Petroglyph National Monument Boundary Adjustment Act of 1997.

24. This does not take into consideration the amount of sand built up in 3,000 years. More petroglyphs may be buried under the area.

25. Conversation with Sonny Weahkee.

26. Ibid.

27. Beneshi Albert, interview by author, July 23, 2003; and interview with anonymous man, July 17, 2003.

28. Laurie Weahkee, co-founder of the Sacred Alliance for Grassroots Equality (SAGE) Council, interview by author, July 17, 2003.

29. Valerie Taliman, "Mayor 'Sneaks In' Petroglyph Road," *Indian Country Today*, September 18, 2002.

30. Kate Nash, "7 Road Foes Arrested," *Albuquerque Tribune*, September 6, 2002.

31. Taliman, "Mayor 'Sneaks In' Petroglyph Road."

32. Mark Graser, "Domenici, Indians Hit Impasse," *Albuquerque Journal*, May 18, 1997.

33. Taliman, "Mayor 'Sneaks In' Petroglyph Road."

34. Brenda Norrell, "Petroglyph Lawsuit Filed against City of Albuquerque," *Indian Country Today*, February 28, 2005; Jan Jonas, "Groups Sue over Paseo Extension," *Albuquerque Tribune*, February 18, 2005; Andrea Schoellkopf, "Mayor Pledges Dec. Start for Paseo; Judge's Ruling Gives Albuquerque a Partial Victory but Says Questions Remain," *Albuquerque Journal*, October 12, 2005.

35. Associated Press, "Apache Members Say Sacred Rocks Shouldn't Be Moved," November 23, 2005; and Erik Siemers, "Paseo Extension on the Way," *Albuquerque Tribune*, October 12, 2005.

36. Siemers, "Paseo Extension on the Way."

37. Erik Siemers, "City Gets Green Light on Moving Petroglyphs from Paseo's Path," *Albuquerque Tribune*, November 22, 2005.

38. Ibid.

39. Associated Press, "Apache Members"; and Erik Siemers, "Exasperated Apache: 100 Feet Incalculable to Rocks' Significance," *Albuquerque Tribune*, November 23, 2005.

40. Taliman, "Protection of Sacred Pueblo Petroglyphs Gains Support."

41. Norrell, "Petroglyph Lawsuit Filed against City of Albuquerque."

42. Rory McClannahan, "Smooth Flow on Paseo Addition; Officials say extent of traffic relief won't be clear for a week," *Albuquerque Journal*, June 22, 2007.

43. For an analysis, see Myla Vicenti Carpio, "(Un)disturbing Exhibitions: Indigenous Historical Memory at the NMAI," *The American Indian Quarterly* 30:3&4 (Summer/Fall 2006): 619–631.

44. Andrea Smith looks at this in more depth in her book, *Native Americans and the Christian Right: The Gendered Politics of Unlikely Alliances* (Durham, NC: Duke University Press, 2008).

45. My upcoming research project explores the shared experiences of federal policies of removal and relocation for both the American Indian and Japanese American communities. In addition, I am currently the co-principal investigator and lead scholar, with the Gila River Indian Community, for an oral history project, "Beyond the Barbed Wire Fence," that was awarded an Arizona Humanities Council research grant in June 2009.

Bibliography

ARCHIVAL SOURCES

Bureau of Indian Affairs, Branch of Relocation Services. Record Group 75, National Archives, Washington, DC.

Bureau of Indian Affairs, Denver Field Relocation Office. Record Group 75, Rocky Mountain Region of National Archives, Denver, Colorado.

Bureau of Indian Affairs, Los Angeles Field Relocation Office. Record Group 75, Laguna-Niguel Region of National Archives, San Pedro, California.

National Indian Youth Council Records. MSS 703, Center for Southwest Research Collection, University Libraries, University of New Mexico, Albuquerque, New Mexico.

New Mexico Collection. Special Collections Library, City of Albuquerque, Albuquerque, New Mexico.

Sophie D. Aberle Papers. MSS 509 BC, Center for Southwest Research, University Libraries, University of New Mexico, Albuquerque, New Mexico.

U.S. GOVERNMENT DOCUMENTS

American Indian Policy Review Commission, Task Force Eight: Urban and Rural Non-Reservation Indians. *Report on Urban and Rural Non-Reservation Indians: Final Report to the American Indian Policy Review Commission.* Washington, DC: U.S. Government Printing Office, 1976.

Armstrong, Troy L., Philmer Bluehouse, Alfred Dennison, Harmon Mason, Barbara Mendenhall, Daniel Wall, James W. Zion, eds. *Finding and Knowing the Gang—Nayee, Field-Initiated Gang Research Project, The Judicial Branch of the Navajo Nation.* Washington, DC: U.S. Department of Justice, Office of Juvenile Justice and Delinquency Prevention, 1995.

Cherokee Nation v. Georgia, 30 U.S. (5 Pet.) 1, 15 (1831).

Indian Health Service. "Overview of the Phoenix Indian Medical Center." Phoenix, AZ: Indian Health Service, Phoenix Indian Medical Center, 2001.

———. "Trends in Indian Health 2000–2001: Part 2 Population Statistics." U.S. Department of Health and Human Services, Indian Health Service, Office of Public Health Office of Program Support Division of Program Statistics, 2004.

———. "Health Care Services Are Not Always Available to Native Americans." U.S. Government Accountability Office, Report to the Committee on Indian Affairs, U.S. Senate, August 2005.

Indian Self-Determination and Educational Assistance Act. Public Law 93–638. *United States Statutes at Large,* 88 (1975): 2203–2214.

Joint Resolution to Provide for the Establishment of the American Indian Policy Review Commission. Public Law 93–580. *United States Statutes at Large,* 88 (1975): 1910.

Office of Civil Rights Evaluation. *A Quiet Crisis: Federal Funding and Unmet Needs in Indian Country.* Washington, DC: U.S. Commission on Civil Rights, July 2003.

Personal Responsibility and Work Opportunity Reconciliation Act of 1996. Public Law 104–193. *United States Statutes at Large* 110 (1996): 2105.

Petroglyph National Monument and Pecos National Historical Park Establishment Act. Public Law 101–313. *United States Statutes at Large* 104 (1990): 272.

U.S. Census Bureau. "American Indian and Alaska Native Alone or in Combination with One or More Other Races and with One or More Tribes Reported for Selected Tribes." Data Set: Census 2000 Summary File 1 (SF 1) 100-Percent Data. Washington, DC: U.S. Census Bureau, 2002.

———. "The American Indian and Alaska Native Population: 2000." Economics and Statistics Administration. Washington, DC: U.S. Census Bureau, 2002.

United States v. McGowan, 302 U.S. 535 (1938).

U.S. Congress. Senate. *S. 633. A Bill to Amend the Petroglyph National Monument Establishment Act of 1990 to Adjust the Boundary of the Monument, and for Other Purposes,* April 29, 1998. 105th Cong., 2nd sess., 1998. S. Rept. 105–176.

U.S. Government Accountability Office. *Welfare Reform: Tribal TANF Allows Flexi-*

bility to Tailor Programs, but Conditions on Reservations Make It Difficult to Move Recipients into Jobs. Washington, DC: GAO, July 2002.

ORAL HISTORIES

Albert, Beneshi. Lead organizer and co-director, Sacred Alliance for Grassroots Equality (SAGE) Council. Interview by author. Albuquerque, NM, July 17, 2003.

Andrews, Grace. Member of Laguna Colony of Albuquerque. Interview by author. Albuquerque, NM, March 12, 2001.

Augustine, Katherine. Member of Laguna Colony of Albuquerque. Interview by author. Albuquerque, NM, March 12, 2001.

English, Sam. Artist and urban Indian advocate. Interview by author. Albuquerque, NM, March 26, 2006.

Felipe, Darrell "Lawrence." Former DJ for The Singing Wire program, KUNM. Interview by author. Albuquerque, NM, March 3, 2001.

Francis, Emmett. Former liaison for Indian affairs to Mayor Jim Baca (1997–2001). Interview by author. Albuquerque, NM, March 13, 2001.

Harris, La Donna. Founding member of the Toyah Band of Comanches, Albuquerque, NM. Telephone interview by author. Albuquerque, NM, March 5, 2001.

Jojola, Theodore. Author and researcher on Indigenous issues. Interview by author. Albuquerque, NM, March 3, 2001.

Loretto, Geri. Former liaison for Indian affairs to Albuquerque Mayor Martin Chavez (1993–1997). Telephone interview by author. Albuquerque, NM, March 8, 2001.

Martin, Larry. Former board member of Albuquerque Indian Center. Interview by author. Albuquerque, NM, January 3, 2001.

Melton, David. Former chairman of Laguna Colony of Albuquerque. Interview by author. Albuquerque, NM, March 12, 2001.

Paisano, Cheryl. Former chairwoman of Laguna Colony. Interview by author. Albuquerque, NM, March 9, 2001.

Paisano, Ulysses. Former chairman of Laguna Colony of Albuquerque. Interview by author. Albuquerque, NM, March 9, 2001.

Ration, Norman. Director of National Indian Youth Council. Interview by author. Albuquerque, NM, August 5, 2008.

Reid-Jojola, Darlene. Director of Urban Indian Advocacy Program and Morning Star House. Interview by author. Albuquerque, NM, July 24, 2008.

Weahkee, Carol. Former director of Albuquerque Indian Center. Interview by author. Albuquerque, NM, March 8, 2001.

Weahkee, Laurie. Co-founder of the Sacred Alliance for Grassroots Equality (SAGE) Council. Interview by author. Albuquerque, NM, July 17, 2003.

Weahkee, Sonny. Co-founder of the Sacred Alliance for Grassroots Equality (SAGE) Council. Interview by author. Albuquerque, NM, July 16, 2003.

PRIMARY SOURCES

Aberle, S.D. "All Indian Pueblo Council and the Albuquerque Indian School Land." October 20, 1969. Sophie D. Aberle Papers, MSS 509 BC, Box 8, Folder 28. Center for Southwest Research, University Libraries, University of New Mexico, Albuquerque, NM.

"Albuquerque Indian Center." Pamphlet. Albuquerque, NM: American Indian Center, 2000.

"Albuquerque Indian Center Focal Point for Urban Indians." *Pueblo News*, February 1978.

Albuquerque Metro Native American Coalition. "APS 2000, 80 day Native American Report Card. Why Are the APS Native American Students Being Left Behind?" Albuquerque, NM: Coalition, February 2001.

Albuquerque Public Schools. Indian Education Department pamphlet. City of Albuquerque. www.aps.edu/APS/IndianEd/ied%20FOLD %20WEB.htm (accessed June 24, 2008).

———. *Storyteller*. Albuquerque Public Schools, Indian Education Newsletter. Albuquerque, NM: Albuquerque Public Schools: March 2007.

Amnesty International. *Maze of Injustice: The Failure to Protect Indigenous Women from Sexual Violence in the USA*. April 2007. www.amnesty.org /en/library/asset/AMR51/035/2007/en/dom-AMR510352007en.html (Accessed August 3, 2009).

"Apache Members Say Sacred Rocks Shouldn't Be Moved." Associated Press, November 23, 2005.

Augustine, Katherine. "From Field to Feast: An Initiative of New Mexico Community Foundation." *Pueblo Horizons: Indian Pueblo Cultural Center Newsletter*, Winter 2008/2009. www.indianpueblo.org/images/pdfs/pueblo _horizons_win08.pdf (accessed July 29, 2008).

———. "Gallup Round House." *Storyteller: Laguna Colony of Albuquerque Newsletter*, 1st quarter edition, 1996, 1–2.

Blatchford, Herb. Correspondence from Chicago Conference Youth Group to

Tentative Charter Membership, July 17, 1961. MSS 703, National Indian Youth Council Records, Box 1, Folder 11. Center for Southwest Research Collection, University Libraries, University of New Mexico, Albuquerque, New Mexico.

———. Correspondence for Chicago Conference Youth Group, July 23, 1961. MSS 703, National Indian Youth Council Records, Box 1, Folder 11. Center for Southwest Research Collection, University Libraries, University of New Mexico, Albuquerque, NM.

———. Letter to Mel Thom, June 28, 1961. MSS 703, National Indian Youth Council Records, Box 1, Folder 11. Center for Southwest Research Collection, University Libraries, University of New Mexico, Albuquerque, NM.

Brookings Institution Institute for Government Research. *The Problem of Indian Administration; Report of a Survey Made at the Request of Hubert Work, Secretary of the Interior, and Submitted to Him, February 21, 1928.* Lewis Meriam, Ray Brown, Henry Rowe Cloud, Edward Everett Dale, and others. Baltimore, MD: The Johns Hopkins Press, 1928.

Brown, Eddie F., Stephen Cornell, Miriam Jorgensen, et al. *Welfare, Work, and American Indians: The Impact of Welfare Reform.* Report to the National Congress of American Indians. St. Louis: Kathryn Buder Center for American Indian Studies, Washington University; Tucson: Native Nations Institute for Leadership, Management, and Policy, University of Arizona, 2001.

Buford, Katie. "Finding Solutions to the Violence." *Albuquerque Journal*, November 26, 2002.

Bureau of Indian Affairs, United Pueblos Agency. "What Relocation Means." N.d. Sophie D. Aberle Papers, MSS 509 BC, Box 22, Folder 18. Center for Southwest Research, University Libraries, University of New Mexico, Albuquerque, NM.

Carlson, Carolyn. "Pueblo Council Awarded Grant; Group Given $1M For Development." *Albuquerque Journal*, July 21, 2007.

"Center for Native American Health Policy and the Indian Pueblo Cultural Center." *Pueblo Horizons: Indian Pueblo Cultural Center Newsletter*, Winter 2008/2009, 6.

"Chronology of the National Indian Youth Council and the Indian Youth Councils Which Preceded It." MSS 703, National Indian Youth Council Records, Box 1, Folder 31. Center for Southwest Research Collection, University Libraries, University of New Mexico, Albuquerque, New Mexico.

City of Albuquerque Human Rights Office. *Review of the City of Albuquerque's Employment Policies Procedures, and Practices, as They Impact Upon Equal*

Employment Opportunities. Includes Attachments 1–61. Albuquerque, NM: City, 1998.

"County GOP Chair Urged to Resign over Comments." Transcript of KOAT News broadcast. KOAT-TV, Albuquerque, NM. www.koat.com/news /17536179/detail.html (accessed September 23, 2008).

Echoing Green. "2005 Fellows: Kara Bobroff. Native American Community Academy." echoinggreen.org/fellows/kara-bobroff (accessed July 26, 2008).

Felshaw, George M. Field Relocation Officer, "Bi-weekly reports to BIA." Los Angeles Field Relocation Office, Employment Trends and Forecast (June 27, 1958) Number 12, Folder 2 721.8 Bi-weekly Reports 1958. Laguna-Niguel Region of National Archives, San Pedro, California.

"The First American: A Dramatic Pageant of Indian Life, 1929." Pamphlet. 1930. New Mexico Collection. Special Collections Library, Albuquerque, New Mexico.

Fonseca, Felicia. "New Mexico Charter School Caters to Urban Indians." *Albuquerque Journal*, August 19, 2006.

Franklin, Keith. "The Tribes' Turn: Urban Indians' Lament." *Albuquerque Tribune*, April 5, 2000, sec. C.

George, M., F. Ortega, and M. Martinez. *Tribal–State Indian Education Summit Report, Developing Relationships and Partnerships Between Tribes and the State to Ensure Equitable Resources and Quality Education for Native American Students.* State of New Mexico, December 19, 2005.

Gibbs, Jason. "Groups Want Probe, Boycott of Oñate Statue." *Albuquerque Tribune*, July 28, 1999, sec. A.

Glover, Cindy. "Gift to Women's Shelter on Hold." *Albuquerque Journal*, June 4, 1997, sec. C.

Graser, Mark. "Domenici, Indians Hit Impasse." *Albuquerque Journal*, May 18, 1997, sec. A.

Hartranft, Michael. "Indian School Site Faces Snags." *Albuquerque Journal*, October 18, 1995, sec. C.

Hoffman, Ian. "A Man of His Times." *Albuquerque Journal*, January 18, 1998, 1.

Holt, Leann. "Cell Phones Donated to Violence Shelters." *Albuquerque Journal*, December 25, 2005, sec. E.

Indian National Finals Rodeo. www.infr.org (accessed March 10, 1999).

Indian Pueblo Cultural Center. Website. www.indianpueblo.org /visit/cafe.html (accessed April 5, 2009).

of Indian Center Task Force." Albuquerque: Indian Center Task Force, March 1990.

Madigan, LaVerne. "The American Indians Relocation Program." The Association on American Indian Affairs, Inc, December 1956, 3, 5. MSS 509 BC, Sophie D. Aberle Papers, Box 27, Folder 123. Center for Southwest Research. University Libraries. University of New Mexico, Albuquerque, NM.

Martin, Larry, and Edward La Croix. *Education and Employment in Albuquerque: A Response to the Mayor's Symposium on Indian Affairs.* Albuquerque: City of Albuquerque, Task Force on Education, 1995.

Mayor's Symposium on Indian Affairs: Final Report. Albuquerque, NM: City of Albuquerque, 1994.

"Metro Watch." *Albuquerque Journal,* October 17, 1995 sec. C.

Miller, Amy. "Bridging the Gap: APS Sees Cultural, Language Programs As a Way to Help Indian Students." *Albuquerque Journal,* April 9, 2006 sec. B.

———. "Charters Facing a Math Problem; Coming up with building funds for both charter and traditional schools is a challenge." *Albuquerque Journal,* November 12, 2006 sec. A.

Myer, Dillon S. "Address by Commissioner of Indian Affairs Dillon S. Myer, Before the Western Governor's Conference at Phoenix, Arizona." December 9, 1952. MSS 509 BC, Sophie D. Aberle Papers, Box 6, Folder 1. Center for Southwest Research, University Libraries, University of New Mexico, Albuquerque, New Mexico.

Nash, Kate. "7 Road Foes Arrested." *Albuquerque Tribune,* September 6, 2002.

National Congress of the American Indian. "Fact Sheet: Violence Against Women in Indian Country." N.d. www.ncai.org/ncai/advocacy/hr/docs/dv-fact_sheet.pdf (accessed August 3, 2009).

"National Indian Council." *Green Letter.* Berkeley, CA, 1987. MSS 703, National Indian Youth Council Records, Box 1, Folder 16. Center for Southwest Research Collection, University Libraries, University of New Mexico, Albuquerque, NM.

"National Indian Council on Aging and the Indian Pueblo Cultural Center." *Pueblo Horizons: Indian Pueblo Cultural Center Newsletter,* Winter 2008/2009, 6. Albuquerque, NM: Indian Pueblo Cultural Center. www.indianpueblo.org/images/pdfs/pueblo_horizons_win08.pdf (accessed July 29, 2008).

"National Indian Youth Council." N.d. MSS 703, National Indian Youth Council

Records, Box 1, Folder 2. Center for Southwest Research Collection, University Libraries, University of New Mexico, Albuquerque, NM.

"National Indian Youth Council, Inc. 1961–1975." Unsigned and undated typed manuscript. MSS 703, National Indian Youth Council Records, Box 1, Folder 11. Center for Southwest Research Collection, University Libraries, University of New Mexico, Albuquerque, NM.

National Park Service. "Petroglyph National Monument New Mexico." National Park Service website. www.nps.gov/petr/ (accessed March 23, 2003).

Native American Community Academy. Website. www.nacaschool (accessed July 19, 2008).

New Mexico Business Weekly Staff. "Albuquerque Hispano Chamber Announces Rodeo Deal." *New Mexico Business Weekly*, June 21, 2004.

Norrell, Brenda. "Petroglyph lawsuit filed against city of Albuquerque." *Indian Country Today*, March 5, 2005.

Norrell, Brenda. "Urban Indian Summit Mirrors Population Shift." *Indian Country Today*, February 11, 2005 sec. A.

Official Report of the Nineteenth Annual Conference of Charities and Correction (1892), 46–59. Reprinted in Richard H. Pratt. *"The Advantages of Mingling Indians with Whites," Americanizing the American Indians: Writings by the "Friends of the Indian" 1880–1900*. Cambridge, MA: Harvard University Press, 1973, 260–271.

Paisano, Ralph. "Laguna Colony's Role in Albuquerque." *Laguna Colony Info Page*, June 20, 1997.

Plevin, Nancy and Ben Neary. "Onate's Foot Cut Off." *The Santa Fe New Mexican*, January 8, 1998 sec. A.

Reed, Ollie Jr. "Oñate Statute Artist Told to Regroup, Try Again." *Albuquerque Tribune*, March 13, 1998 sec. A.

Reed, Ollie Jr. "Passion for Tradition." *Albuquerque Tribune*, April 28, 2001 sec. A.

Rodriguez, Juan-Carlos. "Hub of Activity, Indian Pueblo Cultural Center and Area Undergoing Renovations." *Albuquerque Journal*, May 23, 2008.

Schoellkopf, Andrea. "Mayor Pledges Dec. Start for Paseo; Judge's Ruling Gives Albuquerque a Partial Victory But Says Questions Remain." *Albuquerque Journal*, October 12, 2005.

Schroeder, Kathi. "Pueblos Help Save NM Federal Jobs." *New Mexico Business Weekly*, April 2, 2004, 1.

Siemers, Erik. "City Gets Green Light on Moving Petroglyphs from Paseo's Path."

Albuquerque Tribune, November 22, 2005.

———. "Exasperated Apache: 100 Feet Incalculable to Rocks' Significance." *Albuquerque Tribune*, November 23, 2005.

———. "Paseo extension on the way." *Albuquerque Tribune*, October 12, 2005.

Smallwood, Scott. "Memorial Supporter Hopes for Baca Veto." *Albuquerque Journal*, March 3, 1999 sec. D.

Smith, Toby. "Indian School Brings Sadness, Joy for Alum." *Albuquerque Journal*, November 29, 1996 sec. C.

Solimon, Ronald J. "A Letter from IPCC CEO and President." *Pueblo Horizons: Indian Pueblo Cultural Center Newsletter*, Winter 2008/2009, 1. www .indianpueblo.org/images/pdfs/pueblo_horizons_win08.pdf (accessed July 29, 2008).

Southwest Association for Indian Arts. "Santa Fe Indian Market." April 1, 2002. www.swaia.org/market.php (accessed July 18, 2008).

Steiger, Susan. "Fractured Lives." *Albuquerque Journal*, April 2, 2000.

Taliman, Valerie. "Mayor 'Sneaks In' Petroglyph Road." *Indian Country Today* 22 September 18, 2002 sec. B.

———. "Protection of Sacred Pueblo Petroglyphs Gains Support." *Indian Country Today* September 30, 1996, sec. C.

"Thousands attend Gathering of Nations." Associated Press State & Local Wire, April 30, 2005.

"Urban Indian Advocacy Program." Morning Star House: 2007. Pamphlet in possession of author.

"Urban Indian Center Meal Program Serving Nutrition Needs of Elders." *Pueblo News*, May 1978.

Wagener, Victoria. "Resources for Welfare Decisions: Tribal TANF and Welfare-to-Work Programs." Welfare Information Network (now The Financial Report) 3 (September 1999): 5.

Webb, Andrew. "Indians Fear Census Undercount." *Albuquerque Journal*, February 10, 2001 sec. E.

Wihl, Abby. "APS Dropout Rates Down." *Albuquerque Tribune*, July 13, 2007.

Witt, Shirley Hill. Letter to Mel Thom, June 21, 1961. MSS 703, National Indian Youth Council Records, Box 1, Folder 11. Center for Southwest Research Collection, University Libraries, University of New Mexico, Albuquerque, NM.

169

SECONDARY SOURCES

Dissertations and Theses

Baker, Nancy Roux-Teepen. "American Indian Women in an Urban Setting." PhD dissertation, Ohio State University, 1982.

Carpio, Myla F. Thyrza. "Lost Generation: The Involuntary Sterilization of American Indian Women." Master's thesis, Arizona State University, 1995.

Davis, Julie. "American Indian Movement Survival Schools in Minneapolis and St. Paul, 1968–2002." PhD diss., Arizona State University, 2004.

McKinney, Lillie G. "History of the Albuquerque Indian School." Master's thesis, University of New Mexico, 1934.

Molholt, Stephanie Anne Leu. "Place to Call Home: Examining the Role of American Indian Community Centers in Urban Settings." Master's thesis, University of Arizona, 1996.

Quintana, Penny Ann. "The Early Years of the Albuquerque Indian School, 1879–1928." Master's thesis, Arizona State University, 1992.

Books and Articles

Adams, Richard Newbold. *Community Culture and National Change.* Publication 24. New Orleans, LA: Middle American Research Institute, Tulane University, 1972.

Albers, Patricia, and Beatrice Medicine. *The Hidden Half: Studies of Plains Indian Women.* Washington, DC: University Press of America, 1983.

Allen, Paula Gunn. *Spider Woman's Granddaughters: Traditional Tales and Contemporary Writing by Native American Women.* Boston: Beacon Press, 1989.

Anderson, Douglas, Barbara Anderson, and Southwest Parks and Monuments Association. *Chaco Canyon: Center of a Culture.* Globe, AZ: Southwest Parks and Monuments Association, 1981.

Arbuckle, Justin, Lenora Olsone, Mike Howard, Judith Brillman, Carolyn Anctil, and David Sklar. "Safe at Home? Domestic Violence and Other Homicides Among Women in New Mexico." *Annals of Emergency Medicine* 27 (February 1996): 210–215.

Arndt, Grant P. "Relocation's Imagined Landscape," in Terry Strauss and Grant P. Arndt, eds. *Native Chicago.* Chicago: McNaughton and Gunn Inc., 1998.

Bahr, Howard M, Bruce A. Chadwick, and Robert C. Day, eds. *Native Americans Today: Sociological Perspectives.* New York: Harper & Row, 1972.

Barker, J.C., and B.J. Kramer. "Alcohol Consumption among Older Urban American Indians." *Journal of Studies on Alcohol* 57(1996) 2: 119–124.

Bayer, Laura with Floyd Montoya and the Pueblo of Santa Ana. *Santa Ana: The*

People, the Pueblo, and the History of Tamaya. Albuquerque: University of New Mexico Press, 1994.

Bell, James, and Nicole Lim. "Young Once, Indian Forever: Youth Gangs in Indian Country." *American Indian Quarterly* 29 (Spring & Fall 2005) 3/4: 626–650.

Champagne, Duane. "From Sovereignty to Minority, As American as Apple Pie," *Wicazo Sa Review* 20 (Fall 2005) 2: 21–36.

Chung Simpson, Caroline. *An Absent Presence: Japanese Americans in Postwar American Culture, 1945–1960.* Durham, NC: Duke University Press, 2001.

Cook-Lynn, Elizabeth, Tom Holm, John Redhorse, and James Riding In, Moderator. "First Panel: Reclaiming American Indian Studies." *Wicazo Sa Review* 20, no. 1 (Spring 2005): 169–177.

Dutton, Bertha P. *American Indians of the Southwest.* Albuquerque: University of New Mexico Press, 1983.

Fixico, Donald. *Termination and Relocation: Federal Indian Policy, 1945–1960.* Albuquerque: University of New Mexico Press, 1986.

———. *The Urban Indian Experience in America.* Albuquerque: University of New Mexico Press, 2000.

Forbes, Jack. *Only Approved Indians.* Norman, OK: University of Oklahoma Press, 1995.

———. "The Urban Tradition among Native Americans." *American Indian Culture and Research Journal* 22 (1998) 4:15–27.

Fowler, Melvin L. "Mound 72 and Early Mississippian at Cahokia." In *New Perspectives on Cahokia: Views From the Periphery* edited by James B. Stoltman, 1–28. Madison, WI: Prehistory Press, 1991.

Friese, Kathy. "The Creative Terrain of *Numbe Whageh*: Creating Memory, Leading to Center." *American Indian Culture and Research Journal* 31, no. 3 (2007): 81–98.

Gattuso, John. *A Circle of Nations: Voices and Visions of American Indians.* Earthsong Collection. Hillsboro, OR: Beyond Words, 1993.

Gibson, Daniel. "Reclaiming Our Place." *Native Peoples Magazine.* November/December 2004. www.nativepeoples.com/site/np_nov_dec04/nd04-on_the_wind/nd04-on_the_wind_article.html (accessed July 23, 2010).

Harjo, Joy, and Gloria Bird. *Reinventing the Enemy's Language: Contemporary Native Women's Writing of North America.* New York: W.W. Norton & Company, 1997.

Hodge, William H. *The Albuquerque Navajos.* Tucson: University of Arizona Press, 1969.

Humphrey, Annie. "DNA," from *The Heron Smiled*. Bismarck, ND: Makoche Records, 2000.

Iverson, Peter. *The Navajo Nation*. Albuquerque: University of New Mexico Press, 1981.

———. *"We are Still Here": American Indians in the Twentieth Century*. Wheeling, IL: Harlan Davidson, 1998.

———. *When Indians Became Cowboys: Native Peoples and Cattle Ranching in the American West*. Norman: University of Oklahoma Press, 1994.

Jackson, Helen Hunt. *A Century of Dishonor: A Sketch of the United States Government's Dealings with Some of the Indian Tribes*. Minneapolis, MN: Ross & Haines, 1964.

Jacobs, Sue-Ellen, Wesley Thomas, and Sabine Lang. *Two-Spirit People: Native American Gender Identity, Sexuality, and Spirituality*. Urbana: University of Illinois Press, 1997.

Johnson, Byron. *Old Town, Albuquerque, New Mexico: A Guide to Its History and Architecture*. Albuquerque, NM: City of Albuquerque, 1980.

Johnson, Byron, and Robert Dauner. *Early Albuquerque: A Photographic History, 1870–1918*. Albuquerque, NM: The Albuquerque Journal and the Albuquerque Museum, 1981.

June-Friesen, Katy. "Recasting New Mexico History." *Weekly Alibi* 14 (October 20–26, 2005): 42. http://alibi.com/index.php?story=13065&scn=feature&submit_user_comment=y (accessed on July 23, 2010).

Kantner, John, and Nancy M. Mahoney. *Great House Communities across the Chacoan Landscape*. Anthropological Papers of the University of Arizona, No. 64. Tucson: University of Arizona Press, 2000.

Krisberg, Kim. "Budget Cuts for Urban Indian Programs a Danger to Health." *Nations Health* 36, no. 5 (June/July 2006): 1, 4.

Lobo, Susan, and Kurt Peters. "Introduction: Special Issue; American Indians and the Urban Experience." *American Indian Culture and Research Journal* 22, no. 4 (1998): 1–13.

Luckingham, Bradford. *The Urban Southwest: A Profile History of Albuquerque, El Paso, Phoenix, and Tucson*. El Paso: Texas Western Press, 1982.

Mauzé, Marie. *Present Is Past: Some Uses of Tradition in Native Societies*. Lanham, MD: Oxford University Press of America, 1997.

Miller, Dorothy Lonewolf, and Metropolitan Tucson Commission on Urban Native American Affairs. *Native Americans in Tucson, Our Home—Your City: Report 2, Community Agencies Respond to Native American Needs*. Tucson,

AZ: The Commission, 1991.

Mitchell, Pablo. *Coyote Nation: Sexuality, Race, and Conquest in Modernizing New Mexico, 1880–1920*. Chicago: University of Chicago Press, 2005.

Nagel, Joanne. *American Indian Ethnic Renewal: Red Power and the Resurgence of Identity and Culture*. New York: Oxford University Press, 1996.

Naranjo-Morse, Nora (Santa Clara Pueblo). *Numbe Whageh (Our Center Place)*. 2005. www.nativenetworks.si/edu/eng/orange/numbe_whageh .htm (accessed on July 16, 2010).

Nieto-Phillips, John M. *The Language of Blood: the Making of Spanish-American Identity in New Mexico, 1880s–1930s*. Albuquerque: University of New Mexico Press, 2004.

Officer, James E. "American Indian and Federal Policy." In Jack O. Waddell and O. Michael Watson, eds., *The American Indian in Urban Society*, 8–64. Boston: Little, Brown and Company, 1971.

Opler, Morris E. "Mescalero Apache." In *Smithsonian Handbook of Indians of North America*, Vol. 10, edited by Alfonso Ortiz, 419–439. Washington, DC: Smithsonian Institute, 1983.

Ortiz, Alfonso, ed. *Smithsonian Handbook of Indians of North America*, Vol. 10. Washington, DC: Smithsonian Institute, 1983.

Ortiz, Simon J. *Woven Stone*. Tucson: University of Arizona Press, 1992.

Osterhammel, Jürgen. *Colonialism: A Theoretical Overview*. Trans. Shelley L. Frisch. Princeton, NJ: Markus Wiener Publishers, 1997.

Peters, Kurt. "Continuing Identity: Laguna Pueblo Railroaders in Richmond, California." *American Indian Culture and Research Journal* 22, no. 4 (1998): 187–198.

Philip, Kenneth R. "Dillon S. Meyer and the Advent of Termination: 1950–1953." *Western Historical Quarterly* 19, no. 1 (January 1988): 37–59.

Poupart, Lisa. "A Familiar Face of Genocide: Internalized Oppression Among American Indians." *Hypatia* 18, no. 2 (2003): 86–100.

Ramirez, Reyna. *Native Hubs: Culture, Community, and Belonging in Silicon Valley and Beyond*. Durham, NC: Duke University Press, 2007.

Riding In, James. "The Contracting of Albuquerque Indian School." *The Indian Historian* 11, no. 4 (January 12, 1979): 21–28.

Riley, Carroll L. *Rio del Norte: People of the Upper Rio Grande from Earliest Times to the Pueblo Revolt*. Salt Lake City: University of Utah Press, 1995.

Rusco, Elmer R. "Purchasing Lands for Nevada Indian Colonies, 1916–1917." *The Nevada Historical Quarterly* (Spring 1989): 1–22.

Sando, Joe. *Pueblo Nations: Eight Centuries of Pueblo Indian History*. Santa Fe, NM:

Clear Light Publishers, 1992.

———. *Pueblo Profiles: Cultural Identity through Centuries of Change.* Santa Fe: Clear Light Publishers, 1998.

Schaafsma, Curtis F. "The Tiguex Province Revisited: The Rio Medio Survey." In *Secrets of a City: Papers on Albuquerque Area Archeology, in Honor of Richard A. Bice,* edited by Anne V. Poore and John Montgomery, 6–13. Sante Fe, NM: Ancient City Press, 1987.

Scott, Wakina. "Welfare Reform and American Indians: Critical Issues for Reauthorization." *National Health Policy Forum Issue Brief,* No. 778 (June 17, 2002): 1–17.

Shoemaker, Nancy. "Urban Indians and Ethnic Choices: American Indian Organizations in Minneapolis, 1920–1950." *The Western Historical Quarterly* 19, no. 4 (1988): 431–437.

Simmons, Marc. *Albuquerque: A Narrative History.* Albuquerque: University of New Mexico Press, 1982.

———. *New Mexico: An Interpretive History.* Albuquerque: University of New Mexico Press, 1988.

Smith, Andrea. *Native America and the Christian Right: The Gendered Politics of Unlikely Alliances.* Durham, NC: Duke University Press, 2008.

Sonnichssen, C.L. *The Mescalero Apaches.* 2nd ed. Norman: University of Oklahoma Press, 1972.

Sorkin, Alan L. *The Urban Indian.* Lexington, MA: Lexington Books, 1978.

Stack, Carol. *All Our Kin: Strategies for Survival in a Black Community.* New York: Harper & Row, 1974.

Stanbury, W.T. *Success and Failure: Indians in Urban Society.* Vancouver: University of British Columbia Press, 1970.

Stanley, F. *The Duke City, the Story of Albuquerque, New Mexico: 1706–1956.* Pampa, TX: Pampa Print Shop, 1963.

Strauss, Terry, and Arndt P. Grant, eds. *Native Chicago.* Chicago: McNaughton and Gunn Inc, 1998.

Sturtevant, William C., ed. *Handbook of North American Indians.* 10 vols. Washington, DC: Smithsonian Institution, 1978.

Swann, Brian, and Arnold Krupat. *I Tell You Now: Autobiographical Essays by Native American Writers, American Indian Lives.* Lincoln: University of Nebraska Press, 1987.

Thomas, Wesley, and Sue-Ellen Jacobs. "'. . . And We Are Still Here': From Berdache to Two-Spirit People." *American Indian Culture and Research Journal,* 23, no. 2 (1999): 91–107.

Trask, Haunani-Kay. *From a Native Daughter: Colonialism and Sovereignty in Hawaii.* Honolulu: University of Hawaii Press, 1999.

Tuhiwai Smith, Linda. *Decolonizing Methodologies: Research and Indigenous Peoples.* New York: Zed Books, 1999.

Varien, Mark D. "Communities and the Chacoan Regional System." In *Great House Communities across the Chacoan Landscape.* Anthropological Papers of the University of Arizona, No. 64, edited by John Kantner and Nancy M. Mahoney, 149–156. Tucson: University of Arizona Press, 2000.

Velarde Tiller, Veronica E. *The Jicarilla Apache Tribe: A History.* 2nd ed. Lincoln: University of Nebraska Press, 1992.

———. ed. *Tiller's Guide to Indian Country: Economic Profiles of American Indian Reservations.* Albuquerque, NM: BowArrow Publishing Company, 1996.

Waddell, Jack O. and O. Michael Watson, eds. *American Indian Urbanization.* Purdue University. Institute for the Study of Social Change. Institute Monograph Series, No. 4. Lafayette, IN: Institute for the Study of Social Change, Purdue University, 1973.

———. *The American Indian in Urban Society.* The Little, Brown Series in Anthropology. Boston: Little Brown, 1971.

Weibel-Orlando, Joan. *Indian Country L.A.: Maintaining Ethnic Community in Complex Society.* Urbana: University of Illinois Press, 1991.

Weppner, Robert S. "Urban Economic Opportunities: The Example of Denver." In *The American Indian in Urban Society,* edited by Jack O. Waddell and O. Michael Watson, 244–273. Boston: Little Brown, 1971.

White, Lynn C., and Bruce A. Chadwick. "Urban Residence, Assimilation, and Identity of the Spokane Indian." In *Native Americans Today: Sociological Perspectives,* edited by Howard M. Bahr, Bruce A. Chadwick, and Robert C. Day, 240–248. New York: Harper & Row, 1972.

Young, Biloine Whiting and Melvin L. Fowler. *Cahokia: The Great Native American Metropolis.* Urbana: University of Illinois Press, 2000.

Zerger, Suzanne. *Health Care for Homeless Native Americans.* Nashville, TN: National Health Care for the Homeless Council, February 2004.

Index

Page numbers in *italics* indicate images.

acculturation, xx
Acoma Pueblo, 24, 27, 28, 30, 35, 40,
    44, 45, 52, 90; railroad workers,
    28, 28, *29*, 29, *53*, 53, 98, 99
activism, xxvi, 6, 60, 116–120, 124,
    126. *See also* National Indian
    Youth Council, Petroglyph
    National Protection Coalition,
    SAGE Council
Albuquerque, xxiii, xxv, 23, 27, 38, 40,
    45, 47, 49, 50, 52, 54, 55, *63*, 63,
    73
Albuquerque Cherokees, 60
Albuquerque Indian Center, 58, 60, 75,
    78–85, *81*, 81, *84*, 84
Albuquerque Indian population, 57,
    58, 60, 74, 80; invisibility, *53*, 53,
    55, 55, *56*, 56, 57, 58, 75
Albuquerque Indian School, 41, 42,
    43, 44, 50, 71, 85, 99, 98, 112;
    development, 68–71, *42*, 42, *44*,
    44
Albuquerque Public Schools, 20, 67,
    68, 86, *51*, 51, *68*, 68
Albuquerque Urban Indian Center, 59,
    79, 80, 81

Alburquerque, xxv, 31, 33, 36, 37, 38,
    40
All Indian Pueblo Council, 70–72, 77,
    85–86, 127
All Pueblo Council, 85–86
American Indian studies, xii–xiv, xxiv,
    4
Anasazi, 25
Andrews, Grace, 107, 110
assimilation, xx, xxi, xxiii, xxiv, 15, 42,
    43, 94, 95, 120
Atchison Topeka Railroad Company,
    39, 40
Atlantic and Pacific Railroad Com-
    pany, 39, 40, 97
Atsye, Dan, 106
Augustine, Katherine, 98, 99

Baca, Jim, 22, 49, 57, 60, 122
Bayer, Laura. *See* Santa Ana Pueblo
Bell, James. *See* youth gangs
Blatchford, Herb, 117–119
Bobroff, Kara, 20, 69
Bureau of Indian Affairs, xvii, 9, 10,
    13, 62, 70, 71, 74, 75, 92, 99, 112,
    119. *See also* relocation program

Carlisle Indian Industrial School, 43, 67
census undercount, 22–23
Central New Mexico Community College, 56; TV-I, 51
Champagne, Duane, xxvi
Chavez, Martin, 57, 59, 60, 66, 122, 123, 125
Cherokee Nation v. the State of Georgia, 8
Cherokees of New Mexico, 60, 91, 92, 93, 114
Cherokees of Albuquerque, 77, 96, 114
Cheromiah, Emily, 104–105
City of Albuquerque, xxiii, xxiv, 23, 25, 46, 50, *51*, 51, 54, 58, 59, 61–63, *63*, 70, 79, 80, 82, 84, 108, 117, 120, 121, 126, 127. *See also* Baca, Chavez, Kinney, Saavedra (mayors)
Cochiti Pueblo, *28*, 28, *29*, 29, 52, 53, 117
Cold War, 3, 10, 26, 100
colonialism, 7, 8; European, xviii, xxv, 8, 113, 127; United States, xxv, 4, 24, 38, 113, 127. *See also* colonization
colonization, xxv, 9, 25, 26, 34, 35, 36, 38, 39, 76, 95, 96, 113, 115, 116, 120; Spanish, ix, 31, 34, 113; United States, 95, 113
Commissioner of Indian Affairs, 10
Cook-Lynn, Elizabeth, xxiv

de Vargas, Diego, Don, 36, 65
Diné (Navajo) Nation, xx, 9–10, 28–30, 31, 40–43, 45, 50, 55, 57, 67, 69, 74, 85; Alamo Navajo Chapter, 86; Navajo Club, 109, 28, *29*; reservation, 9, *16*, 16, *55*, 55; To'hajiilee, 52

English, Sam, 79, 80
ethnic enclaves, xx

federal relocation program, 13, 54, 57
federal trust responsibility, 8, 10, 11, 14, 15, 54, 94
Felipe, Darryl, 70, 71, 90
First American Pageant, 46
First Nations Community Health Source, 19, 60, 83, 84
Fixico, Donald, xviii, 74
Forbes, Jack, xviii
Francis, Emmett, 22, 57, 60

Gathering of Nations, 52, 77–78

Harris, La Donna, 91–92
Harvey, Fred, 45, 46
historical memory, xxiv, 49, 115, 128

identity, xxi, xxii, xxiii, xxv, xxvi, 3, 4, 49, 50, 69, 74, 76, 85, 93, 95, 96, 113, 115, 117, 128; pan-Indian, xxiii, xxvi, 74, 96, 115; Spanish, 39
imperialism, 8, 26, 113
Indian Health Service (IHS), 62, 74, 75, 80, 83, 92, 99, 115; eligibility, 17, 80, 84; funding, *16*, 16, 18–19
Indian middle class, 74, 91
Indian National Finals Rodeo, 54
Indian Pueblo Cultural Center, 71, 77, 85, 87–90; museum, 87; restaurant, *86*, 86, 87, *88*, 88, *89*, 89
Indian Pueblos Federal Development Corporation, 70, 71
Indigenous urbanization/cities, xviii; Cahokia, xix; Chaco Canyon, xix; Huhugam, xix; Mesa Verde, xix
Isleta Pueblo, xvii, xviii, *28*, 28, *29*, 29, 36, 52, *53*, 53

Japanese American internment, 10, 128

Jemez Pueblo, 19, 27, *28*, 28, *29*, 29, 36, 42, 52, *53*, 53, 84, 85, 109
Jicarilla Apaches, xvii, xviii, 28, *29*, 29, 30, 31, 126, 127
Jojola, Theodore, 22–23

Kewa (formerly Santo Domingo), *28*, 28, *29*, 29, 35, 36, 42, 52, *53*, 53
King, Bruce, 79
Kinney, Harry, 59, 79
Kiva Club, 117
KUNM, 90, 91

Laguna Colony of Albuquerque, xxvi, 41, 60, 77, 96, 128; officers, 103–105; Arts and Crafts Committee, 105, 107; Christmas dinner, 103, 105, 106; Education Committee, 105, 107; Social Committee, 105; State Fair booth, 107, 109; State Fair Committee, 105, 107; Sunshine Committee, 105
Laguna Pueblo, xviii, 24, *28*, 28, *29*, 29, 40, *53*, 53, 91, 97, 100, 101, 104, 111, 112
Laguna railroad colonies, 41, 97, 98, 99, 111
Land of Enchantment, 25
Lim, Nicole. *See* youth gangs
Loretto, Geri, 57, 58, 60, 80

Martin, Larry, xiii, 43, 45, 83, 119
Melton, David, 102, 103, 112
Meriam Report, 8–9
Mescalero Apaches, 28, *29*, 29, 30, 42, 109
Meyer, Dylan S., 10, 11
Miss Indian World, 78
Mitchell, Pablo, 42–43
Montoya, Floyd. *See* Santa Ana Pueblo
Morning Star House, 64–66. *See also* Urban Indian Advocacy Program

Nambe Pueblo, *28*, 28, *29*, 29
National Indian Youth Council, 19, 20, 60, 61, 89, 117, 119–120; Indian Youth Council, 118
Native American Community Academy, 20, 69
New Mexico, ix, xii, 24, 26–31, *28*, 28, *29*, 29, 33–35, 37, 39, 48–50, 52, 54
Nieto-Phillips, John, 39

Officer, James E., xviii
de Oñate, Juan, Don, ix, 33–35, 48; statue, 48, 49
Oke Owinge (formerly San Juan Pueblo), *28*, 28, *29*, 29, 33, 35

Paak'u, xxv, 26–28
Paisano, Cheryl, 104, 106, 107, 109, 110, 112
Paisano, Ulysses, 100, 101, 104, 107
petroglyphs, 120–127
Petroglyph National Monument, 121–123, *123*
Petroglyph National Monument Boundary Adjustment Act, 122, *124*, 124. *See also* colonization
Petroglyph National Protection Coalition, 121, 124, 125
Picuris Pueblo, *28*, 28, *29*, 29, 31, 35, 36, 126
Pojoaque Pueblo, *28*, 28, *29*, 29
Popé, 35
Poupart, Lisa, 95, 96, 116
powwow, xxiii, 6, 52, 54, 75, 77, 78, 82, 90, 96, 109, 118. *See also* Gathering of Nations
Public Law 93–638, 16–18, 70
Pueblo Revolt, 31, 35, 36

Ramirez, Renya, 76
Ration, Norman, 19, 60
Reid-Jojola, Darlene, 66, 67

178

relocation: success of, xx, xxi, 12, 95;
 failure of, xx, xxi, 95
relocation centers, xxv
relocation periods, 5–6; first wave, 5,
 20; second wave, 6; third wave 5,
 6
relocation policy, xxiv, 5, 6, 8–15, 54,
 74, 94; dilemmas, 4, 14; dilemmas–health care, 15–19, 62;
 dilemmas–welfare, 19–22
relocation program, xvii, xxi, xxiv, xxv,
 6, 9, 11, 12, 13, 57, 74, 94, 95; officers, xx, xxiv, 11–13; propaganda,
 xvii, *xxii*, xxii, 12
Roberts, Elizabeth, 44

Saavedra, Louis, 59, 80, 81
SAGE Council, xxvi, 120, 124–126
San Felipe, *28*, 28, *29*, 29, 41, 52, *53*,
 53
San Ildelfonso, *29*, 29, *28*, 28
Sandia Pueblo, *28*, 28, *29*, 29, 52, *53*,
 53, 84, 85
Sando, Joe, 32, 85
Santa Clara Pueblo, ix, *28*, 28, *29*, 29,
 36
Sherman Institute, 43, 45, 67
Simmons, Marc, 31
Singing Wire, 70, 90, 91
Southwestern Indian Polytechnic
 Institute, 19, 56, 62, 80, 91
sovereignty, xii, xxiv, 4, 8, 14, 37, 72,
 116

Tamaya (Santa Ana Pueblo), 25, 27,
 28, 28, *29*, 29, *53*, 53, 52, 84, 90,
 91
Taos Pueblo, x, *28*, 28, *29*, 29, 31, 35,
 36, 52, 90

termination policy, 10, 11, 12, 94
Tesuque Pueblo, *28*, 28, *29*, 29
tourism, 40–46, 52, 72
Toyah band of Comanches, 77, 91–93,
 96, 114, 128
Tri-cultural state, 25, 48, 49, 108, 109

urban divide, 5
Urban Indian Advocacy Program, 66,
 67. *See also* Morning Star House
urban Indian health centers, 17, 18.
 See also First Nations Community
 Health Source
urban Indians, xxiii, xxiv, xxvi, 5, 22,
 23, 73, 75, 77, 95, 115
urban migrations, xix, 3, 6, 9, 45
urbanization, xviii, xix, xxiv, 5, 8–14,
 113, 117

violence against American Indian
 women, 63–67

War Relocation Authority, 10, 12
Weahkee, Bill, 126
Weahkee, Carol, 58, 81, 82
Weahkee, Laurie, 124. *See also* SAGE
 Council, Petroglyph National Pro-
 tection Coalition
welfare reform, xxiii, 7, 20–22, 75;
 Temporary Aid for Needy Fami-
 lies (TANF), 20
Weppner, Robert, xxi
World War II, xviii, 3, 10, 12, 13, 128

youth gangs, 7

Zia Pueblo (Tsiiya), 27, *28*, 28, *29*, 29,
 35, 52, *53*, 53, 84
Zuni Pueblo, *28*, 28, 28, *29*, 29, 32, 109

About the Author

MYLA VICENTI CARPIO is a citizen of the Jicarilla Apache Nation and is also Laguna and Isleta Pueblo. An assistant professor in the American Indian Studies program at Arizona State University, she lives in Tempe, Arizona.